MC

000

396

Small
Antennas

ELECTRONIC & ELECTRICAL ENGINEERING RESEARCH STUDIES

ANTENNAS SERIES

Series Editor: **Professor J. R. James,** *The Royal Military College of Science, Shrivenham, Wiltshire, England*

Kyohei Fujimoto (pictured left) and Kazuhiro Hirasawa in the laboratories of the Institute of Applied Physics, University of Tsukuba, Japan

Ann Henderson and Jim James in the Wolfson RF Engineering Centre, RMCS, England

The Authors

Professor K. Fujimoto, DEng
Institute of Applied Physics,
University of Tsukuba, Japan

Dr Ann Henderson, PhD
Wolfson RF Engineering Centre,
Royal Military College of Science, Shrivenham, England

Professor K. Hirasawa, PhD
Institute of Applied Physics,
University of Tsukuba, Japan

Professor J. R. James, DSc
Wolfson RF Engineering Centre,
Royal Military College of Science, Shrivenham, England

Small
Antennas

K. Fujimoto

A. Henderson

K. Hirasawa

and

J. R. James

RESEARCH STUDIES PRESS LTD.
Letchworth, Hertfordshire, England

JOHN WILEY & SONS INC.
New York · Chichester · Toronto · Brisbane · Singapore

RESEARCH STUDIES PRESS LTD.
58B Station Road, Letchworth, Herts. SG6 3BE, England

Marketing and Distribution:

Australia, New Zealand, South-east Asia:
Jacaranda-Wiley Ltd., Jacaranda Press
JOHN WILEY & SONS INC.
GPO Box 859, Brisbane, Queensland 4001, Australia

Canada:
JOHN WILEY & SONS CANADA LIMITED
22 Worcester Road, Rexdale, Ontario, Canada

Europe, Africa:
JOHN WILEY & SONS LIMITED
Baffins Lane, Chichester, West Sussex, England

North and South America and the rest of the world:
JOHN WILEY & SONS INC.
605 Third Avenue, New York, NY 10158, USA

Library of Congress Cataloging in Publication Data

Small antennas.
  (Electronic & electrical engineering research
studies. Antennas series; 7)
  Includes bibliographical references and index.
  1. Antennas (Electronics) I. Fujimoto, K. (Kyōhei),
1929–   . II. Series.
TK871.6.S565 1987   621.38′028′3   86-26198
ISBN 0 471 91413 4 (Wiley)

British Library Cataloguing in Publication Data

Small antennas.——(Electronic & electrical
  engineering research studies. Antennas
  series; 7)
  1. Antennas (Electronics)
  I. Fujimoto, K. II. Series
  621.38′028′3   TK7871.6

  ISBN 0 86380 048 3

  ISBN 0 86380 048 3 (Research Studies Press Ltd.)
  ISBN 0 471 91413 4 (John Wiley & Sons Inc.)

Printed in Great Britain by Short Run Press Ltd., Exeter

Editorial Preface

Small is beautiful—Anon
小さい それは素晴らしいことだ

The need for smaller antennas has become increasingly important in recent years because the effect of large scale integration of electronic components generally isolates the antenna as the most bulky, heavy and obtrusive part of the equipment. The topic of small antennas is however extraordinary in many ways because the physical problems are well known but solutions have not been established with confidence and design techniques vital to the successful manufacture of modern communication equipment are seldom recorded in the literature. In fact to my knowledge no book has ever been published that is devoted to the design concepts of small antennas. A text on small antennas is thus long overdue.

In 1981 I made contact with Professor Kyohei Fujimoto and Dr Kazuhiro Hirasawa and found our interest in small antennas had much in common. Dr Ann Henderson and I had specialised mainly on material loaded techniques while Professor Fujimoto had carried out much significant research on wire structures. This division of the topic turned out to be quite logical because despite the multitude of small antenna types, resonance in a size reduced wire structure is maintained either by adding more wire in some shape or loading with materials/lumped components. While this may seem an over-simplification it is in fact the source of much existing confusion about the merits of one sort of small antenna as opposed to another. There are very few generic types of small antennas and to assist designers in their choice, a glossary of known types is given in the first chapter. We have not intended to review the basic theory of antennas and the book focusses on recent advances with ample references given to established fundamental antenna theory. Small antennas are often required to function on small mobile ground planes or platforms and here lies another source of confusion because antenna performance then relates to the size and shape of the host equipment. The recent advances in computing these effects are therefore an important part of this text.

Coauthoring this book has indeed been a rewarding experience for us in bringing together specialist knowledge from two distant lands and we have all enjoyed the exchange visits and family meetings.

Lastly, I will expect the book to be of interest to anyone connected with the design of antennas but it will be of considerable value to designers of mobile systems or indeed any equipment demanding an antenna of constrained size or shape. A particular feature of the book concerns the use of computational methods in design and postgraduates and specialists in electromagnetics will find the book useful and a rich source of configurations for further analysis.

J.R. James

Foreword

Piquant though small

The proverb says that the Japanese pepper tastes very hot although it is as small as a tiny seed. This implies "smart though small". The expression seems to fit the small antenna case exactly in the same sense; "good performance, though small". The physical size of the radio communication equipment and electronic devices on which antennas are installed has become smaller and smaller in recent years, and small-sized antennas with size appropriate to the equipment and efficient electrical performance in spite of this smallness, are urgently needed. The development of such "piquant though small" antennas is one of the significant objectives for antenna engineers.

This monograph introduces some of the techniques to realize small antennas in practice. The fundamental theory of small antennas is not treated here; primarily the analysis and design of practical antennas are presented.

It should be noted that the term "small antennas" does not mean only "electrically small" here, but that smallness is defined in terms of the physical structure and the function of the antennas. Low profile antennas are categorized as physically constrained small antennas, since they have either a flush-mountable structure or a height as low as a fraction of the wavelength and their structure is partly constrained to an electrically small size.

The functionally small antennas are shown in the monograph by taking dipole antennas as the examples. A dipole antenna designed with a

X

beam-shifting function, which would usually be obtained by an array of dipole elements, is classified as a functionally small antenna, since the dipole antenna has a smaller size than an array antenna system with the same antenna function. The functionally small antenna is introduced here for the first time. The importance of this concept will be recognized by noting that there is an increasing tendency to use antenna systems having such functions as beam control and beam shaping, and size reduction in these antenna systems is required in most cases.

One of the techniques to make antenna systems small is integration or loading, by which an antenna system can be designed to have either a modified function or an improved performance. In the text, various integration techniques are introduced that use electronic devices such as electromagnetic materials, reactance components, and transistor circuitry. Various examples of material loading to antenna elements are shown in Chapter 3 to realize small antennas with plenty of practical design data.

In practical situations, there exist many cases where materials adjacent to the antenna element cannot be separated electromagnetically, so that the radiation current flows on adjacent conducting materials, and this affects the antenna performance significantly. This is a problem often encountered in practice, especially when the antenna size becomes small and the size of the adjacent conducting materials is comparable to that of the antenna element. But this situation may be utilized intentionally to improve antenna performance. The concept exactly corresponds to the integration technique. Some examples are described for the cases where a rectangular loop antenna is used for a pocket-size receiver and a wire antenna element is placed on a rectangular conducting box.

The examples shown in the monograph are of course limited in number, but can be applied to various other types of antennas. The way of application depends upon the objective, for example, improving the antenna performance or enhancing the antenna function. Because small antennas are particularly required in mobile systems for which smallness and light weight are imperative, various examples described in this monograph are concerned with mobile systems. However, the principles are applicable generally to other antenna systems, wherever demands for small sizing arise.

It was in 1981 when Professor J.R.James proposed to Prof. K.Hirasawa and me that we join with him and Dr. Ann Henderson in writing this monograph. As I have long been working on small antenna problems, there was good reason for accepting Prof. James' offer and our collaboration with them started. It is quite meaningful and significant for us to work together internationally on small antennas.

I hope that this monograph will be helpful and useful to researchers and engineers in the fields of antennas and also of communications as well.

I would like to express my sincere appreciation to everyone who in any way worked for us to publish this book. Thanks to Prof. James, who gave us the opportunity of creating this book and assisted us in each stage of the publishing process; to Dr. Henderson, who examined our manuscript in detail and made many improvements; to Professor J.W. Higgins of University of Tsukuba, who kindly checked the text in the early stage of writing; to several secretaries, who expertly typed the draft of the text, and finally to Mr. Toshimitsu Kakeida, who was most cooperative and helpful in arranging and managing the typing process.

Kyohei Fujimoto

Contents

CHAPTER 3 - MATERIAL LOADED ANTENNAS

CHAPTER 4 - SMALL ANTENNAS ON OR NEAR A CONDUCTING BODY

CHAPTER 1
Introduction

INTRODUCTION

Antennas are now commonplace objects in everyday life and since
their inception, there has been continuing interest in reducing their
physical size. Some of the earliest examples of reduced height antennas were the low frequency broad cast antennas, first used at the
turn of the century (Belrose et al., 1959). Because of the long wavelength of transmission involved, a full size antenna was often too
costly to erect and by necessity, one solution to this problem was to
construct L-shaped and other types of top-loaded antennas using supporting towers; this in effect reduced the height of the antenna.

Other types of reduced height and constrained size antennas were devised during the World Wars to satisfy various operational requirements at higher frequencies. Since then, there have been increasing
demands for small antennas to fulfil a variety of specifications. In
general, the need for a small antenna arises because there is insuffi-
cient space to fit a conventional one. This is the most common requirement which often arises because the 'platform' or object onto
which the antenna is to be mounted, is itself physically small and in
many cases it will be electrically small. It is thus not possible to
address the topic of small antennas without consideration being given
to the effect of small platforms.

Other reasons for the growing demand for small antennas are numerous
and include requirements for low aerodynamic drag on aircraft, covert-
ness and concealment in vehicles, protection against vandalism as in

police patrol cars, reduction in the radar and/or optical signature on platforms, the incorporation of several antennas into a limited space such as on ships and aircraft, and finally the need for miniaturised or low profile robust radiators, sometimes with the capability of working at elevated temperatures as on the space shuttle. Of all the diverse and highly specialised small radiators the ubiquitous ferrite rod antenna, (Van Suchtelen, 1952), deserves special mention being the most common electrically small antenna used in domestic radio sets today, for medium and long-wave reception.

More recently the astronomical progress in miniaturising electronic equipment, brought about by advances in integrated semiconductor circuits, has often isolated the antenna as the most bulky and heavy component in a system, even at VHF and UHF frequencies. In the commercial market, the antennas on FM/VHF radio receivers and on portable TV sets are particularly cumbersome in relation to the size of the equipment involved.

The reduction in antenna size presents problems to the system designer due to the performance penalties in antenna bandwidth and efficiency that generally arise. These penalties have to be absorbed into the overall system performance of the equipment, which could result in very poor reception in low signal areas. If, for example, the quarter-wave VHF whip antenna on a portable radio set was to be reduced significantly in length, then there would have been not only a narrowing of the antenna bandwidth but in the past it would have been necessary to fit the antenna with some sort of matching unit. This would incur significant power losses and reduce the general efficiency of the receiver as well as increasing equipment costs. Today more efficient matching techniques are available - for example, by using both passive and active lumped components within the antenna structure itself, it is possible to achieve self-resonance without the need for an external matching circuit and this aspect will be discussed later. A reduction in overall efficiency is still incurred however but the failure to incorporate matching techniques could lead to even worse system penalties.

The trade-off between antenna size and performance is in general difficult to predict for practical situations, particularly where matching units are involved and evaluations tend to be experimental. For these reasons, designers in many sectors of the market are now demanding more precision in small antenna design, so that any performance penalties incurred can be minimised.

The incorporation of the antenna inside the receiver itself is an attractive proposition which has been investigated lately with some success for certain hand-held radio applications and this also will be discussed in depth.

To date, there are many fragmentary reports on small antennas published but to our knowledge, there is no general text or design guide. The renewed interest in evaluating small antenna performance for defence applications was illustrated by the 1976 ECOM-ARO workshop, held in the USA. The proceedings of this workshop (Goubau, 1976) were a comprehensive account of the state-of-the-art in small antenna design and indicated the areas where research effort was thought to be needed at that time.

This present monograph is concerned with advances made in small antenna design in recent years and, as can be seen from the text, many of the applications relate to man-pack radio equipment. In view of the highly specialised nature of the book, it will be assumed that the reader is familiar with advanced electromagnetic theory in its application to antenna structures. In this Chapter we have, however, included a summary of established principles relating to the design of small antennas with section 1.1 summarising fundamental issues and section 1.2 giving a pictorial glossary of small antenna types. There is no limit to the number of variants that can be derived from what in reality is a very small number of generic types. An exhaustive designers' "catalogue" has not been compiled but groups of antennas do have properties broadly in common. It is useful to draw attention to these common features bearing in mind the limitations of taking the classification too rigidly and some grouping of types into tables has been undertaken.

It is interesting to note at this point the usage and definition of the terms 'small' and 'electrically small' in antenna structures.

• <u>an electrically small</u> antenna is one that can be physically bounded by a sphere having a radius equal to $\lambda/2\pi$ where λ is the free-space wavelength. A very short dipole is an example of this.

• <u>a physically constrained</u> antenna is one which is not necessarily electrically small but is shaped in such a way that considerable size reduction is achieved in one plane. Conformal antennas fall into this category.

• <u>functionally small</u> antennas do not necessarily satisfy the above two definitions but apply where additional performance has been achieved without increasing the antenna size. Antennas with extensive beam control and adaptiveness brought about by signal processing are included here.

• <u>physically small</u> antennas may not fall into any of the above categories yet their dimensions are regarded as small in a relative sense. A millimetre-wave horn antenna is an example.

These definitions cannot be analytically formulated in practical situations because the platform and the feeder cables can strongly influence the performance of the antenna structure and can contribute to the radiation. For instance, a quarter-wave monopole on a spherical shell of small radius, say $\lambda/16$, has a markedly different performance to the same monopole on a large flat ground-plane and these aspects are discussed in Chapters 2 and 4.

It will be evident from the pictorial glossary of small antenna types in section 1.2 that variants of the wire monopole and the loop are most common It is thus to be anticipated that the improved calculation and design of small wire antennas has received the most attention recently and is the subject of Chapter 2 where advances in helical antennas, inverted L antennas, small dipoles and loops using both active and passive loading techniques are reported. A less common method of size reduction for wires is material loading and this is extensively treated in Chapter 3 and includes many variants. With the advent of new materials with controlled electrical properties, this loading technique has increased in significance.

Finally the important practical situation of the electrically small ground-plane is addressed in Chapter 4 which often occurs with present day communications equipment and other small platform applications.

1.1 Summary of fundamental properties

1.1.1 Early work

A glance at the glossary of antennas in section 1.2 confirms the diverse nature of the various physical configurations of small antennas. When these variations are compounded with the multitude of differing system requirements it is not surprising to find that there are no simple laws to predict the general behaviour of these antennas and each antenna has to be examined on its own merits for a particular system requirement. There are however some well established trends in behaviour which indicate the nature of the various penalty factors and benefits that are likely to be experienced in a trade-off of design parameters. For instance, it is an accepted fact that electrically smaller antennas have narrower bandwidths and poorer efficiencies than their larger counterparts. Whatever the antenna type, one can therefore expect some trade-off between efficiency, bandwidth and size and for this reason several attempts have been made in the past to establish guidelines.

One of the earliest attempts at quantifying small antennas was made by Wheeler in 1947 who used a figure of merit called the radiation power factor, p, defined as

$$p = \frac{\text{resistance of antenna}}{\text{reactance of antenna}}$$

The essence of Wheeler's work was the equivalent lumped circuit approach to an electromagnetic radiator and the attractive feature was that it included, admittedly in a simplistic fashion, the generator and its circuit components. As such p represented the product of the efficiency and bandwidth of the antenna when matched by a simple tuned circuit. As the antenna size decreases, the radiation resistance of the antenna decreases in comparison to the ohmic losses in both the antenna and the matching elements, which results in a loss of overall system efficiency. Wheeler demonstrated that the matching of a small antenna can be done efficiently for a narrow bandwidth, but if a wider system bandwidth is required then the total efficiency will decrease due to the additional losses in the matching unit. This point was illustrated with an example of a small FM loop antenna for a portable radio. This antenna, typically 20 cm^3 in volume, can be tuned to a single channel for a circuit loss of 4dB, but for usage over the entire 88-108MHz band, then 12-15dB loss would be necessarily incurred by the matching unit indicating the importance of a well-defined system requirement.

Wheeler was one of the first to recognise the effect of material loading on antennas and his circuit approach to small loaded capacitors and inductors is seen to embody the rudimentary properties. He deduced that if the permittivity of a dielectric-loaded capacitor-plate antenna is increased then 'p' will decrease. On the other hand, if a ferrite were to be loaded into an inductor then 'p' would increase with permeability due to a lowering of the Q factor of the antenna. This indicated that there could be some advantage in using magnetic material-loaded inductors but results apparently do not apply to small antenna structures in general (Galejs, 1962) and this emphasises the need for more specialised treatments.

A more generalised analysis by Chu (1948) enabled the equivalent circuit components to be derived from the fields surrounding an arbitrarilyshaped radiator. He quantified the minimum Q factor that can be achieved for omnidirectional antennas in relation to their volume and the results can be applied to small antenna structures. Spherical harmonic wave expansions were taken to represent the field outside a sphere containing the antenna; this enables calculation of the minimum theoretical Q factor that can be achieved. He found that an antenna which generated the field of a simple dipole has the smallest Q of all possible antenna types and is given by

$$Q = \frac{1 + 3k^2a^2}{k^3a^3(1+k^2a^2)}$$ (1.1.1)

where $k=2\pi/\lambda$ and 'a' is the radius of the sphere that can contain the antenna. As the antenna size is reduced to less than $\lambda/2\pi$, the Hankel functions in the field expansions behave essentially as imaginary quantities giving an excessive amount of energy stored in the near-field of the antenna and resulting in a massive increase in Q. Theoretically as the antenna size is reduced to zero, the Q factor goes to infinity but in practice the intense fields in the near-field will generate high ohmic losses and lower the Q factor predicted by Chu.

Although the analysis of Chu gives a useful worst case solution for Q, it does not account for losses in the antenna and cannot relate to the conditions at the input terminals.

1.1.2 More recent work

The analysis of Chu was further extended in 1960 by Harrington to include the effects of ohmic losses on the antenna Q factor for an idealised lossy metal sphere. Hansen (1981) in a more recent review presented the results of Harrington's analysis, given below in Fig.1. 1.1 which clearly demonstrates the trade-off between efficiency η and

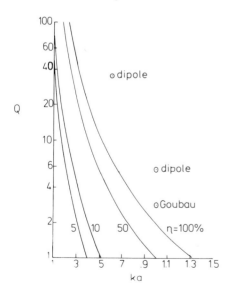

Fig.1.1.1 Theoretical trade-offs between efficiency η and Q factor for an idealised lossy metal sphere (Hansen, 1981) © IEEE.

Q factor for this particular antenna. In practice, other small antenna types do not achieve the Q factors shown above and three such cases are given on the graph, including two short dipoles and a top-loaded monopole structure by Goubau (1976).

The information on small antennas given in Harrington's work is necessarily incomplete since it does not include matching losses. As pointed out by Wheeler (1947), these can significantly affect the overall system performance and further analysis by Smith (1977) has laid down the basic rules for the design of matching circuits using dissipative elements. The overall system efficiency η_s is a product of the efficiencies of the antenna η_a and its matching unit η_m

$$\eta_s = \eta_a \cdot \eta_m$$

The resistance of an antenna can be resolved into two distinct components, namely the radiation resistance r_r and the loss resistance r_{loss}, and depends upon the relative values of these two resistances as below

$$\eta_a = \frac{r_r}{r_r + r_{loss}} \qquad\qquad (1.1.2)$$

and for small antennas r_r/r_{loss} is usually a small quantity giving a low antenna efficiency. η_m is a relatively more complicated quantity depending on the input impedance of the antenna and on the losses within the components of the matching unit. For small antennas, it is reasonable to assume that

$$\eta_m \simeq \frac{\eta_a}{1 + Q_a/Q_m}$$

where Q_a is the Q factor of the antenna and Q_m is that of the matching components, assuming that they are all of the same order in value. In practice, η_a and Q_a are obtained by measurement and there are two simple techniques that give useful results. Firstly, the Q-method suggested by Newman et al. (1975) is based on the deductions made by Chu (1948) described earlier, whereby the Q of a lossless small dipole-like antenna has a minimum value Q_{min} given by eqn(1.1.1). It is assumed here that the ratio of the measured Q value of the test antenna to Q_{min} gives the efficiency of the antenna. Clearly this technique is only approximate but is useful during the initial design stage.

Secondly, the 'Wheeler can' method (Wheeler, 1959) provides an esti-mate of the efficiency by measuring the input resistance of the an-tenna, with and without an enclosing metal can. The near-field of a small antenna is chiefly contained within a spherical region of radius $\lambda/2\pi$ as shown by Chu (1948) and the presence of a metal can of that size should eliminate any radiation effects, without disturbing the near-field. In this way, the dissipative loss resistance of the an-tenna r_{loss} can be measured separately from the total resistance $r_r + r_{loss}$ and the efficiency is estimated from eqn(1.1.2).

It is evident from the above that no generalised analytical treat-ment has been established which includes the antenna geometric fac-tors, the losses and the physical characteristics of the feed circuits (Wheeler, 1983). Wasylkuisky and Kahn (1970) have presented generali-sed formulations but we are not aware of their general application to specific antenna structures. It is likely that further progress will only result by specific rather than generalised approaches and the specialised analysis of a coated wire monopole in Chapter 3 is one of the few examples where both the physical characteristics of the feed and radiating elements are included.

1.2 Glossary of antenna types

The fundamental theory of electrically small radiation sources as summarised above, readily identifies the nature of the practical dif-ficulties and performance problems associated with small antennas. The theories give little or no indication as how to design a reduced size antenna to fulfil given system criteria with physical constraints and it is not surprising therefore that a multitude of seemingly dif-ferent types of electrically small antennas have been developed over the years for various applications. A glossary of these principal an-tenna types is given and a description of the main features of each antenna is accompanied by a source of references for further detailed study together with a simple diagram to illustrate the antenna shape.

Although it is not possible to subdivide the antennas into distinct groups, some broad trends in shape and performance are evident and two tables are now presented which aim to give some degree of guidance in choosing a small antenna type for a given application.

Table 1.2.1 Most likely operating frequency band for small antenna types. The numbers refer to the glossary of antennas.

Frequency	ELF 3–30kHz	VLF–LF 30kHz–3MHz	HF 3–30MHz	VHF 30–300MHz	UHF >300MHz
Antenna reference number	14 24 25	1, 2, 4, 5, 10, 12, 13, 31	1, 2, 4, 5, 6, 8, 9, 10, 12, 13, 15, 18, 22, 23, 28, 30, 32, 33, 34, 35	1, 3, 6, 7, 8, 11, 13, 15, 16, 17, 18, 19, 20, 22, 26, 28, 29, 30, 33, 34, 35	1, 11, 18, 19, 20, 22, 26, 27, 28, 29, 30, 34, 36

Table 1.2.2   Some principal uses of small antenna types.   The numbers refer to the Glossary.

Antenna type	Platform	Reasons for using small antenna techniques	Antenna reference number
Small monopoles and loops	Man-pack radio sets and pagers	Concealment and ease of use when on portable equipment	1, 18, 19, 20, 21, 22, 26, 31, 32, 33, 34, 35
Low profile	Aircraft	Low drag and the minimisation of damage to antenna	2, 3, 11, 12, 27
	Vehicles	To minimise damage by vandals and environmental effects when in transit. Concealment.	2, 3, 7, 8, 9, 11, 12, 22, 27
	Ships	Limited size of platform for number of antennas required.	13, 23
Low-frequency	Submarines	Choice of ELF necessary due to dissipative medium	2, 4, 5, 6, 10, 13, 23
	Ground-based	Small towers needed due to cheapness or concealment	2, 4, 5, 6, 10, 13, 23

The simple thin monopole has a low radiation resistance $r \sim 40\pi^2(h/\lambda)^2$ and is highly capacitive (Jasik, 1952, p3-2). When tuned and matched at the input, a low efficiency generally results due to power losses in the matching circuits. Typically for $h/\lambda \sim 0.05$, efficiencies of 30-70% for bandwidths of 10-1% are attainable after matching (Seeger, 1959; Schroeder and Soo Hoo, 1976). The short dipole has twice the value of r_r and requires a balanced feeder arrangement. See also inductively-loaded monopole (Glossary No 18).

On top loading a short monopole, the current distribution tends to become more uniform along its length and this increases the radiation resistance. The inverted L antenna is the simplest form of top loaded antenna and is used at HF and below (Pierce, 1920; Harrison, 1958; King and Harrison, 1949; Prasad and King, 1961). Simpson (1969, 1971) quotes an input impedance of about 5 ohms for $h/\lambda \sim 0.05$: the input impedance can be brought to resonance by adjusting ℓ so that $h + \ell \sim \lambda/4$. The inverted L- antenna is mentioned again under transmission-line loaded antennas (Glossary No 12)(Guertler, 1977).

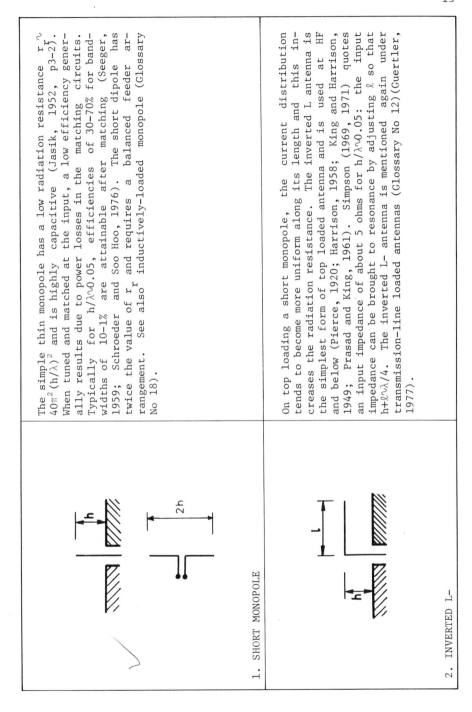

1. SHORT MONOPOLE

2. INVERTED L-

14

The transistor-loaded inverted L- antenna has been treated by Hiroi and Fujimoto (1970) and Fujimoto (1970) and shown to be useful in shifting the direction of the maximum in the antenna pattern by varying the bias supply to the Tr-circuit. The application of these devices in VHF receivers is considered in Section 2.4.2. Further examples of active antennas are given later and the concept of integrated antenna systems is described by Fujimoto (1970).

Simpson (1971) has calculated the input impedance of several multi-element top-loaded monopoles. These antennas have approximately the same radiation resistance as the inverted L but are usually operated below self-resonance and consequently need tuning and matching circuits.

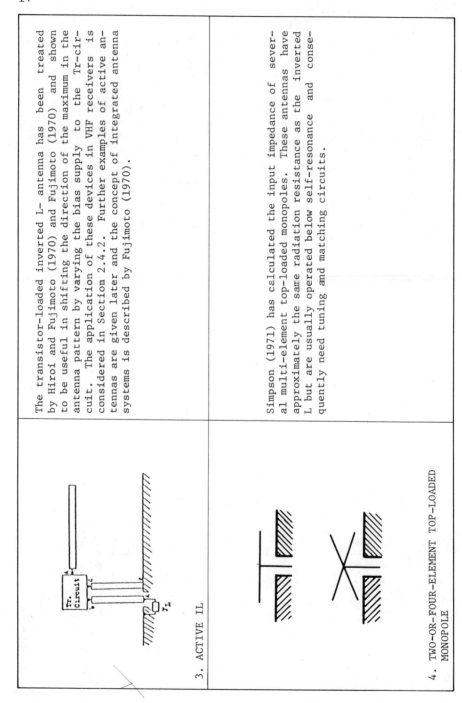

3. ACTIVE IL

4. TWO-OR-FOUR-ELEMENT TOP-LOADED MONOPOLE

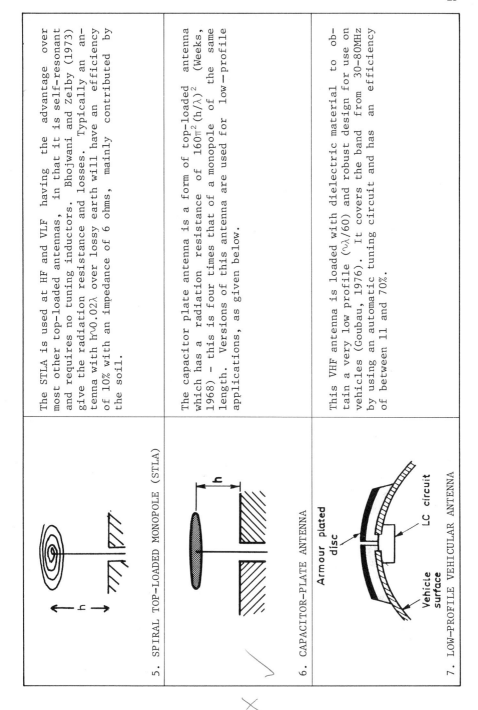

5. SPIRAL TOP-LOADED MONOPOLE (STLA)

The STLA is used at HF and VLF having the advantage over most other top-loaded antennas, in that it is self-resonant and requires no tuning inductors. Bhojwani and Zelby (1973) give the radiation resistance and losses. Typically an antenna with $h \sim 0.02\lambda$ over lossy earth will have an efficiency of 10% with an impedance of 6 ohms, mainly contributed by the soil.

6. CAPACITOR-PLATE ANTENNA

The capacitor plate antenna is a form of top-loaded antenna which has a radiation resistance of $160\pi^2 (h/\lambda)^2$ (Weeks, 1968) – this is four times that of a monopole of the same length. Versions of this antenna are used for low-profile applications, as given below.

7. LOW-PROFILE VEHICULAR ANTENNA

This VHF antenna is loaded with dielectric material to obtain a very low profile ($\sim \lambda/60$) and robust design for use on vehicles (Goubau, 1976). It covers the band from 30-80MHz by using an automatic tuning circuit and has an efficiency of between 11 and 70%.

This antenna is also based on the disc-loaded monopole but some increase in bandwidth has been achieved by mutual coupling between elements (Goubau, 1976). The top disc has been segmented into four sections and each is excited by a small monopole. The radiation resistance is increased to 50 ohms by this means.

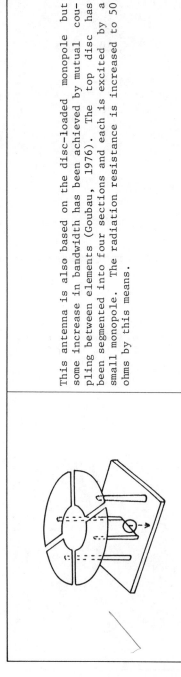

8. MULTI-ELEMENT TOP-LOADED MONOPOLE

A similar low-profile antenna to the above has been developed by Tokumaru (1976) and consists of two metal plates. The lower plate is connected to the ground and the upper plate is connected to the lower. The size of the lower plate determines the lowest operating frequency whereas the upper plate determines the VSWR characteristics. Typically a VSWR of 1.4 can be obtained between 1.2 and 2GHz.

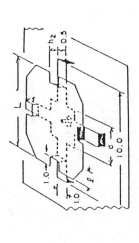

9. MULTI-PLATE

Mainly used as a VLF or LF antenna when low cost and low wind resistance are important. The guy wires act as a top loading and can increase the radiation resistance to 10 ohms for h~0.1λ (Gangi et al, 1965). The antenna is usually operated below resonance but can readily be made resonant by adjusting the length of the guy wires. The radiation efficiency is similar to that of the T and L type antennas but requires only one tower for installation (Goubau, 1976).

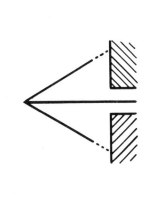

10. UMBRELLA TOP-LOADED MONOPOLE

The cavity-backed slot is particularly used on aircraft and on vehicles at VHF and UHF where a flush surface is required. The radiating annular slot is matched to the coaxial feed by means of a tuning capacitor and a coupling loop. It has a radiation resistance of about 100 ohms for a 0.5λ diameter (Cumming and Cormier, 1958).

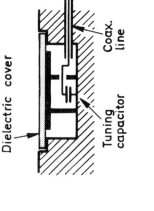

Dielectric cover

Coax. line

Tuning capacitor

11. CAVITY-BACKED ANNULAR SLOT

The inverted L- is a special case of the transmission-line antenna (or 'tranline') where $Z_L = \infty$. Tranlines exist in a wide variety of forms and have been used as missile or vehicle antennas where the body constitutes the ground-plane (King et al., 1960). More recently (Goubau, 1976, p129), tranlines fitted with automatic tuning for use on helicopters have achieved efficiencies of between 90 and 8% in the 2-5MHz band, for $\ell \sim \lambda/50$. In this particular case the dipole mode is excited in the helicopter frame thus increasing the efficiency at low frequency.

Impedance loading Z_L

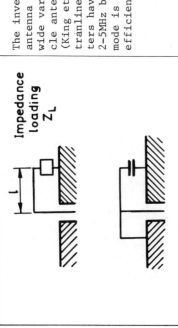

12. TRANSMISSION LINE LOADED

Fenwick (1965) describes a variety of flat half-wave windings of small height, which are simple to manufacture and easy to deploy. They are essentially wound tranlines of $\lambda/2$ in total length and have a tuned input impedance. Bandwidths of about 0.2%, efficiencies up to 10% and impedances up to 6 ohms for $h \sim 0.01\lambda$ have been measured.

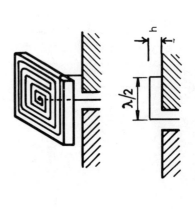

13. PLANAR HALF-WAVE WOUND TRANSMISSION-LINE

For long range ELF reception in submarines, the antennas are necessarily electrically very small with very low signal to noise ratios. To reduce hull noise, the antennas take the form of tranline cables which are trailed through the water. Electrodes provide the earthing points into the sea-water (Burrows, 1978; Fessenden and Cheng, 1974). Because the antenna has an electric dipole pattern, nulls in coverage occur and helical loops have been considered to improve performance (Burrows, 1978 and Cafaro et al.,1974).

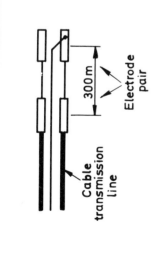

Cable transmission line

300m

Electrode Pair

14. TRAILING ELECTRODE PAIR

The Hula-hoop was originally devised by Boyer (1963) and later analysed by Burton and King (1963) and Egashira (1975). Measurements by Boyer indicated that the antenna gain was only 2-3dB lower than a $\lambda/4$ mast at 4MHz and a good match was obtained by means of a stub. Egashira gives the radiation resistance as

$$r_r \sim 320\pi^2 (h/\lambda)^2$$

without the matching stub, which is twice that of the top-loaded monopole.

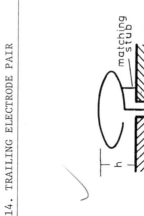

matching stub

h

15. HULA-HOOP

This antenna consists of a doubly fed, air-cored coaxial line folded back upon itself, and is basically a transmission-line type. Only small height reductions are claimed (Rahman and Maclean, 1978) with input resistances comparable to that of a monopole of the same height. The short-circuit version is much more narrowband than the open-circuit version.

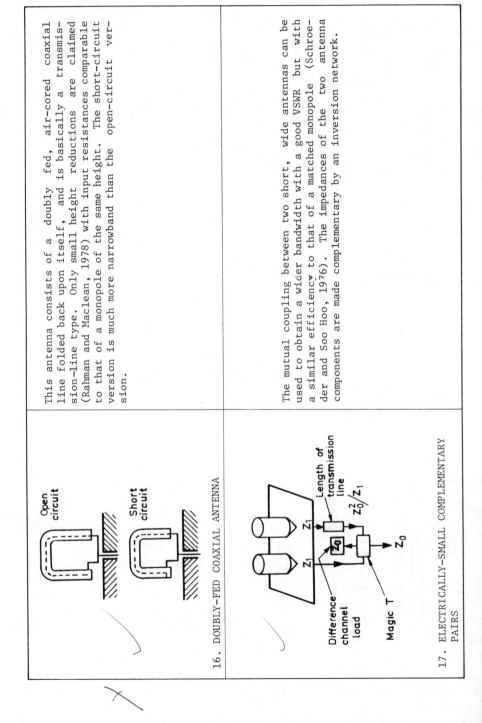

Open circuit

Short circuit

16. DOUBLY-FED COAXIAL ANTENNA

The mutual coupling between two short, wide antennas can be used to obtain a wider bandwidth with a good VSWR but with a similar efficiency to that of a matched monopole (Schroeder and Soo Hoo, 1976). The impedances of the two antenna components are made complementary by an inversion network.

Length of transmission line

Z_1

Z_1

Z_0

Z_0^2/Z_1

Z_0

Difference channel load

Magic T

17. ELECTRICALLY-SMALL COMPLEMENTARY PAIRS

The inductively loaded monopole was first measured by Walters in 1954 and analysed more recently by Harrison (1963), Hansen (1973 and 1975) and Fujimoto (1968). There appears to be some advantage in positioning the inductor half-way along the monopole rather than at the base as in a tuning circuit (Fournier and Pomerleau, 1978). An efficiency of 50-70% can be obtained for $h \sim 0.1\lambda$ and by choosing the Q of the coil, appropriately, the bandwidth can be increased to about 2% and the radiation resistance from 4 to 23 ohms (Goubau, 1976, p50).

18. INDUCTIVELY LOADED MONOPOLE

A folded version of the above has been suggested by Walters (1955) and gives a wider bandwidth and larger impedance by varying the ratio of the diameters of the two arms.

19. FOLDED VERSION OF (18)

Lamensdorf (1973) has used capacitive tuning for a folded dipole over a band of 573-1270MHz. Diodes were chosen as capacitive components. No efficiency values were given.

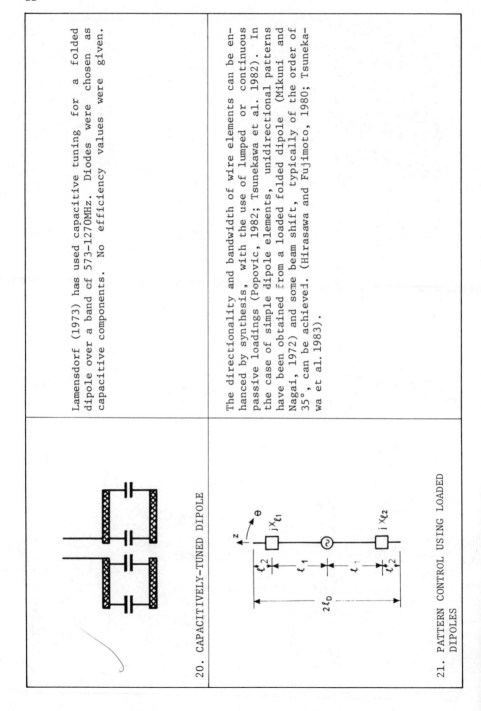

20. CAPACITIVELY-TUNED DIPOLE

The directionality and bandwidth of wire elements can be enhanced by synthesis, with the use of lumped or continuous passive loadings (Popovic, 1982; Tsunekawa et al. 1982). In the case of simple dipole elements, unidirectional patterns have been obtained from a loaded folded dipole (Mikuni and Nagai, 1972) and some beam shift, typically of the order of 35°, can be achieved. (Hirasawa and Fujimoto, 1980; Tsunekawa et al. 1983).

21. PATTERN CONTROL USING LOADED DIPOLES

The helix can be made to resonate at a shorter length than the monopole provided that the total length of wire in the helix is about $\lambda/2$ (Weeks, 1968). The pattern is that of the electric dipole and the radiation resistance is typically that of a monopole of the same height. The impedance can be increased by a shunt feed or by a bifilar winding or by certain loading techniques (Hansen 1961; Ramsdale and Mac-lean, 1971). The efficiency in the VHF region has been analysed by Hiroi and Fujimoto (1976) showing that 80% can be achieved for a length of 0.05λ. Further analysis is given in Section 2.2 of this book.

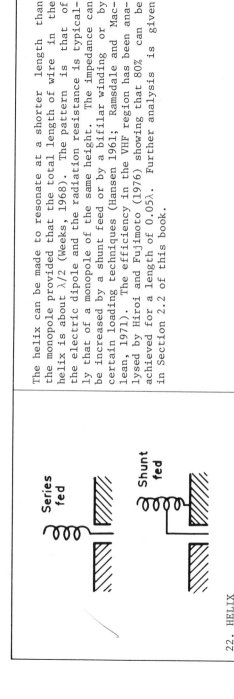

Series
fed

Shunt
fed

22. HELIX

The MTL has a low radiation resistance

$$r_r \sim 320\pi^6 n^2 (b/\lambda)^4$$

and relatively high ohmic losses, giving low efficiency and a high Q. The ohmic losses are affected by the proximity of the loops (Smith, 1972) and limit the radiation efficiency even if n is increased. Matching circuits reduce the efficiency even further. A MTL has been developed for HF ship-board applications, and the pattern was basically that of a horizontal magnetic dipole (Goubau, 1976, p10).

n turns

2b

23. MULTI-TURN LOOP (MTL)

24

It has been shown by Walker and Haden (1969) and Adachi (1976) that an electrically small antenna in a superconducting state can have both a high Q and a high radiation efficiency. Super directionality in antenna arrays has been reported by Walker et al.(1977) and Adachi et al. (1980). One of the applications of the cooling technique is to ELF reception in submarines (Davis et al,1977).

24. SUPER-CONDUCTING ANTENNAS

A small magnetic loop has a very low radiation resistance and efficiency (typically 0.0001% for a 0.001λ diameter coil at 1MHz). Consequently they can be only used for receiving. By cooling the device the signal to noise ratio can be improved by up to 1000x at the expense of reduced bandwidth. Super-cooled loops are now being used with SQUIDS as highly sensitive sideband magnetometers (Goubau 1976) and for ELF reception in submarines (Burrows 1978). The loop is typically 10cm in diameter and is inductively coupled to a 2mm diameter SQUID super-conducting loop.

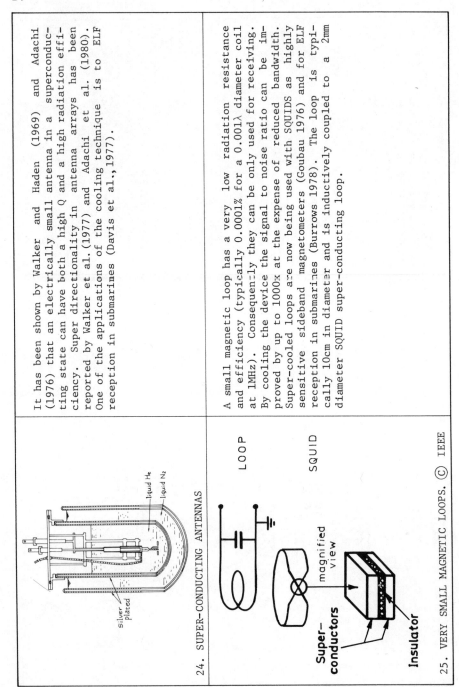

LOOP

SQUID

Super-conductors

magnified view

Insulator

25. VERY SMALL MAGNETIC LOOPS. © IEEE

Small wire loops have been used successfully in VHF and UHF pocket-size receivers by Ito, Haruki and Fujimoto (1973) and Haruki (1974) and further design data is given in Section 2.3. Some gain improvement can be achieved at UHF by loading with ferrite materials (Tsukiji, 1978) and further increase in efficiency can be obtained by coupling with a long wire (Hiroi and Fujimoto, 1978). Such coupling effects can arise in practice from any conductors within the receiver and play a fundamental role in the loop's overall perfor- amnce. The radiation pattern can be varied by loading re- active components onto the loop as shown by Hirasawa (1978).

Loops have also been used in HF mobile applications by Ire- land (1978).

Cavity-backed slots can be reduced in size using dielectric or ferrite materials. The experimental results of Lyon (Goubau, 1976, p205) conform to the general behaviour of material-loaded monopoles, in that a ferrite-loaded slot gives a better impedance match and bandwidth than a dielect- ric-filled slot. Dielectric-filled slots are now being used with microwave thermographs in medical applications (Hindin, 1976).

26. VHF/UHF MAGNETIC LOOPS

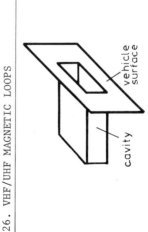

vehicle surface

cavity

27. MATERIAL-LOADED CAVITY-BACKED SLOTS

26

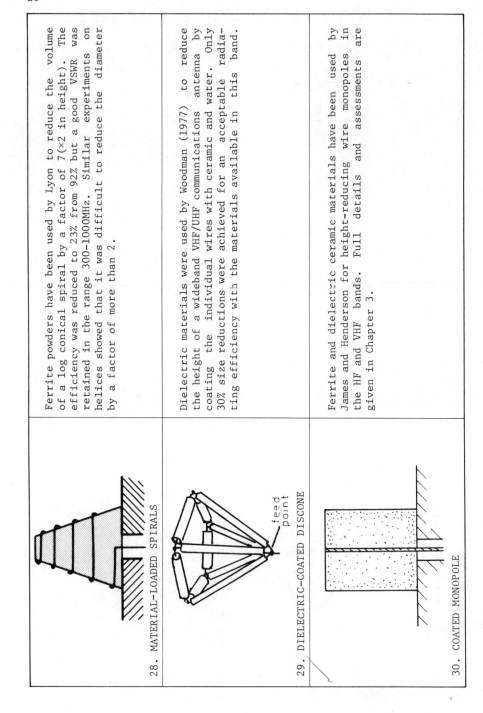

Ferrite powders have been used by Lyon to reduce the volume of a log conical spiral by a factor of 7(×2 in height). The efficiency was reduced to 23% from 92% but a good VSWR was retained in the range 300-1000MHz. Similar experiments on helices showed that it was difficult to reduce the diameter by a factor of more than 2.

28. MATERIAL-LOADED SPIRALS

Dielectric materials were used by Woodman (1977) to reduce the height of a wideband VHF/UHF communications antenna by coating the individual wires with ceramic and water. Only 30% size reductions were achieved for an acceptable radiating efficiency with the materials available in this band.

feed point

29. DIELECTRIC-COATED DISCONE

Ferrite and dielectric ceramic materials have been used by James and Henderson for height-reducing wire monopoles in the HF and VHF bands. Full details and assessments are given in Chapter 3.

30. COATED MONOPOLE

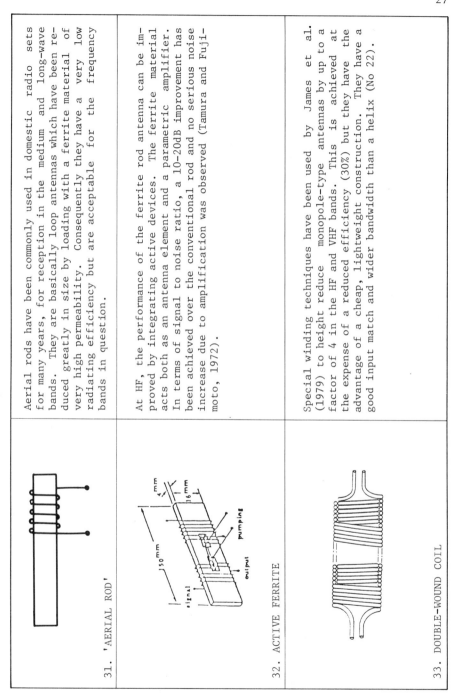

Aerial rods have been commonly used in domestic radio sets for many years, for reception in the medium and long-wave bands. They are basically loop antennas which have been reduced greatly in size by loading with a ferrite material of very high permeability. Consequently they have a very low radiating efficiency but are acceptable for the frequency bands in question.

At HF, the performance of the ferrite rod antenna can be improved by integrating active devices. The ferrite material acts both as an antenna element and a parametric amplifier. In terms of signal to noise ratio, a 10-20dB improvement has been achieved over the conventional rod and no serious noise increase due to amplification was observed (Tamura and Fujimoto, 1972).

Special winding techniques have been used by James et al. (1979) to height reduce monopole-type antennas by up to a factor of 4 in the HF and VHF bands. This is achieved at the expense of a reduced efficiency (30%) but they have the advantage of a cheap, lightweight construction. They have a good input match and wider bandwidth than a helix (No 22).

31. 'AERIAL ROD'

32. ACTIVE FERRITE

33. DOUBLE-WOUND COIL

28

The problems of matching the feed to a short monopole for $h << \lambda$ can be avoided by integrating an active network (N) with the antenna and many forms of these antennas have been developed (Meinke, 1966). Large reductions in height can be achieved at the expense of some degree of non-reciprocal action; optimisation of signal to noise ratio and minimisation of cross-modulation effects are some of the main design issues (Rangole and Saini, 1975; Ramsdale, 1971). Beam control using transistor elements with dipoles and dipole arrays has been discussed in the literature and some successful results reported (Copeland et al., 1964; Hiroi and Fujimoto, 1971, 1972).

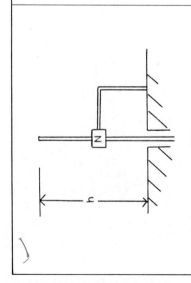

34. ACTIVE MONOPOLE/DIPOLE ANTENNAS

Very short monopoles, with normally very low signal to noise ratios, can achieve a much wider bandwidth of useful operation by employing transistor circuits at the feed. The trade-offs between the antenna height reduction, bandwidth and signal to noise ratio in a receiving system have been studied by Lindenmeier (1976) (a) and (b).

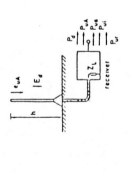

35. NOISE MATCHED SHORT MONOPOLE

29

Experimental superdirective arrays have been designed by Newman and Schrote (1982) achieving reasonable directivity from an electrically small array. Super suppression of sidelobes and increased directivity have been achieved by Anderson et al. (1981) using a microstrip array. In both cases, complex feed networks are required which result in a reduced overall efficiency and susceptance to tolerance errors. A superdirective Yagi was developed by Bacon and Medhurst (1969) by configuring the elements in a novel fashion and avoiding loss of efficiency.

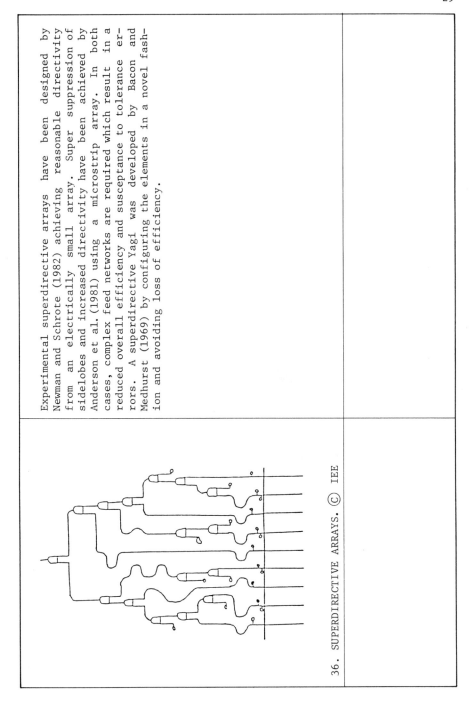

36. SUPERDIRECTIVE ARRAYS. © IEE

30

REFERENCES

Adachi, S. et al. (1976). An experiment on superconducting antennas.
Trans. of IECE Japan, J59-B, 299-300 (in Japanese).

Adachi, S. et al. (1980). Superconducting dipole array antenna.
Trans. of IECE Japan, J63-B, 916-923 (in Japanese).

Anderson, A.P., Dawoud, M.M. and Patel, P.D. (1981). Supersuppression
of side lobes in linear arrays.
Second International IEE Conference on Antennas and Propagation, York,
England, 15-19.

Bacon, J.M. and Medhurst, R.G. (1969). Superdirective aerial array
containing only one fed element.
Proc. IEE, 166, 365-372.

Belrose, J.S. et al. (1959). The engineering of communication systems
for low radio frequencies.
Proc.IRE, 47, 661-680.

Bhojwani, H.R. and Zelby, L.W. (1973). Spiral top-loaded antenna:
Characterisation and design.
IEEE Trans. AP-21, 293-298.

Boyer, J.M. (1963). Hula-hoop antennas. A coming trend?
Electronics, January 11, 44-46.

Burrows, M.L. (1978). ELF communication antennas. IEE Electromagnetic Waves Series 5, Peter Peregrinus Ltd, England.

Burton, R.W. and King, R.W.P. (1963). Theoretical considerations and
experimental results for the Hula-hoop antenna.
Microwave Journal, November, 89-90.

Cafaro, A.D. et al. (1974). Stress-induced noise in magnetic-cored
H-field antennas.
IEEE Trans. COM-22, 543-548.

Chu, L.J. (1948). Physical limitations of omni-directional antennas.
J. Appl. Phys., 19, 1163-1175.

Copeland, J.R. et al. (1964). Antennafier arrays.
IEEE Trans., AP-12, 227-233.

Cumming, W.A. and Cormier, M. (1958). Design data for small annular slot antennas.
IRE Trans., AP-6, 210-212.

Davis, J.R. et al. (1977). Development of a superconducting ELF receiving antenna.
IEEE Trans., AP-25, 223-231.

Egashira, S. and Iwashige, J. (1975). Analysis of Hula-hoop antenna and consideration of its radiation resistance.
IEEE Trans., AP-23, 709-713.

Fenwick, R.C. (1965). A new class of electrically small antennas.
IEEE Trans., AP-13, 379-383.

Fessenden, C.T. and Cheng, D.H.S. (1974). Development of a trailing-wire E-field submarine antenna for ELF reception.
IEEE Trans., COM-22, 428-437.

Fournier, M. and Pomerleau, A. (1978). Experimental study of an inductively loaded short monopole antenna.
IEEE Trans., VT-27, 1-6.

Fujimoto, K. (1968). A loaded antenna system applied to VHF portable communication equipment.
IEEE Trans., VT-17, 6-12.

Fujimoto, K. (1970). A treatment of integrated antenna systems.
IEEE AP-S International Symposium, 120-123.

Galejs, J. (1962). Dielectric loading of electric dipole antennas.
J. of Research, NBS, 66D, 557-562.

Gangi, A.F., Sensiper, S. and Dunn, G.R. (1965). The characteristics of electrically short, umbrella top-loaded antennas.
IEEE Trans., AP-13, 864-871.

Goubau, G. and Schwering, F. (Editors) (1976). Proceedings of the ECOM-ARO Workshop on electrically small antennas, 6-7 May, Fort Monmouth.

Guertler, R.J.F. (1977). Isotropic transmission-line antenna and its toroid-pattern modification.

32

IEEE Trans., AP-25, 386-392.

Hansen, L.H. (1961). A new helical ground-plane antenna for 30 to 50
Mc.
IRE Trans., VC-10, 36-39.

Hansen, R.C. (1973). Efficiency transition point for inductively
loaded monopole.
Electronics Letters, 9, 117-118.

Hansen, R.C. (1975). Optimum inductive loading of short whip antennas.
IEEE Trans., VT-24, 21-29.

Hansen, R.C. (1981). Fundamental limitations in antennas.
Proc IEEE, 69, 170-182.

Harrington, R.F. (1960). Effect of antenna size on gain, bandwidth
and efficiency.
J. Research, NBS, 64D, 1-12.

Harrison Jr, C.W. (1958). Theory of inverted L-antenna with image.
Sandia Corp., Albuquerque, New Mexico, Tech Memo 11-58 (14).

Harrison, C.W. (1963). Monopole with inductive loading.
IEEE Trans. AP-11, 394-400.

Haruki, H. et al. (1974). A small-loop antenna for pocket-size VHF-
UHF radio equipment.
Paper of Technical Group, TGAP 73-29, IECE Japan, 7-12 (in Japanese).

Hindin, H.J. (1976). Microwave probe for cancer cells.
Microwaves, 15, 10-14.

Hirasawa, K. (1978). Design of arbitrarily shaped thin wire antennas
by passive impedance loadings.
Electronics and Communications in Japan, 61-B, 55-63.

Hirasawa, K. and Fujimoto, K. (1980). On electronically-beam-con-
trollable-dipole antenna.
IEEE AP-S International Symposium, 692-695.

Note: IECE: Institute of Electronic and Communication Engineers

Hiroi, Y. and Fujimoto, K. (1970). Active inverted-L antenna.
Paper of Technical Group, TGAP 70-29, IECE Japan, 1-12 (in Japanese).

Hiroi, Y. and Fujimoto, K. (1971). Receiving pattern of a transistor-loaded-active antenna.
International Symposium on Antennas and Propagation, Japan, 69-70.

Hiroi, Y. and Fujimoto, K. (1972). Analysis and design of the electronically-beam-controllable antenna.
IEEE AP-S International Symposium, 241-244.

Hiroi, Y. and Fujimoto, K. (1976). Practical usefulness of normal mode helical antenna.
IEEE AP-S International Symposium, 238-241.

Hiroi, Y. and Fujimoto, K. (1978). Improvement of small loop antenna efficiency by using adjacent dipole element.
International Symposium on Antennas and Propagation, Japan, 117-120.

Ireland, W. (1978). High frequency mobile loop antenna.
Ibid., 69-72.

Ito, H., Haruki, H. and Fujimoto, K. (1973). A small-loop antenna for pocket-size VHF radio equipment.
National Technical Report, 19(2), 145-154. (Published by Matsushita Electric Ind. Co. Osaka, Japan) (in Japanese).

James. W., Drewett, R. and James, J.R. (1979). Experimental investigation of a new type of electrically small VHF antenna.
RMCS Tech. Report RT114, prepared for NRDC, Great Britain.

Jasik, H. (1952). Antenna engineering handbook. McGraw-Hill Book Company, New York.

King, R.W.P. et al.(1960). Transmission-line missile antennas.
IRE Trans. AP-8, 88-90.

King, R.W.P. and Harrison, C.W. Jr. (1949). The inverted L-antenna; current and impedance.
Sandia Crop., Albuquerque, New Mexico, Tech Memo 353-59(4).

Lamensdorf, D. (1973). Capacitively tuned dipole.
Electronics Letters, 9, 445-446.

34

Lindenmeier, H.K. (1976a). Design of electrically small broadband
receiving antennas under consideration of nonlinear distortions in amplifier elements.
IEEE AP-S International Symposium, 242-245.

Lindenmeier, H.K. (1976b). Relation between minimum antenna height
and bandwidth of the signal-to noise ratio in a receiving system.
Ibid., 246-249.

Meinke, H. (1966). Aktive antenna.
NTZ, 19, 697-705.

Mikuni, Y. and Nagai, K. (1972). Unidirectional two conductor antenna.
Trans. of IECE Japan, 55-B, 52-59 (in Japanese).

Newman, E.H., Bohley, P., Walter, C.H. (1975). Two methods for the
measurement of antenna efficiency.
IEEE Trans., AP-23, 457-461.

Newman, E.H. and Schrote, M.R. (1982). A wide-band electrically small
superdirective array.
IEEE Trans., AP-30, 1172-1176.

Pierce, G.W. (1920). Electric oscillations and electric waves. Mc-
Graw-Hill, New York.

Popovic, B.D., Dragovic, M.B. and Djordjevic, A.R. (1982). Analysis
and synthesis of wire antennas. Research Studies Press, England.

Prasad, S. and King, R.W.P. (1961). Experimental study of inverted
L-, T- and related transmission-line antennas.
J. of Research, NBS, 65D, Sept/Oct.

Rahman, F. and Maclean, T.S.M. (1978). Doubly-fed coaxial antennas.
Electronics Latters, 14, 178-179.

Ramsdale, P.A. and Maclean, T.S.M. (1971). Active loop-dipole aerials.
Proc. IEE, 118, 1697-1710.

Ramsdale, P.A., (1971). Active loop-dipole aerials.
Proc. IEE, 8, 1968-1710.

Rangole, P.K. and Saini, S.P.S. (1975). Transistor configuration in integrated transistor antennas.
Radio and Electronic Engineer, 45, 95-104.

Schieffer, G. (1962). A small ferroxcube aerial for VHF reception.
Philips Tech. Rev., 24, 332-336.

Schroeder, K.G. and Soo Hoo, K.M. (1976). Electrically small complementary pair(ESCP) with interelement coupling.
IEEE Trans., AP-24, 411-418.

Seeger, J.A. et al.(1959). Antenna miniaturization.
Electronic Design, 64-69.

Simpson, T.L. (1969). Top-loaded antennas, a theoretical and experimental study.
PhD dissertion, Harvard University, Cambridge, Mass.

Simpson, T.L. (1971). The theory of top-loaded antennas: Integral equations for the currents.
IEEE Trans., AP-19, 186-190.

Smith, G.S. (1972). Radiation efficiency of electrically small multiturn loop antennas.
IEEE Trans., AP-20, 656-657.

Smith, G.S. (1977). Efficiency of electrically small antennas combined with matching networks.
IEEE Trans., AP-25, 369-373.

Tamura, K. and Fujimoto, K. (1972). A parametric- excitation- integrated-ferrite antenna.
IEEE Trans., MAG-8, 384, and IEEE Intermag Conference Digest, 17, 2.

Taylor, Y.T. (1948). A discussion of the maximum directivity of an antenna.
Proc. IRE, 36, 1135.

Tokumaru, S. (1976). Multiplates: Low profile antennas.
IEEE AP-S International Symposium, 379-382.

Tsunekawa, K. et al. (1982). Three dimensionally beam controllable antennas by reactance loading.

Paper of Technical Group, TGAP 82-91, IECE Japan, 123-128 (in Japanese).

Tsunekawa, K. et al. (1983). Sidelobe reduction of linear arrays by reactance loading.
National Convention Record of IECE Japan, 735 (in Japanese).

Tsukiji, T. (1978). Experimental studies on ferrite loaded rectangular loop antenna.
International Symposium on Antennas and Propagation, Japan, 121-124.

Van Suchtelen, H. (1952). Ferroxcube aerial rods.
Electronic Applications Bulletin, 13, 88-100.

Walker, G.B. and Haden, C.R. (1969). Superconducting antenna.
Journal of Applied Physics, 40, 2035-2039.

Walker, G.B. et al. (1977). Superconducting superdirectional antenna arrays.
IEEE Trans., AP-25, 885-887.

Walters, A.W. et al. (1954). Small antenna study.
NOLC Report 184.

Walters, A.W. et al. (1955). Small antenna study.
NOLC Report 304, Annual Report.

Wasylkuisky, W., Kahn, W.K. (1970). Scattering properties and mutual coupling of antennas with prescribed radiation pattern.
IEEE Trans., AP-18, 741-752.

Weeks, W.L. (1968). Antenna engineering. McGraw-Hill Book Co, New York.

Wheeler, H.A. (1947). Fundamental limitations of small antennas.
Proc. IRE, 35, 1479-1484.

Wheeler, H.A. (1959). The radiansphere around a small antenna.
Proc.IRE, 47, 1325-1331.

Wheeler, H.A. (1983). The wideband matching area for a small antenna.
IEEE Trans., AP-31, 364-367.

Woodman, K.F. (1977). Dielectric-clad discone.
Electronics Letters, 13, 264-265.

CHAPTER 2

Wire Antennas

INTRODUCTION

Some of the most important demands for small antennas arise from mobile applications such as on vehicles and on portable equipment. Antennas of small size are essential for such applications, for either mechanical reasons or due to the miniaturization of electronic components in general as in the case of portable radios and pagers.

It is well known that, as the size of an antenna is reduced, the efficiency tends to degrade and the bandwidth becomes narrower. For a size-reduced antenna, matching to the load becomes important to make the antenna practically useful. One of the effective ways to accomplish efficient matching is to attain self-resonance of the antenna. This is because a self-resonant antenna is purely resistive at the frequency of operation and no conjugate circuit between the antenna and the load is necessary. The loss existing in such a circuit could seriously degrade the antenna gain and is best avoided. This self-resonance can sometimes be achieved using the antenna element itself such as with the normal mode helical antenna, or by integrating passive reactive loadings or active devices into the antenna structure. The inclusion of these loadings can also be used to improve the bandwidth of the antenna and to control the radiation pattern.

This chapter deals with four types of small antennas, namely, the normal mode helical antenna (or NMHA), the small loop, the inverted -L antenna (or ILA) and the loaded dipole antenna, all of which have practical applications to portable and vehicular radio equipment.

The NMHA and the rectangular loop antenna are examples of electrically small antennas which are designed for the self-resonance condition, sometimes by using reactive loadings. Acceptable efficiencies can be obtained by this means in the VHF and UHF region where these antennas are now in extensive use commercially, for mobile applications. The small loop is particularly useful in small pager systems where the antenna is usually arranged inside the receiver case. Due to the proximity of the internal circuitry and the receiver box itself, the antenna has to be carefully designed. In practice the pager antenna described here has three notable features in its design. The first one is that the antenna structure is devised to attain a resonance condition so that the use of the lossy circuit element is avoided and the efficiency of the antenna system can be kept sufficiently high for the practical operation. The second one is the generation of the unbalanced mode within the antenna structure and the nearly omnidirectional radiation pattern on the horizontal plane which can be obtained as the combination of the loop radiation and the unbalanced mode radiation patterns. This is very important since the omnidirectional pattern is inevitably needed in mobile communications. The third feature is rather unique in contrast to the usual system design concept when the equipment is operated very near to a human body. Here the human body proximity effect is utilized for increasing the system gain by so arranging the antenna placement inside the equipment that the field produced by the image antenna due to the human body can be added to that produced by the actual antenna in front of the human body, when the equipment is operated in the bearer's pocket. In practice, it has been found that the scattering and loading effects of the circuitry, the box and the closeness of the human operator can be used to advantage, giving a near omni-directional coverage and an increase in the sensitivity of the pager system.

All these design methods are examined here in detail both analytically and practically. The concept introduced here has a wider application to other types of portable equipment.

Inverted -L antennas (ILA) are examples of 'physically constrained' antennas because their heights are very low electrically, typically only 0.01 wavelengths. The ILA is useful on portable equipment due to its low profile but here again the equipment box plays an important role in the system design. Improved signal to noise ratios (S/N) can be achieved by loading active devices into the structure and some degree of electronic beam steering obtained.

In mobile applications, the direction of the incoming signal varies as the equipment is transported about and it is highly desirable that the antenna beam should have the capability of following the incoming direction electronically, rather than mechanically. This is possible to some degree by using two unloaded dipole antennas but more attractively, this can now be achieved in a smaller volume using a single loaded dipole antenna. As such, the dipole antenna when integrated with either passive or active devices can perform a similar function to a larger antenna and is introduced here as an example of a 'functionally small' antenna.

A detailed analysis of all these antenna structures is made in order to derive the important antenna design criteria, such as bandwidth, gain and radiation pattern. Section 2.1 is devoted to deriving an integral equation method for this purpose and this is based initially on finding the currents on an arbitrarily-bent thin conducting antenna. Although integral equations can be solved by the method of moments with subsectional or entire domain functions, the method chosen here is piecewise (subsectional) sinusoidal expansion with weighting functions this being more suitable for the modelling of a conducting body by grid wires as demonstrated in Chapter 4. Near and far field expressions are then obtained using the computed current distributions for arbitrarily-bent wire antennas, which are then applied to the particular antenna types in later sections. The analysis and design of these antennas is described for cases with and without passive or active loadings. Impedance loading is treated in Section 2.1 by using network parameters, and an analytical expression to find the absolute optimum antenna performance with one independent passive impedance load is obtained.

Instead of using the method of moments, some simple alternative treatments are used for finding impedances and radiation patterns of certain antennas such as the ILA, small loop, and active dipole. These treatments apply the theories of circuits, transmission lines, and radiation from wires to an antenna system. This offers the advantage that the physical significance of the functions underlying antenna performance can be understood in the process of analysis, which is seldom the case when only numerical results are obtained by computer. The treatment is given in each section where the antennas concerned are discussed.

In Section 2.2, the NMHA is analysed by slightly modifying the analysis presented in Section 2.1 to take into account the complex helical structure and in Section 2.3, the electrically small rectangular loop antenna is presented. Firstly, the basic design data of the loop element are given and then the conditions for self-resonance and the efficiency are evaluated. Problems arise when the loop element is built into the equipment box and when the box is placed in the operator's pocket - both these situations are extensively treated. By making use of the image effect produced by the human body, which is considered here as a VHF reflector, the sensitivity of the receiver when operated in the pocket was found to be nearly double that in free-space and a nearly omnidirectional pattern on the horizontal plane was obtained - a result that could not be obtained by the loop element alone.

In Section 2.4, the impedances of ILA and inverted-F antenna (IFA) are calculated for various antenna dimensions. The self-resonance condition is easily obtained by arranging the antenna configuration to form an inverted-F. A simplified analysis of the radiation patterns is given, using zeroth-order current approximations. Some modified structures of ILA, including IFA, are introduced. An application of ILA to portable equipment, taking advantage of its low-profile structure, is discussed for a case where the antenna is mounted on the surface of the equipment body. Radiation patterns of the antenna system, in which the equipment body is included as a part of the antenna system, are shown for various sizes of the equipment body. The active ILA loaded with a transistor circuit is also introduced. The objectives of making the ILA active are to achieve (1) electronic beam shifting and (2) replacement of a long wire antenna by a small sized ILA, with undegraded or increased S/N performance in a receiver system. Actually, better S/N performance was observed in a portable receiver system with a very small size active ILA than with a quarter-wavelength monopole antenna. This was achieved by making use of the transistor circuit as an impedance transformer and an amplification device simultaneously within the antenna structure.

In Section 2.5, dipoles integrated with either passive or active devices are shown as examples of functionally small antennas. The purpose of this type of antenna is primarily shaping or control of the receiving pattern by electronic means. The passive component integration is discussed to show the fundamental treatment of this type of antenna and the passive component can be replaced by active devices for achieving variable control of beam direction and shape.

Theoretical treatment of the dipole integrated with either passive or active devices is presented and the performance of the beam shifting achieved is discussed. This type of antenna has a potential application to beam control for following the direction of the incident wave when used for mobile communications.

All of these antennas described in this chapter are discussed primarily from the viewpoint of mobile applications, and the examples presented may appear to be restricted to systems in particularly selected applications. The concept, however, is common to the treatment of small antennas when they are applied to systems other than mobile communications.

2.1 Method of Analysis

Let us consider antennas in regions of permittivity ε and permeability μ which are linear, homogeneous and isotropic. If not indicated otherwise, free space permittivity ε_0 and permeability μ_0 are used throughout the monograph.

To obtain wire antenna characteristics computationally, currents on each wire have to be determined. To do this, the integral equation for the current on a perfectly conducting wire is derived from the boundary condition on the surface of the wire, and is solved by the method of moments (Harrington, 1968). The method for solving Hallen's integral equation in the work of King, Mack and Sandler (1968) is mentioned also. The integral equation thus obtained for a perfectly conducting wire is then modified to treat wire antennas with an imperfect conductor or a load, and the terminal relation between a feed point and a load point is derived. Finally an impedance loading technique to optimize an antenna performance such as input impedance and gain is described.

2.1.1 Matrix Method

It is assumed that the wire radius is very thin compared with the wavelength, and the current on the wire flows only in the direction of the wire axis. Then the electric field $\underline{E}^s$ produced by the current $\underline{J}$ on the wire is expressed in terms of a vector potential $\underline{A}$ as

$$\underline{E}^s = -j\omega\mu\underline{A} + \frac{1}{j\omega\varepsilon} \nabla \ (\nabla \cdot \underline{A}), \tag{2.1.1}$$

where

$$\underline{A}(\underline{r}) = \frac{1}{4\pi} \int_{wire} \underline{J}(\underline{r}') \ \frac{e^{-jk|\underline{r}-\underline{r}'|}}{|\underline{r}-\underline{r}'|} \ dt' \tag{2.1.2}$$

The wave number $k=2\pi/\lambda$ where λ is the operating wavelength. The $\underline{J}(\underline{r}')$ is the unknown current to be determined, and is assumed to be the finite sum of the expansion function $\underline{J}_m(\underline{r}')$ as

$$\underline{J}(\underline{r}') = \sum_{m=1}^{M'} I_m \underline{J}_m(\underline{r}') \tag{2.1.3}$$

Once the unknown coefficient I_m is determined, the parameters of interest such as input impedances and electric fields can be calculated.

The piecewise sinusoidal expansion function first introduced by Richmond and Geary (1970) is used:

$$J_m(\underline{r}') = \begin{cases} \hat{t}_{m-1} \cdot \dfrac{\sin\{k(\Delta t_{m-1}+t(r')-t_i)\}}{\sin(k\Delta t_{m-1})} & \\[2em] \hspace{3em} (t_{i-1} \le t \le t_i) & \\[1em] \hat{t}_m \cdot \dfrac{\sin\{k(\Delta t_m-t(\underline{r}')+t_i)\}}{\sin(k\Delta t_m)} & \\[2em] \hspace{3em} (t_i \le t \le t_{i+1}) & \\[1em] 0 & \text{elsewhere,} \end{cases} \qquad (2.1.4)$$

where as shown in Fig.2.1.1, Δt_{m-1} and Δt_m are the lengths of the sub-sections from t_{i-1} to t_i and from t_i to t_{i+1}, respectively. $\hat{t}_{m-1}$ and $\hat{t}_m$ are the unit vectors of the corresponding subsections.

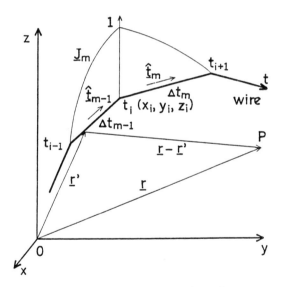

Fig.2.1.1.　Current on a wire element.

By designating the known electric field at the feed point as $\underline{E}^f$, the boundary condition on the surface of the wire is written by

$$\hat{\underline{n}} \times [\underline{E}^s(\underline{r}) + \underline{E}^f(\underline{r})] = 0, \qquad (2.1.5)$$

where $\hat{\underline{n}}$ is the unit normal to the surface of the wire. This is Pocklington's integral equation with respect to $\underline{J}(\underline{r})$.

The numerical solution of eqn.(2.1.5) is obtained by the method of moments where the weighting function is chosen to be the same as the expansion function in eqn.(2.1.4). Then the unknown quantity I_m is written as

$$[I] = [Y][V], \quad [Y] = [Z]^{-1}, \qquad (2.1.6)$$

where [V], a voltage matrix, is a column vector and all the elements are zero except the ones corresponding to the feed point voltages. [Z] is an M' x M' impedance matrix and the evaluation of the elements is done by the method given in Harrington (1968).

The electric field $\underline{E}(P)$ at an arbitrary point P outside the wire element due to the induced current $\underline{J}(\underline{r}')$ is obtained by a procedure similar to Jordan and Balmain (1968).

$$\underline{E}(P) = \sum_{m=1}^{M'} (\hat{\underline{n}}_{m-1} E'_{m-1} + \hat{\underline{t}}_{m-1} E''_{m-1} + \hat{\underline{n}}_m E'_m + \hat{\underline{t}}_m E''_m), \qquad (2.1.7)$$

where $\hat{\underline{n}}_{m-1}$ is the unit vector in the plane of the three points t_{i-1}, t_i and P, and normal to $\hat{\underline{t}}_{m-1}$. Also, $\hat{\underline{n}}_m$ is defined similarly. E'_{m-1} E'_m, E''_{m-1} and E''_m are

$$E'_{m-1} = \frac{-30I_m}{r_i \sin\theta_i^{m-1}} \left[\{1 + j \cos\theta_i^{m-1} \cot(k\Delta t_{m-1})\} e^{-jkr_{i-1}} - j \frac{\cos\theta_{i-1}^{m-1} e^{-jkr_{i-1}}}{\sin(k\Delta t_{m-1})} \right]$$

$$E'_m = \frac{30I_m}{r_i \sin\theta_i^m} \left[\{1 - j \cos\theta_i^m \cot(k\Delta t_m)\} e^{-jkr_{i+1}} + j \frac{\cos\theta_{i+1}^m e^{-jkr_{i+1}}}{\sin(k\Delta t_m)} \right]$$

$$E''_{m-1} = \frac{j30I_m}{\sin(k\Delta t_{m-1})} \left[\frac{\cos(k\Delta t_{m-1})}{r_i} e^{-jkr_i} - \frac{e^{-jkr_{i-1}}}{r_{i-1}} \right] \qquad (2.1.8)$$

$$E''_m = \frac{j30I_m}{\sin(k\Delta t_m)} \left[\frac{\cos(k\Delta t_m)}{r_i} e^{-jkr_i} - \frac{e^{-jkr_{i+1}}}{r_{i+1}} \right]$$

where θ_{i-1}^{m-1} is the angle between $\hat{\underline{t}}_{m-1}$ and $\underline{r}_{i-1}$, and θ_i^{m-1}, θ_i^m and θ_{i+1}^m are defined similarly (Fig.2.1.2).

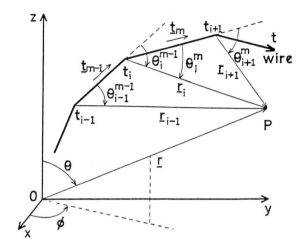

Fig.2.1.2   Wire element coordinates.

Equation (2.1.8) becomes simpler for the far field point $P(r,\theta,\phi)$ as

$$E'_{m-1} = \frac{-30I_m e^{-jkr}}{rsin\theta_i^{m-1}} \left[\{(1+jcos\theta_i^{m-1}cot(k\Delta t_{m-1}))\}e^{jk\alpha_i} - j\frac{cos\theta_i^{m-1}e^{jk\alpha_{i-1}}}{sin(k\Delta t_{m-1})}\right]$$

$$E'_m = \frac{30I_m e^{-jkr}}{rsin\theta_i^m} \left[\{1-jcos\theta_i^m cot(k\Delta t_m)\}e^{jk\alpha_i} + j\frac{cos\theta_i^m e^{jk\alpha_{i+1}}}{sin(k\Delta t_m)}\right]$$

$$E''_{m-1} = \frac{j30I_m e^{-jkr}}{rsin(k\Delta t_{m-1})} \left[cos(k\Delta t_{m-1})e^{jk\alpha_i} - e^{jk\alpha_{i-1}}\right]$$

$$E''_m = \frac{j30I_m e^{-jkr}}{rsin(k\Delta t_m)}[cos(k\Delta t_m)e^{jk\alpha_i} - e^{jk\alpha_{i+1}}] \qquad (2.1.9)$$

where α_i becomes

$$\alpha_i = (x_i cos\phi + y_i sin\phi)\ sin\theta + z_i cos\theta \qquad (2.1.10)$$

with $t_i(x_i,\ y_i,\ z_i)$. α_{i-1} and α_{i+1} are obtained similarly. For the far field point P, $\theta_{i-1}^{m-1} = \theta_i^{m-1}$ and $\theta_{i+1}^m = \theta_i^m$. Then we get

$$\cos\theta_i^{m-1} = (\alpha_i - \alpha_{i-1}) \,/\, \Delta t_{m-1,} \tag{2.1.11}$$

where $\cos\theta_i^m$ is obtained similarly, and from these values $\sin\theta_i^{m-1}$ and $\sin\theta_i^m$ are calculated easily.

Where there are N' straight wire antennas which are all less than $\frac{5}{4}\lambda$ in length and center-fed, the current can also be obtained from the solution of Hallen's integral equation by King, Mack, and Sandler (1968). In their work three expansion functions on each wire are assumed as

$$\underline{J}(\underline{r}') = \sum_{m=1}^{N'}\sum_{p=1}^{3} I_{mp} J_{mp}(\underline{r}') \,\hat{\underline{t}}_m, \tag{2.1.12}$$

where (see Fig.2.1.1)

$$\left.\begin{aligned} J_{m1}(\underline{r}') &= \sin\{k(\Delta t_m - |t(\underline{r}') - t_i|)\} \\[4pt] J_{m2}(\underline{r}') &= \cos\{k(t(\underline{r}') - t_i)\} - \cos(k\Delta t_m) \\[4pt] J_{m3}(\underline{r}') &= \cos\{\tfrac{1}{2}k(t(\underline{r}') - t_i)\} - \cos(\tfrac{1}{2}k\Delta t_m) \end{aligned}\right\} \tag{2.1.13}$$

The antenna is fed at the ith point, and the i-1 and i+1 points correspond to the ends of the antenna. Also it is assumed that $\Delta t_{m-1} = \Delta t_m$. The unknown coefficients I_{mp} are found from the solution of the N' simultaneous integral equations. The details of the method are shown in King, Mack, and Sandler (1968).

2.1.2 General Theory of Loading

When the wire surface is not a perfect conductor, or an impedance is loaded on the wire, the tangential electric field is related to the current $\underline{J}(\underline{r})$ as

$$\hat{\underline{n}} \times [\underline{E}^s(\underline{r}) + \underline{E}^f(\underline{r})] = Z^i(\underline{r}) \, \underline{J}(\underline{r}) \tag{2.1.14}$$

where $Z^i(\underline{r})$ is the internal impedance of the conductor per unit length.

Reducing eqn.(2.1.14) to a matrix equation by the method of moments yields

$$[I] = [Y][V'], \quad [Y] = [Z]^{-1}. \tag{2.1.15}$$

which is similar to eqn.(2.1.6). The quantity from the right-hand side of eqn.(2.1.14) is included in a voltage matrix $[V']$ where the voltage (or the current) at the load is unknown.

Accordingly the elements of $[V']$ are zero except at the feed point or the load point, and we get the relation between the feed and load terminals from eqn.(2.1.15) as

$$\begin{bmatrix} [i_1] \\ [i_2] \end{bmatrix} = \begin{bmatrix} [y_{11}][y_{12}] \\ [y_{21}][y_{22}] \end{bmatrix} \begin{bmatrix} [v_1] \\ [v_2] \end{bmatrix}, \tag{2.1.16}$$

where the subscripts 1 and 2 stand for the feed and load terminals, respectively.

In terms of the impedance parameters, eqn.(2.1.16) is rewritten as

$$\begin{bmatrix} [v_1] \\ [v_2] \end{bmatrix} = \begin{bmatrix} [z_{11}][z_{12}] \\ [z_{21}][z_{22}] \end{bmatrix} \begin{bmatrix} [i_1] \\ [i_2] \end{bmatrix}, \tag{2.1.17}$$

where

$$\begin{bmatrix} [z_{11}][z_{12}] \\ [z_{21}][z_{22}] \end{bmatrix} = \begin{bmatrix} [y_{11}][y_{12}] \\ [y_{21}][y_{22}] \end{bmatrix}^{-1}. \tag{2.1.18}$$

Denoting the load impedance matrix by $[Z_\ell]$, we have

$$[v_2] = -[Z_\ell][i_2], \tag{2.1.19}$$

where $[Z_\ell]$ is the diagonal matrix.

Then the current coefficient $[i_2]$ can be expressed by the current $[i_1]$ from eqns.(2.1.17) and (2.1.19) as

$$[i_2] = -[Z_\ell + z_{22}]^{-1}[z_{21}][i_1]. \tag{2.1.20}$$

We shall use eqns.(2.1.17) and (2.1.20) to calculate the antenna performance in the next section.

From eqns.(2.1.7), (2.1.9) and (2.1.15) the θ and ϕ components of the radiation field can be given as

$$E_q = [\Phi_q][Y][V'] \tag{2.1.21}$$
$$= [B_q][v_t], \tag{2.1.22}$$

where

$$[\tilde{v}_t] = [[\tilde{v}_1][\tilde{v}_2]].$$
(2.1.23)

Here ~ denotes the transpose of a matrix, and the subscript q stands for the θ or the ϕ component. The element of the row matrix $[\Phi_q]$ is from eqn. (2.1.7)

$$\Phi_{qm} = \frac{1}{I_m}\hat{\underline{u}}_q \cdot (\hat{\underline{n}}_{m-1}E'_{m-1} + \hat{\underline{t}}_{m-1}E''_{m-1} + \hat{\underline{n}}_m E'_m + \hat{\underline{t}}_m E''_m).$$
(2.1.24)

The unit vector $\hat{\underline{u}}_q$ is either θ or ϕ directed. The matrix $[B_q]$ is obtained from the elements of the row matrix $[\Phi_q][Y]$ corresponding to the feed and load voltages.

2.1.3 Optimum Loading

One of the most simple and powerful techniques to improve small antenna performance is impedance loading which has been extensively studied by Harrison (1963), Hansen (1975), etc. As a design problem, the question arises as to where the loading should be placed, and what values of impedance should be used in order to achieve the desired antenna performance index. The latter question can be solved analytically for one load whose position is fixed. This is done for a straight wire antenna by Fujimoto (1968), Lin et al (1970), Strait and Hirasawa (1970), for a circular antenna by Kagoshima and Sekiguchi (1973), and for various antennas by Hirasawa (1978 a, b, 1979). The former question can be solved by repeatedly changing the position and finding the impedance value.

If it is desired to improve the antenna performance by multiple loadings, the method by Hirasawa (1980) could be used. This is an extension of the work by Hirasawa (1978 b) and may be a faster-convergent and more reliable technique compared with the general non-linear optimization methods used by Hirasawa and Strait (1971), Popovic (1982) and Harrington (1978).

The analytical method (Hirasawa, 1978 b) to optimize an arbitrarily shaped wire antenna performance index by using one impedance load is given in this section, and the application of the method to some examples is also shown. Alternative procedures involve time-consuming optimization methods with two variables (sometimes with a constraint), and the convergence is not always guaranteed.

(1) Optimization of a Function of Two Variables with a Constraint

Before we proceed to optimize an antenna performance by impedance loading, consider an optimization problem to find the minimum of the following function f with variables R_ℓ and X_ℓ with a constraint $R_\ell \geq R_c \geq 0$.

$$f = K_f \frac{(R_\ell + a_1)^2 + (X_\ell + c_1)^2 + d_1}{(R_\ell + a_2)^2 + (X_\ell + c_2)^2} \tag{2.1.25}$$

where K_f is a positive constant, and a_1, a_2, c_1, c_2 and d_1 are real. It is assumed that f is not negative with the constraint on R_ℓ. Since reflection coefficient, radiation field ratio and the inverse of power gain considered later in 2.1.3.(3) to (5) will be expressed as the form of eqn.(2.1.25) with respect to a loading impedance $(R_\ell + jX_\ell)$ (the details are shown in the corresponding section), it is useful to find the minimum f with the constraint $R_\ell \geq R_c \geq 0$.

Let f_m, R_m, and X_m stand for the minimum f and the corresponding R_ℓ and X_ℓ. To find R_m and X_m, eqn.(2.1.25) is rewritten as

$$f = K_f \frac{(R_f + e_1)^2 + (X_f + e_2)^2 + d_1}{R_f^2 + X_f^2} \ , \tag{2.1.26}$$

where

$$R_f = R_\ell + a_2, \quad X_f = X_\ell + c_2 \ ,$$

$$e_1 = a_1 - a_2 \text{ and } e_2 = c_1 - c_2 \ . \tag{2.1.27}$$

Since there is no constraint on X_ℓ, X_m can be found from the solution of $\partial f/\partial X_\ell = 0$. Then substituting X_m into eqn.(2.1.26) we get f with respect to R_ℓ only, and R_ℓ for f_m can be found from the solution of $df/dR_\ell = 0$ with the constraint on R_ℓ.

When $e_2 \neq 0$, X_m becomes

$$X_m = - \frac{D_f + \sqrt{D_f^2 + 4e_2^2(R_m+a_2)^2}}{2e_2} - c_2 \quad,$$ (2.1.28)

where

$$D_f = e_1^2 + e_1^2 + 2e_1(R_m+a_2) + d_1 \quad.$$ (2.1.29)

When $d_1 \geq 0$, f is always non-negative with any R_ℓ. Therefore we have

$$R_m = \left\{ \begin{array}{ll} R_0 & \text{for} \quad R_0 > R_c \\ R_c & \text{for} \quad R_0 \leq R_c \end{array} \right. ,$$ (2.1.30)

where

$$R_0 = -e_1 \left(1 + \frac{d_1}{e_1^2 + e_2^2}\right) - a_2 \quad.$$ (2.1.31)

When $d_1 < 0$, $f(R_\ell, X_m)$ varies as shown in Fig.2.1.3. For $e_1^2 + e_2^2 + d_1 \leq 0$, f reaches minus-infinity at $R_\ell = R_0$, and for $e_1^2 + e_2^2 + d_1 > 0$, f becomes minimum at $R_\ell = R_0$. Since f is non-negative with $R_\ell \geq R_c \geq 0$, we get

$$R_m = R_c .$$ (2.1.32)

Once we get R_m and X_m, f_m can be easily obtained by substituting them into eqn.(2.1.26).

So far it is assumed that R_ℓ and X_ℓ can be changed independently, but it is sometimes desired to find the optimum f when R_ℓ and X_ℓ are related as

$$R_\ell = \frac{|X_\ell|}{Q} \quad,$$ (2.1.33)

where Q is the positive constant. When eqn.(2.1.33) holds, eqn.(2.1.25) becomes

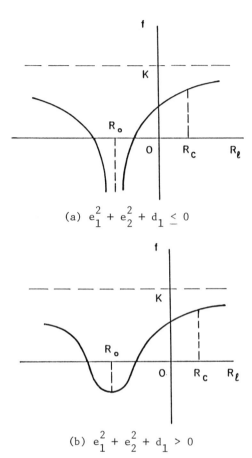

(a) $e_1^2 + e_2^2 + d_1 \leq 0$

(b) $e_1^2 + e_2^2 + d_1 > 0$

Fig.2.1.3. $f-R_\ell$ characteristics.

$$f = \frac{X_\ell^2 + aX_\ell + b}{X_\ell^2 + cX_\ell + e} ,$$ (2.1.34)

where

$$a = 2(c_1 \pm \frac{a_1}{Q})(\frac{Q^2}{1 + Q^2}), \quad b = (d_1 + a_1^2 + c_1^2)(\frac{Q^2}{1 + Q^2}),$$

$$c = 2(c_2 \pm \frac{a_2}{Q})(\frac{Q^2}{1 + Q^2}) \text{ and } e = (a_2^2 + c_2^2)(\frac{Q^2}{1 + Q^2}).$$ (2.1.35)

The sign $\pm$ becomes $+$ when $X_\ell \geq 0$, and $-$ when $X_\ell < 0$.

The value X_m for f_m is obtained from the solution of $df/dX_\ell = 0$. For $a \neq c$

$$X_m = \frac{e - b - \sqrt{(e-b)^2 - (a-c)(cb-ae)}}{a - c} \qquad (2.1.36)$$

Then the value R_m is obtained from eqn.(2.1.33). Note that the assumed sign $+$ or $-$ of $\pm$ in eqn.(2.1.35) must correspond to $X_m > 0$ or $X_m < 0$, respectively. Otherwise $X_m = 0$.

(2) Optimization of Input Impedance

Using eqns.(2.1.17) and (2.1.20), we get the input impedance Z_i ($= R_i + jX_i$) as

$$Z_i = \frac{v_1}{i_1} = z_{11} - \frac{z_{12}z_{21}}{z_{22} + Z_\ell} \quad , \qquad (2.1.37)$$

where Z_ℓ ($= R_\ell + jX_\ell$) is a loading impedance. Let the real number Z_0 denote the characteristic impedance of the feeder. The feeder impedance matches that of the antenna if

$$R_i = Z_0, \text{ and } X_i = 0. \qquad (2.1.38)$$

The matching condition eqn.(2.1.38) can hardly be satisfied with one passive load. Since the feeder is easily matched to the antenna if $X_i = 0$, we determine X_ℓ to satisfy this requirement instead of the two conditions of eqn.(2.1.38). Setting

$$\begin{aligned} z_{11}z_{22} - z_{12}z_{21} &= a_3 + jb_3 \\ z_{11} = a_4 + jb_4, \; z_{22} &= a_5 + jb_5 \end{aligned} \Biggr\} \qquad (2.1.39)$$

in eqn.(2.1.37), we get the requirement for $X_i = 0$ when $b_4 \neq 0$, that

$$(R_\ell - \frac{a_4 b_5 - a_5 b_4 - b_3}{2b_4})^2 + (X_\ell - \frac{a_3 - a_4 a_5 - b_4 b_5}{2b_4})^2$$

$$= \frac{(a_4 b_5 + a_5 b_4 - b_3)^2 + (a_3 - a_4 a_5 + b_4 b_5)^2}{4(b_4)^2} \qquad (2.1.40)$$

Therefore, Z_ℓ stays on a circle given by eqn.(2.1.40). If the circle stays in the region $R_\ell < 0$, an active load must be used to achieve X_i = 0. If the circle touches or intersects the X_ℓ axis, X_i = 0 can be satisfied with R_ℓ = 0.

If the loading is lossy, the efficiency η has to be considered, and is given as

$$\eta = 1 - \frac{R_\ell |i_2|^2}{R_i |i_1|^2} \qquad (2.1.41)$$

which can be calculated easily once we know R_ℓ and X_ℓ.

When R_ℓ and X_ℓ are related by eqn.(2.1.33), R_ℓ in eqn.(2.1.40) is replaced by eqn.(2.1.33), and X_ℓ for X_i = 0 is obtained from the solution of the quadratic equation.

As an example, consider a loaded monopole antenna over an infinite perfectly conducting ground plane as shown in Fig.2.1.4. Ten piecewise sinusoidal expansion functions in eqn.(2.1.4) with the same weighting functions are used to analyze this problem by the method of moments. The circles in Fig.2.1.4 show the load impedance which makes the input impedance real for different load positions. In this problem a passive impedance could be used to achieve X_i = 0. Fig.2.1.4 is a useful chart for finding a practical loading impedance value and its position for X_i = 0.

(3) Minimization of VSWR

The VSWR ρ at the feed point is given in terms of the reflection coefficient $|\Gamma|$ as

$$\rho = \frac{1 + |\Gamma|}{1 - |\Gamma|} \ , \qquad (2.1.42)$$

where from eqn.(2.1.37) with $Z_\ell = R_\ell + jX_\ell$

$$|\Gamma|^2 = \left| \frac{Z_i - Z_0}{Z_i + Z_0} \right|^2$$

$$= \left| \frac{z_{11} - Z_0}{z_{11} + Z_0} \right|^2 \cdot \frac{(R_\ell + a_1)^2 + (X_\ell + c_1)^2}{(R_\ell + a_2)^2 + (X_\ell + c_2)^2} \ . \qquad (2.1.43)$$

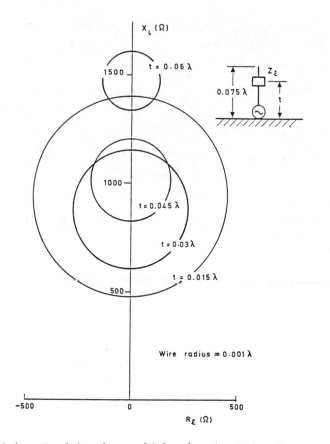

Fig.2.1.4.   Load impedance which makes input impedance real.

Here $z_{11} \neq Z_0$ is assumed, and

$$a_1 + jc_1 = \frac{z_{11}z_{22} - z_{12}z_{21} + z_{22}Z_0}{z_{11} + Z_0} \quad ,$$

$$a_2 + jc_2 = \frac{z_{11}z_{22} - z_{12}z_{21} - z_{22}Z_0}{z_{11} - Z_0} \quad .$$

(2.1.44)

When we have

$$R_\ell = -a_1, \text{ and } X_\ell = -c_1,$$

(2.1.45)

$|\Gamma|$ becomes zero, and the VSWR ρ becomes unity. When $-a_1 \geq 0$, R_ℓ becomes passive.

When a passive load is desired and $-a_1 < 0$, equation (2.1.45) for R_ℓ and X_ℓ cannot be satisfied, and ρ is always larger than 1. Then the minimum VSWR ρ_{min} is achieved with $R_\ell = 0$, and X_ℓ for ρ_{min} is the same as the one for the minimum $|\Gamma|^2$. This is because

$$\frac{d\rho}{dX_\ell} = \frac{1}{|\Gamma|(1-|\Gamma|)^2} \frac{d|\Gamma|^2}{dX_\ell} \qquad (2.1.46)$$

and whenever $\dfrac{d|\Gamma|^2}{dX_\ell}$ is zero, $\dfrac{d\rho}{dX_\ell}$ becomes zero. Note that we only con-sider the range $1 < \rho < \infty$ (i.e. $|\Gamma| \neq 1$).

The load impedance Z_m for the minimum $|\Gamma|^2$ (i.e. ρ_{min}) can be ob-tained from eqns.(2.1.28) and (2.1.30), or eqns.(2.1.33) and (2.1.36) with $d_1 = 0$.

As an example, consider again a loaded short monopole antenna over an infinite perfectly conducting ground plane as shown in Fig.2.1.5. Ten piecewise sinusoidal expansion and weighting functions are used to analyze this problem by the method of moments. The minimum VSWR and the efficiency are plotted in Fig.2.1.5 for different load positions and quality factors Q. In this problem the minimum VSWR becomes unity when there is no constraint on quality factors, and the efficiency for $\rho = 1$ is plotted for different load positions.

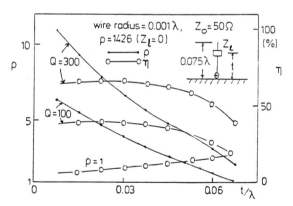

Fig.2.1.5.   Minimum VSWR and efficiency.

(4) Minimization of Radiation Field Ratio

The ratio FR of the radiation field components E_1 and E_2 in the two directions (θ, ϕ) and (θ', ϕ') is defined as

$$FR = \left| \frac{E_1(\theta', \phi')}{E_2(\theta, \phi)} \right|^2 . \tag{2.1.47}$$

In eqn.(2.1.22) we put

$$
\begin{aligned}
[B(\theta, \phi)] &= [b_1 \ b_2] \\
[B(\theta', \phi')] &= [b_1' \ b_2']
\end{aligned}
\tag{2.1.48}
$$

where the subscript θ or ϕ of $[B]$ is dropped, since $[B]$ may be for the θ or the ϕ component. From eqns.(2.1.17), (2.1.20), and (2.1.22) with $Z_\ell = R_\ell + jX_\ell$ we find

$$FR = \left| \frac{b_1' z_{11} + b_2' z_{21}}{b_1 z_{11} + b_2 z_{21}} \right|^2 \cdot \frac{(R_\ell + a_1)^2 + (X_\ell + c_1)^2}{(R_\ell + a_2)^2 + (X_\ell + c_2)^2} , \tag{2.1.49}$$

where

$$
a_1 + jc_1 = \frac{b_1'(z_{11} z_{22} - z_{12} z_{21})}{b_1' z_{11} + b_2' z_{21}} ,
$$

and

$$
a_2 + jc_2 = \frac{b_1(z_{11} z_{22} - z_{12} z_{21})}{b_1 z_{11} + b_2 z_{21}} .
$$

\tag{2.1.50}

Here $b_1' z_{11} + b_2' z_{21} \neq 0$ and $b_1 z_{11} + b_2 z_{21} \neq 0$ are assumed. In this case the load impedance Z_m for the minimum FR can be obtained from eqns.(2.1.28) and (2.1.30), or eqns.(2.1.33) and (2.1.36) with $d_1 = 0$.

As an example, consider a monopole antenna with a loaded wire 0.15 λ apart over an infinite perfectly conducting ground plane as shown in Fig.2.1.6. Twenty piecewise sinusoidal expansion and weighting func- tions are used to analyze this problem by the method of moments. The minimum radiation field ratio and the efficiency are plotted in Fig.2. 1.6 for different load positions and quality factors. Note that the matrix $[Y]$ in eqn.(2.1.15) is calculated only once and is repeatedly used to calculate the field ratio and the efficiency for different load positions and quality factors. This procedure is very important

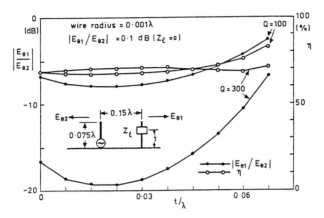

Fig.2.1.6.   Minimum field ratio and efficiency.

for saving computation time when the size of the matrix [Y] in eqn.(2.
1.15) is very large.

(5) Maximization of Power Gain

The power gain in the (θ, ϕ) direction is given by

$$G_p = 4\pi r^2 \frac{|E(\theta, \phi)|^2}{120\pi P_i} , \tag{2.1.51}$$

where P_i is the input power and r is the distance to the radiation
field from the origin. Although only one component of the radiation
field is considered here, two components can be treated similarly.

From eqn.(2.1.37) we get

$$P_i = \text{Re}(v_1 i_1^*)$$

$$= \text{Re}\left(z_{11} - \frac{z_{12}z_{21}}{z_{22} + Z_\ell}\right)|i_1|^2 , \tag{2.1.52}$$

where Re and * denote the real part and complex conjugate, respectively. Using eqns.(2.1.17), (2.1.20), and (2.1.22), we get

$$|E(\theta, \phi)|^2 = \left|\frac{b_1(z_{11}z_{22}-z_{12}z_{21}) + (b_1 z_{11}+b_2 z_{21})Z_\ell}{z_{22} + Z_\ell}\right| \cdot |i_1|^2 . \tag{2.1.53}$$

Then from eqn.(2.1.52) and (2.1.53) with $Z_\ell = R_\ell + jX_\ell$ the power gain

58

becomes, for $b_1 z_{11} + b_2 z_{21} \neq 0$,

$$G_p = \frac{r^2 \cdot |b_1 z_{11} + b_2 z_{21}|^2}{15(z_{11} + z_{11}{}^*)} \cdot \frac{(R_\ell + a_2)^2 + (X_\ell + c_2)^2}{(R_\ell + a_1)^2 + (X_\ell + c_1)^2 + d_1} , \qquad (2.1.54)$$

where

$$a_1 + jc_1 = z_{22} - \frac{z_{12} z_{21}}{z_{11} + z_{11}{}^*} ,$$

$$a_2 + jc_2 = \frac{b_1(z_{11} z_{22} - z_{12} z_{21})}{b_1 z_{11} + b_2 z_{21}} , \qquad (2.1.55)$$

and

$$d_1 = |z_{22}|^2 - \frac{z_{12} z_{21} z_{22}{}^* + z_{12}{}^* z_{21}{}^* z_{22}}{z_{11} + z_{11}{}^*} - a_1{}^2 - c_1{}^2 .$$

In eqn.(2.1.55) it can be shown easily that d_1 is negative whenever $z_{12} z_{21} \neq 0$. Therefore the denominator of eqn.(2.1.54) may become negative if $R_\ell < 0$.

Noting that d_1 is negative, the loading passive impedance Z_m required to minimize $1/G_p$ is obtained from eqns.(2.1.28) and (2.1.32) or from eqns.(2.1.33) and (2.1.36).

As an example, consider a monopole antenna with a loaded wire 0.15 λ apart over an infinite perfectly conducting ground plane as shown in Fig.2.1.7. Twenty piecewise sinusoidal expansion functions with the

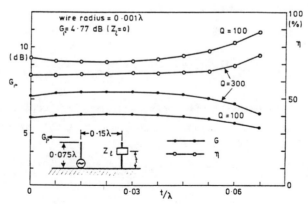

Fig.2.1.7.   Maximum gain and efficiency.

same weighting functions are used to analyze this problem by the method of moments. The maximum absolute power gain and the efficiency are plotted in Fig.2.1.7 for different load positions and quality factors.

2.2 Normal Mode Helical Antennas

A normal mode helical antenna (NMHA) is an antenna which radiates in the direction normal to the helical axis and the radiation pattern of the short NMHA is essentially the same as that of a short dipole (Kraus, 1950). The dimensions of the helix are much smaller than a wavelength, the length of an individual turn being a small fraction of a wavelength and the axial length being much less than a quarter wavelength. The inductive impedance is increased by these turns and as a result, self-resonance can be easily obtained even when the antenna length (in the axial direction) is considerably shorter than that of a conventional resonant-monopole or dipole antenna.

By utilizing the self-resonance property of the helical structure, the efficiency of an antenna system may be made higher than that of a non-helical antenna of the same dimensions. For this reason the NMHA is especially attractive for mobile communications and a monopole or a dipole, usually used for portable equipment, can be replaced by a NMHA which is shorter than the monopole or the dipole, yet has a higher efficiency. In addition, the mechanical structure of the NMHA may be made more flexible and less easily breakable than a conventional thin-wire antenna element, since the helical winding of the conducting wire has a spring-like structure which flexes and is fairly resistive to the hard shocks often encountered in field use.

In this chapter, particular emphasis is paid to the analysis and design problems of the NMHA. One of the latest design developments is the application of integration techniques to the NMHA. The integration technique, essentially the loading of one or more reactance components at intermediate positions on the helical winding, is demonstrated to be useful for either efficiency improvement or bandwidth increase. The bandwidth of the NMHA is usually not very wide, but the integration technique can be applied to an NMHA to overcome this disadvantage.

The first part of this section is a general treatment of the NMHA, and the reactance-component-integrated NMHA is discussed later in section 2.2.3.

2.2.1 NMHA Analysis

The analysis of an NMHA can be done by the method of moments described in section 2.1. The expansion function to be used in this section is that introduced by Inagaki (1971). The schematic structure of an NMHA is shown in Fig.2.2.1, with the coordinate system and antenna parameters such as helix diameter D_h, radius of wire a, pitch of helical winding p, helix one-turn length $\ell_0 = \sqrt{(\pi D_h)^2 + p^2}$, and segment number m. A segment consists of two whole turns of helical structure taken at an arbitrary place on the antenna, shown as the section enclosed by the dotted box in Fig.2.2.1. The dimensions of one segment are shown in Fig.2.2.2.

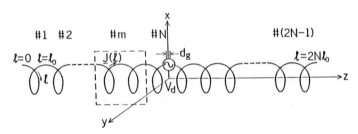

V_d : driving point voltage
$J(\ell)$: current flowing on wire at the point ℓ $(= J(\ell) \; \underline{\hat{a}}(\ell))$
$\underline{\hat{a}}(\ell)$: unit vector at ℓ in the direction of wire axis
d_g : gap distance at the driving point
m   : number of segment

Fig.2.2.1. NMHA and the coordinate system.

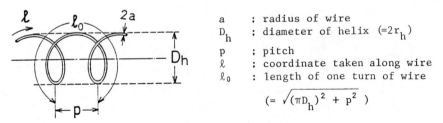

a   : radius of wire
D_h : diameter of helix $(= 2r_h)$

p   : pitch
ℓ : coordinate taken along wire
ℓ_0 : length of one turn of wire

$$(= \sqrt{(\pi D_h)^2 + p^2}\,)$$

Fig.2.2.2. One segment and its dimensions.

The integral equation with respect to the current distribution $\underline{J}(\ell)$ is expressed by

$$[\underline{E}^S(\ell)]_\ell = -\frac{V_d}{d_g} \Pi(\frac{\ell - N\ell_0}{d_g}), \tag{2.2.1}$$

where $\underline{E}^S(\ell)$ is a function of $\underline{J}(\ell)$ and is obtained by using eqns.(2.1.1) and (2.1.2) in section 2.1. In the above equation $[\ ]_\ell$ means the wire axis component and V_d and d_g, respectively, are the voltage and the gap distance at the driving point where m = N. The coordinate is taken along the wire and denoted by ℓ, starting from the left end of the helical structure as shown in Fig.2.2.1. $\Pi(\frac{\ell-N\ell_0}{d_g})$ indicates a function of ℓ which has a rectangular shape with an amplitude of unity, width of d_g, and is centered at $\ell = N\ell_0$. The antenna is not necessarily driven at the centre of the helical structure, but may be driven at an intermediate point where m $\neq$ N.

Rigorous calculation of eqn.(2.2.1) is not easy. With the assumption that ℓ_0 is much smaller than the wavelength, an approximate calculation can be made by dividing the helical wire into small segments of length $2\ell_0$, as shown in Fig.2.2.2. Each segment is redrawn as shown in Fig.2.2.3 and the integral is performed with respect to a new

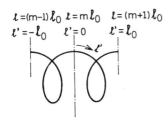

$$\ell=(m-1)\ell_0 \quad \ell=m\ell_0 \quad \ell=(m+1)\ell_0$$
$$\ell'=-\ell_0 \quad \ell'=0 \quad \ell'=\ell_0$$

Fig.2.2.3. One segment of NMHA and its coordinate.

coordinate system defined on the segment by taking a parameter ℓ' along the wire. The current distribution function $f(\ell')$ on the segment here is taken as $f(\ell') = \cos^2(\frac{\pi\ell'}{2\ell_0})$. The current distribution $J(\ell')$ on the helical wire can be obtained in a scalar form as the summation of currents on all segments as follows;

$$J(\ell') = \sum_{m=1}^{2N-1} I_m f(\ell''), \tag{2.2.2}$$

62

where $\ell'' = \ell' - m\ell_0$ and I_m is the coefficient to be determined. The coefficient I_m can be obtained by the method of moments and be expressed, by using impedance matrix $[Z]$ as in eqn.(2.1.6), to be

$$I_m = \sum_{m=1}^{2N-1} Y_{mn} V_d \delta_{Nn},\qquad (2.2.3)$$

where Y_{mn} is an element of an admittance matrix $[Y] = [Z]^{-1}$, and δ denotes Dirac delta function ($\delta_{Nn} = 0$ for $n \neq N$ and $= 1$ for $n = N$).

When an impedance Z_ℓ is integrated or loaded symmetrically on intermediate positions on the helical structure as shown in Fig.2.2.4, the element Z_{nm} is modified to include Z_ℓ as (Hiroi, Fujimoto, 1974)

$$Z_{nm'} = \begin{cases} Z_{nm} & \text{for } n \neq m, \text{ or } n = m \neq (N \pm m_\ell') \\ (Z_{nm} + Z_\ell) & \text{for } n = m = (N \pm m_\ell'). \end{cases} \qquad (2.2.4)$$

Here, m' is the number of turns counted from the centre of the helical structure and m_ℓ' indicates the turn on which the impedance Z_ℓ is loaded.

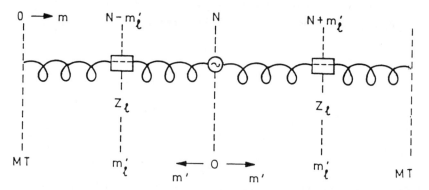

Fig.2.2.4   NMHA integrated with impedances Z_ℓ.

When the loss impedance Z_{loss} exists parasiticaly in the helical structure, it may be included in Z_{nm} as in the case of the discrete loadings Z_ℓ by assuming that Z_{loss} is the loss impedance existing in one segment of helical winding and is concentrated at the centre of the segment.

The conventional expression for Z_{loss} is

$$Z_{loss} = \frac{1 + j}{\pi \sigma d_s} , \tag{2.2.5}$$

where σ is the conductivity of the wire and d_s is the skin depth, given by

$$d_s = \sqrt{\frac{2}{\omega \mu_0 \sigma}} . \tag{2.2.6}$$

2.2.2 Design Considerations

(1) Current distributions

The current distributions along the length of the helical wire are calculated and the variation depending on MT (one half of the total number of turns) is shown in Fig.2.2.5, where relative values normalized by the maximum value at each MT are used. As can be seen from

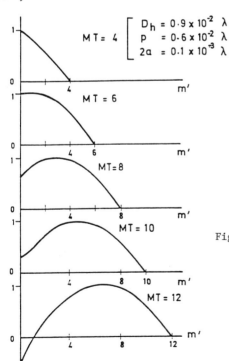

Fig.2.2.5.   Current distributions (relative values) vs. m'.

64

Fig.2.2.5, the phase of the current is reversed as MT is increased, although for a small MT the current distribution resembles that of a linear antenna. Note that even with a large MT, such as 12, the axial length of the helical antenna is only about 0.07 λ, which is still electrically short.

(2) Input impedance and efficiency

The input impedance Z_i of an antenna having the same parameters given in Fig.2.2.5 varies with MT as shown in Fig.2.2.6.

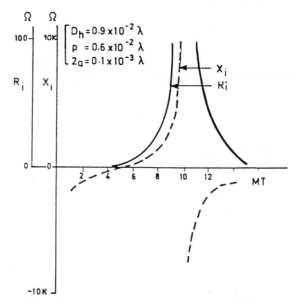

Fig.2.2.6. Input impedances Z_i near resonance and anti-resonance.

Both resistive and reactive components of the impedance change very slowly when MT is less than the number required for resonance, but start increasing rather rapidly after passing the resonance condition where MT $\doteqdot$ 6. The resistive component at the resonance point is fairly low, less than 10 ohms.

When a copper wire with a conductivity $\sigma = 5.8 \times 10^7$ S/m is used for the helical winding, the resistive component R_i in the input impedance increases as shown in Fig.2.2.7 due to the inclusion of lossy compo-

nents. In Fig.2.2.7, variations in resistive components with and without loss component R_i' and R_i are shown against MT. The reactance
component X_i is not affected by the existence of the loss in this antenna structure.

Utilizing this result, the antenna efficiency η was calculated and
is shown in Fig.2.2.8, where experimental results are also shown for
comparison.

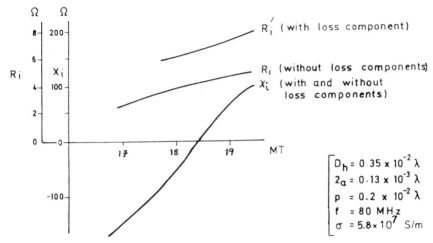

Fig.2.2.7.   Input impedance Z_i with and without loss component.

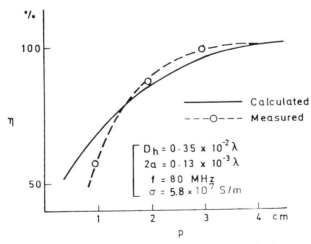

Fig.2.2.8.   Efficiency η vs. pitch p.

(3) Resonance condition and efficiency

The relationship between the pitch p of the helical structure and
the diameter D_h of the helix is shown in Fig.2.2.9, where in (a) MT
needed for resonances is taken as the parameter and in (b) the radiation resistances at the resonance condition can be read. These results
are from Inagaki. et al. (1971).

One example of efficiency η as a function of MT is shown in Fig.2.2.
10, in which the resonance point is observed at about MT = 8. The

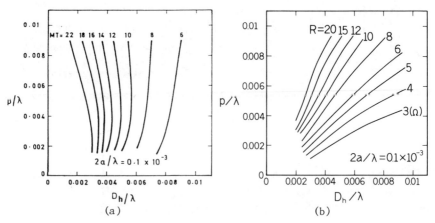

Fig.2.2.9.   Number of turns MT and radiation resistance R_r at the
resonance in relation with pitch p and diameter D_h of helix.

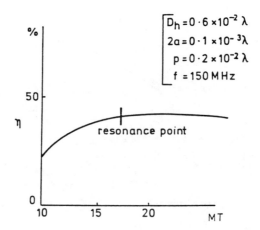

Fig.2.2.10.   Efficiency η vs. numbers of turns MT.

efficiency reaches a maximum value at the resonance point although the variation in efficiency is very small in that region.

The input impedance Z_i increases rapidly beyond the resonance point as shown earlier in Fig.2.2.6. This is shown more precisely in Fig.2.2.11, which shows values for MT in excess of the resonance. In the Figure, the R_i' curve is the case where a loss component R_{loss} exists in the helical structure. If the input resistance R_i' is desired to be 50 Ω for direct matching to a load of 50 Ω, MT is selected as 23. The value of the reactance X_i for this condition is 2,000 Ω, indicating that for matching a capacitor of 2,000 Ω is required. If the quality factor Q of the capacitor is 1,000, the loss resistance is estimated at 2 Ω and no serious degradation of antenna efficiency would be observed (approximately from 80% to 77%). In a practical application, however, an NMHA selected for the resonance condition would be more appropriate, since no additional reactance component at the input is necessary to get resonance and only an impedance transformer would be required, which would incur very little further loss.

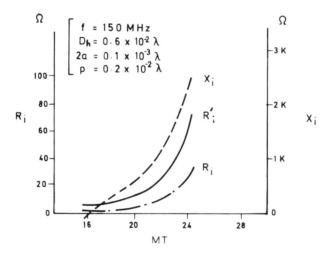

Fig.2.2.11.   Input impedance Z_i near resonance shown in detail.

(4) Comparison of an NMHA with a short dipole

It has been shown that an NMHA can be made resonant for a very short

68

length, and yet its efficiency is higher than that of a dipole of the same length. Here a comparison of an NMHA with a dipole having the same length is given (Hiroi, Fujimoto, 1976 b).

As an example, take a short antenna of length 0.05 λ, as shown in Fig.2.2.12. Table 2.2.1 shows comparisons of two antennas in terms of input impedance Z_i and efficiency η. The input impedance Z_{ih} of the NMHA is 11.7 Ω + j0 (at the resonance condition), while that of the dipole antenna Z_{id} is 0.49 - j 900 Ω. (King, 1956). If a copper wire

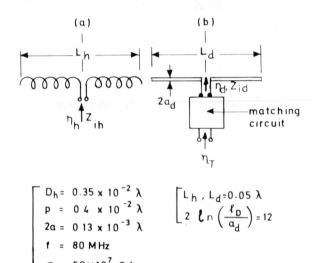

$$\begin{bmatrix} D_h = 0.35 \times 10^{-2}\ \lambda \\ p = 0.4 \times 10^{-2}\ \lambda \\ 2a = 0.13 \times 10^{-3}\ \lambda \\ f = 80\ MHz \\ \sigma = 5.8 \times 10^7\ S/m \end{bmatrix} \quad \begin{bmatrix} L_h , L_d = 0.05\ \lambda \\ 2\ \ln\left(\frac{\ell_D}{a_d}\right) = 12 \end{bmatrix}$$

Fig.2.2.12.   Dimensions of NMHA and short dipole; (a) NMHA (b) dipole

Table 2.2.1   Comparison of an NMHA and a dipole with the same length 0.05λ.

	NMHA	Dipole	
Z_i [Ω]	11.7 + j00	0.49 - j 900	
η [%]	80	91	at feed point
η_T [%]	75 (with matching circuit for 50Ω)	5	Q_c = 100
		18	Q_c = 400

with conductivity $\sigma = 5.8 \times 10^7$ S/m is used for the antenna element and the load of 50 Ω is connected to the antenna terminals, the NMHA would have an efficiency η_h of about 80%, while that of the dipole η_d would be 91 %. In practice, however, a dipole of 0.05 λ could not have such high efficiency, because its efficiency is degraded by losses existing in the matching circuit between the antenna and the 50 Ω load. If the Q of the inductance +900 Ω in the matching circuit is 100, then the efficiency η_d of the antenna system would drop to only 5 %. If a higher Q, for example, as high as 400, could be used, the efficiency η_d would be raised to 18 %, which is still fairly low.

Although an impedance transformer is required to match 11 Ω of the NMHA resistive component to the load of 50 Ω, the reduction of efficiency due to the insertion of the transformer would be only around 5 %. This calculation shows the striking advantage of the NMHA over the dipole of the same length.

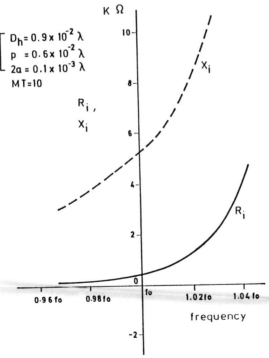

Fig.2.2.13.   Variation of input impedance Z_i with frequency.

70

One more important factor to be noted in the NMHA is that the band width is not very wide, which can be disadvantageous for some communications applications. As an example the variation of the input impedance Z_i with frequency is shown in Fig.2.2.13. Both resistive and reactive components vary as the frequency varies and only a 4% change in the frequency causes an impedance variation of four times or more. The inclusion of a load in the NMHA can improve this performance and this will now be discussed.

2.2.3 Reactance-loaded NMHA

Self-resonance condition in an NMHA is easily achieved by integration of the reactance component into the helical structure. When a reactance component is placed at an intermediate position on the helical winding (Fig.2.2.4), variations in the current distribution on the helical wire and in the input impedance are observed (Hiroi, Fujimoto 1976 a).

For the current distributions shown in Fig.2.2.5, the calculated loading susceptance B_ℓ to obtain the self-resonance condition on an NMHA is shown in Fig.2.2.14. MT is taken as the parameter and the

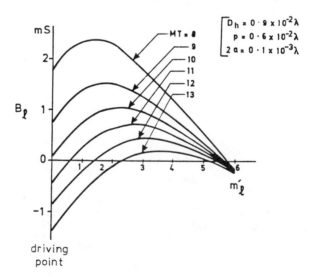

Fig.2.2.14. Loading susceptance B_ℓ necessary to obtain self-resonance.

susceptance B_ℓ, necessary to obtain self-resonance, is plotted with respect to the position m'_ℓ where the susceptance component is located. For a large MT such as 11, 12, 13, the sign of the susceptance component reverses as the loading position m'_ℓ approaches the antenna driving point.

The variations of the input resistance R_i against the loading positions m'_ℓ are shown in Fig.2.2.15 for MT = 8 and 10.

The current distributions as a function of m' depend upon the loading position m'_ℓ and are shown in Fig.2.2.16, where MT is fixed at 10 and the values of the loading reactance component are taken from Fig. 2.2.14.

As the loading position m'_ℓ moves from the driving-point toward the end of the helical structure, the values of the currents fall significantly, especially beyond the loading position m'_ℓ. When MT is varied and the loading position m'_ℓ is fixed, say at $m'_\ell = 4$, the current distributions vary as shown in Fig.2.2.17. For this case, MT values have been chosen as 8, 10 and 12.

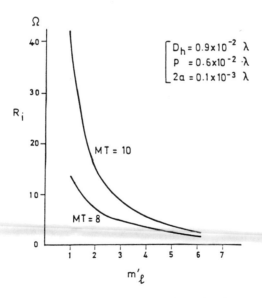

Fig.2.2.15.   Input resistance R_i against loading position m'_ℓ.

72

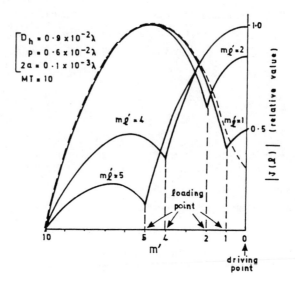

Fig.2.2.16.   Current distributions (relative values) vs. m', where MT=
10.

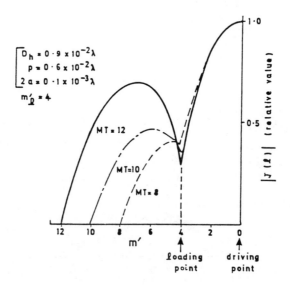

Fig.2.2.17.   Current distributions (relative values) vs. m', where
loading position $m'_\ell = 4$.

The current distribution depends upon frequency and its characteristics for frequency variations up to ±5 % are shown in Fig.2.2.18,
where MT is set at 10 and a capacitance C_ℓ = 2pF is assumed to be
loaded at the position m' = 2.

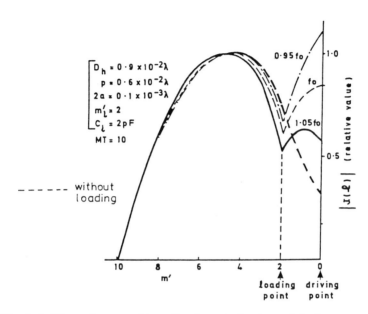

Fig.2.2.18.   Current distribution variation with frequency.

As the frequency changes, the value of the loading susceptance B_ℓ
does of course change, so that if the resonance condition should be
satisfied, B_ℓ should be changed so as to realize zero reactance in the
input impedance Z_i. In an ideal case, as Fig.2.2.19 shows, for attaining resonance over a frequency range of ±5 % or more the value of
B_ℓ should increase as the frequency is increased, as the curve B_ℓ
shows; this implies that a negative capacitance is required as a loading impedance component. The curve R_i illustrates the input resistance component at resonance for each frequency. However, if the perfect resonance condition is not required, a negative capacitance need
not necessarily be used for improvement of frequency characteristics. Fig.2.2.20 illustrates a comparison between the input impedances Z_i' and Z_i for a loaded antenna and a non-loaded antenna. With-

74

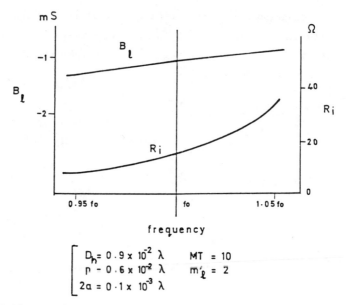

$$\begin{bmatrix} D_h = 0.9 \times 10^{-2}\, \lambda & MT = 10 \\ p - 0.6 \times 10^{-2}\, \lambda & m'_\ell = 2 \\ 2a = 0.1 \times 10^{-3}\, \lambda \end{bmatrix}$$

Fig.2.2.19.   Value of loading susceptance B_ℓ necessary for resonance and resistance component R_i at resonance.

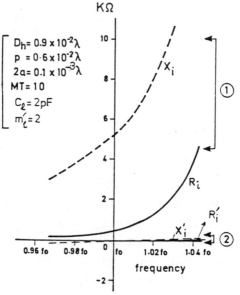

$$\begin{bmatrix} D_h = 0.9 \times 10^{-2}\lambda \\ p = 0.6 \times 10^{-2}\lambda \\ 2a = 0.1 \times 10^{-3}\lambda \\ MT = 10 \\ C_\ell = 2pF \\ m'_\ell = 2 \end{bmatrix}$$

Fig.2.2.20.   Input impedance with and without loading, $Z_i' = R_i' + jX_i'$ and $Z_i = R_i + jX_i$, as a function of frequency.

out loading, the input impedance Z_i varies greatly with frequency, as the curves 1 show, but when loaded with a reactive component, C_ℓ=2pF, Z_i' does not vary very much and is almost flat with the frequency as the curves 2 show for the frequency band of ±4 %.

2.3 Small Rectangular Loop Antennas

Small loop antennas have mostly been employed in the past for low frequency applications. In this section, however, the use of loop antennas for VHF and UHF receivers is introduced. The size of antenna considered here is small enough to fit pocket-size equipment, and is usually smaller than one-tenth of a wavelength – the antenna can thus be classified as an electrically small antenna.

Rectangular or modified-shaped loops have more recently been used in VHF and UHF portable equipment, including paging receivers, and there still exists a high potential for these small antennas in portable equipment, as the demand for personal communications increases.

The reason for treating a rectangular structure here is that it may be typical, since most portable equipment boxes have a rectangular structure and a built-in antenna may follow the inner shape of the box.

In this section, special attention is paid to application of the rectangular loop to the pocket-size paging receivers in VHF and UHF bands. The design data are provided first and problems related to the built-in case and the effects of the human body are discussed next. These problems are rather common in antennas used on small equipment.

Special considerations taken in the design of this antenna are (1) to match the antenna impedance efficiently to the load, by using the loop element itself, without any other potentially lossy circuits, (2) to utilize the human body effect, which usually degrades antenna efficiency, to actually increase the sensitivity of the pager when the equipment is operated inside a bearer's pocket and (3) to arrange the unbalanced component of the current existing in the antenna system to supplement the loop antenna performance, so that the receiver sensitivity is kept unchanged during operation outside a pocket.

Although the efficiency of a small loop antenna cannot be very high, its usefulness has been confirmed by its adoption for practical paging receivers in the 150 MHz and 250 MHz bands (Itoh, et al., 1973). Experiments have demonstrated that similar performances could also be achieved in the 400 MHz bands (Haruki, 1974) and design examples in both VHF and UHF are provided here. It is considered that a similar performance level may also hold for 900 MHz band applications, since the efficiency of the small loop antenna tends to increase as the frequency becomes higher. It should be noted, however,that the influence of adjacent materials on the antenna performance becomes larger as the frequency becomes higher. It may be interesting to know the results here; for the small loop antenna, the efficiency obtained is high enough for operation both inside and outside the bearer's pocket, and the receiving pattern is nearly omnidirectional in the horizontal plane, which cannot be obtained by a single loop element.

Comparisons have been made with other types of antennas such as the small dipole and the ferrite antenna, but the small loop was found to be the most effective antenna among them when used in an operator's pocket.

In practice, the loop element is made with either a thin wire or a thin plate. Both are very simple, compact, light weight, low-cost, and unbreakable, yet can provide performances superior to other types of antennas. The serious problem to consider is the effect of adjacent materials, such as the circuit element and components, on antenna performance. The degradation of antenna efficiency increases as the frequency becomes higher.

Problems discussed in the design of this antenna not only are concerned with the pager receiver introduced here, but also are important to any similar equipment in mobile communications. As the demand for small equipment increases, the concept discussed here may well become more important and be applied toward solution of problems of small mobile equipment such as handheld, portable, book-size equipment.

2.3.1 Design parameters

(1) Antenna structure

The antenna structure considered here is a rectangular loop composed of either a thin wire or a thin plate element. The equipment in which the antenna is installed has a rectangular shape, and the loop which is to be installed inside the equipment follows this shape. The model used for analysis and design is shown in Fig.2.3.1 along with dimensional notation.

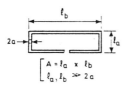

Fig.2.3.1.   Thin-wire loop antenna model.

(2) Loop impedance

The impedance of a small loop antenna can be expressed equivalently by using circuit parameters as shown in Fig.2.3.2, where R_r denotes

Fig.2.3.2.   Equivalent circuit expression of a small loop antenna.

the radiation resistance, R_{loss} the loss resistance, and L the self-inductance of the loop structure. The loop impedance Z_i is then given by

$$Z_i = R_r + R_{loss} + j\omega L. \tag{2.3.1}$$

R_r and R_{loss} are expressed (Weeks, 1968) as

$$R_r = 20 \, (\beta^2 A)^2, \tag{2.3.2}$$

and

$$R_{loss} = \frac{1}{\pi a} \, (\ell_a + \ell_b) \, R_s , \tag{2.3.3}$$

78

where $\beta = 2\pi/\lambda$, $A = \ell_a \times \ell_b$ (the area of the loop), a is the wire radius, and $R_s = \sqrt{\pi f \mu_0 / \sigma}$ (σ is conductivity of the loop element and f is the frequency of operation). L can be obtained by calculating the inductance of the loop, in which the mutual inductance of two parallel wires is taken into consideration, as follows;

$$L = \frac{\mu_0}{\pi}[\ell_b \ln \{\frac{2A}{a(\ell_b+\ell_c)}\} + \ell_a \ln \{\frac{2A}{a(\ell_a+\ell_c)}\}$$
$$+ 2 \{a + \ell_c - (\ell_a + \ell_b)\}], \tag{2.3.4}$$

where

$$\ell_c = \sqrt{\ell_a^2 + \ell_b^2}$$

Calculated values of R_r and R_{loss} are shown in Figs.2.3.3 to 2.3.6,

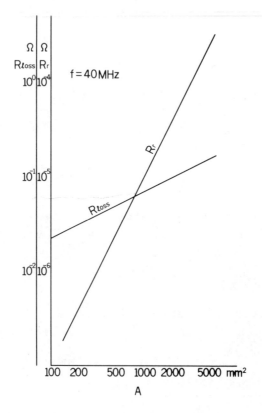

Fig.2.3.3.   Radiation and loss resistances vs. loop area at 40 MHz.

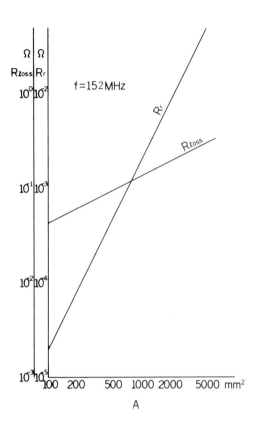

Fig.2.3.4.   Radiation and loss resistances vs. loop area at 152 MHz.

80

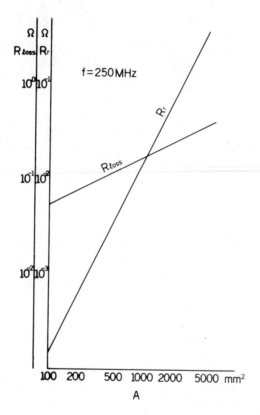

Fig.2.3.5.   Radiation and loss resistances vs. loop area at 250 MHz.

81

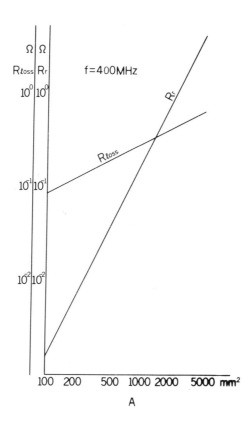

Fig.2.3.6.   Radiation and loss resistances vs. loop area at 400 MHz.

for frequencies of 40, 152, 250 and 400 MHz, respectively. In these calculations it is assumed that ℓ_b = 4ℓ_a and 2a = 1.2 mm.

Fig.2.3.7 shows the calculated inductance L : (a) to (d) as a function of the width ℓ_b for various values of the length ℓ_a, and (e) to (h) as a function of the wire radius a.

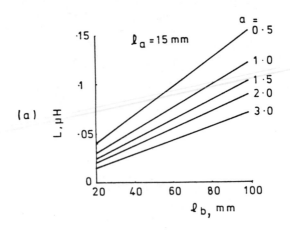

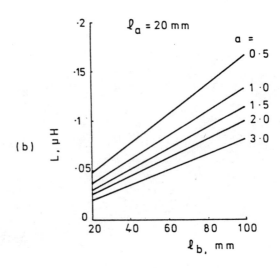

Fig.2.3.7.   Inductance of a small loop antenna.

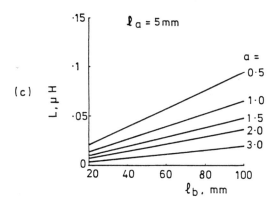

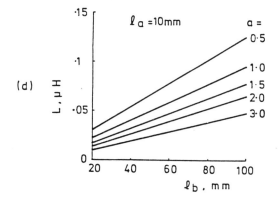

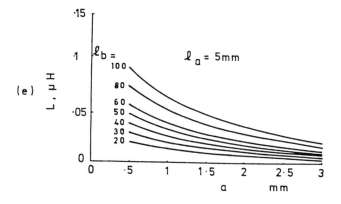

Fig.2.3.7.   Inductance of a small loop antenna.

84

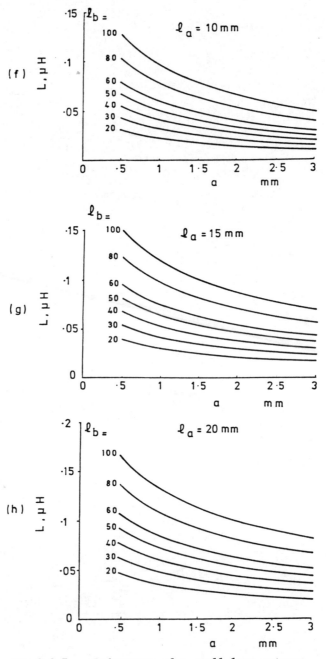

Fig.2.3.7.   Inductance of a small loop antenna.

(3) Efficiency and gain

Antenna efficiency η is given by

$$\eta = \frac{R_r}{R_r + R_{loss}} \, . \qquad (2.3.5)$$

The system gain G_L of a loop antenna is expressed by using η as

$$G_L = G_D \cdot \eta \cdot \gamma, \qquad (2.3.6)$$

where G_D stands for the directive gain with respect to the standard half-wave dipole and γ is the mismatch factor. G_D of a small loop antenna is -0.39 dB and η can be calculated by using values in Fig.2.3.3 to Fig.2.3.6. The gain G_L calculated by eqn.(2.3.6) as a function of frequency is shown in Fig.2.3.8, where the loop area A is taken as the parameter. In these calculations, γ is assumed to be unity, that is, the antenna is matched to the source.

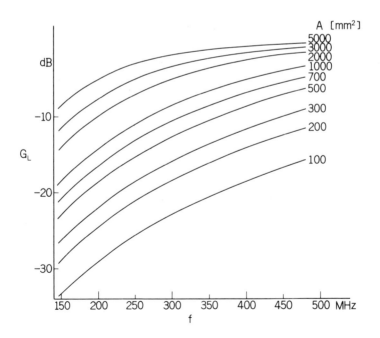

Fig.2.3.8.   System gain vs. frequency.

(4) Resonance and loop admittance

In general, the matching between an antenna and a receiver requires a coupling circuit to transform the antenna impedance to the receiver impedance, say 50 ohms. As the size of the loop antenna considered here is very small compared with the wavelength, the radiation resistance R_r is much smaller than the loss resistance R_{loss}, as shown in Figs.2.3.3 to Fig.2.3.6. If a transformer circuit is used between the antenna and receiver, any loss existing in the circuit will cause the efficiency to be degraded to some extent. To avoid this loss in the coupling circuit, the loop element itself is utilized, because it is inherently an inductance component and a tap at an intermediate point on the loop element is taken to form a transformer as shown in Fig.2. 3.9 (a); the tapping point is indicated as T_ℓ at a distance t from the input terminal of the loop. To achieve resonance a capacitor C_ℓ is used, and is also shown in the Figure. On using the circuit parameters given in Fig.2.3.2 this antenna is expressed by the circuit shown in Fig.2.3.9 (b). In the Figure, e is the induced voltage due to the incoming field, L_1 the inductance of the part of the loop with length t, L_2 the inductance of the rest of the loop, and M the mutual inductance existing between L_1 and L_2.

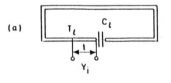

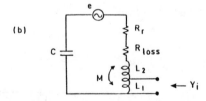

Fig.2.3.9. Matching circuit arrangement of a small loop antenna in VHF and its equivalent circuit.

The input admittance Y_i of the loop is then given by

$$Y_i = \frac{\omega^2 (R_r + R_{loss})(L_1 + M)^2}{[\omega^2 (L_1 + M)^2 + \omega L_1 (\omega L_T - \frac{1}{\omega C_\ell})]^2}$$

$$+ j \frac{\omega L_T - \frac{1}{\omega C_\ell}}{\omega^2 (L_1 + M)^2 + \omega L_1 (\omega L_T - \frac{1}{\omega C_\ell})} \, , \qquad (2.3.7)$$

where $L_T = L_1 + L_2 + 2M$, and ωL_T and $\frac{1}{\omega C_\ell}$ are assumed to be much greater than $(R_r + R_{loss})$. At a resonance condition, where $\omega L_T = \frac{1}{\omega C_\ell}$, the input admittance $Y_i \big|_{res}$ becomes

$$Y_i \big|_{res} = \frac{R_r + R_{loss}}{(L_1 + M)^2} \cdot L_T C_\ell . \qquad (2.3.8)$$

The input admittance Y_i varies with the value of the tuning capacitance C_ℓ and also with the tapping point t. Fig.2.3.10 illustrates the trend in the behavior of the input impedance Z_i with increasing C_ℓ and t values.

By varying the tapping point t, $Y_i \big|_{res}$ will have values within a range given by

$$\frac{(R_r + R_{loss})}{L_T} \cdot C_\ell < Y_i \big|_{res} < \infty. \qquad (2.3.9)$$

When the operating frequency is relatively low, it is sufficient to place one tuning capacitor C_ℓ in parallel to the inductance of the loop. However, as the operating frequency becomes higher, the inductive impedance of the loop increases, so that the capacitance C_ℓ cannot be small enough to obtain the resonance condition, because of its residual capacitance. Thus another capacitor $C_{\ell 2}$ for the higher frequency case is placed in series to the inductance in addition to the tuning capacitor $C_{\ell 1}$, as shown in Fig.2.3.11, in which (a) shows the location of capacitors $C_{\ell 1}$ and $C_{\ell 2}$, and (b) the equivalent circuit.

88

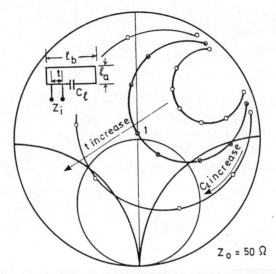

Fig.2.3.10. Variation of input impedance of a small loop antenna against variation in tuning capacitance C_ℓ and tapping position t.

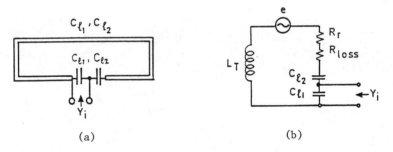

(a)   (b)

Fig.2.3.11. Matching circuit arrangement of a small loop antenna at UHF and its equivalent circuit representation.

At resonance, $Y_i\big|_{res}$ becomes

$$Y_i\big|_{res} = \frac{(R_r + R_{loss})}{L_T} \cdot C_\ell' \cdot \left(\frac{C_{\ell1} + C_{\ell2}}{C_{\ell2}} \right)^2 , \qquad (2.3.10)$$

where $C_\ell' = C_{\ell1}C_{\ell2}/(C_{\ell1} + C_{\ell2})$.

By selecting values of $C_{\ell1}$ and $C_{\ell2}$, $Y_i\big|_{res}$ may take values in the following range:

$$\frac{(R_r + R_{loss})}{L_T} C_\ell' < Y_i \big|_{res} < \infty \quad , \tag{2.3.11}$$

enabling a good match to be made by an appropriate choice of $C_{\ell 2}$, $C_{\ell 1}$, and t.

(5) Quality factor, bandwidth, and efficiency of antenna system

When a loop is resonant and matched to a load, the quality factor Q_L of a built-in antenna is given by

$$Q_L = \frac{\omega L_T}{2(R_r + R_{loss})} = \frac{1}{2} Q, \tag{2.3.12}$$

where Q is the unloaded quality factor. When Q_L is fairly high, the bandwidth W of a loop antenna at an operating frequency f_0 may be obtained from

$$W = \frac{f_0}{Q_L} \quad . \tag{2.3.13}$$

When an antenna element is placed near conducting materials in the equipment box, the antenna efficiency degrades due to the adjacent body effects, R_{loss} increases to R'_{loss} and Q_L decreases to $Q'_L = \omega L_T/2$ $(R_r + R'_{loss})$. The antenna efficiency η' is then expressed by

$$\eta' = R_r/(R'_{loss} + R_r)$$

$$= 2R_r Q'_L / (\omega L_T). \tag{2.3.14}$$

2.3.2 Built-in antenna system

(a) Antenna structure

Fig.2.3.12 illustrates an example of the antenna installation inside a practical pager equipment case. With this structure, the antenna system is expressed by the combination of a loop element and a thin conducting plate (the hatched part) shown in Fig.2.3.13. Here the pager circuit is represented simply by a thin rectangular conducting plate, since the surface of the printed circuit board is almost covered by the ground circuit and has a variety of metallic electronic com-

90

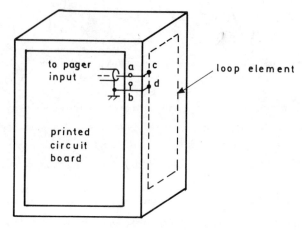

Fig.2.3.12.   Loop element installation in pager equipment.

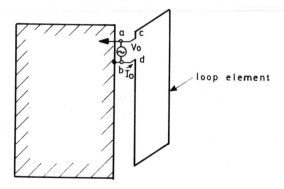

Fig.2.3.13.   Pager antenna model composed of loop element and pager circuit.

ponents connected to it. The induced voltage at the terminals (a-b) of the loop element is denoted as V_0 and the current flowing there as I_0. At the terminals (a-b), because the balanced input of the loop is connected directly to the unbalanced receiver input circuit as shown in Fig.2.3.13, there exist both balanced and unbalanced currents, I_b and I_u, respectively (see the theoretical treatment in Appendix A 2. 1,p184).This terminal structure can be divided into two system; balanced and unbalanced, as shown in Fig.2.3.14. In this Figure, (a) illustrates the balanced system where the balanced mode voltage V_b and current I_b are taken at the terminals (a-b) (refer to Fig.A.2.1.3.(a)), (b) shows the unbalanced system, where the terminals (a-b) and (c-d) are shorted because the potentials at a and b and those at c and d, respectively, are equal to each other. Hence the unbalanced mode voltage V_u is taken at the terminals (a-b)-(c-d), that is to say, between the equivalent rectangular conducting plate and the loop element. The unbalanced mode current $1/2\ I_u$ flows on the loop element as shown in the Figure (refer to Fig.2.1.3. (b)). The current I_u on the equivalent conducting plate may be represented essentially by two components, I_{uV} and I_{uH}, the vertical and horizontal components of I_u, as shown in the Figure. These two components are important when the radiation pattern of the antenna system is considered. This problem is discussed in Section 2.3.2(c).

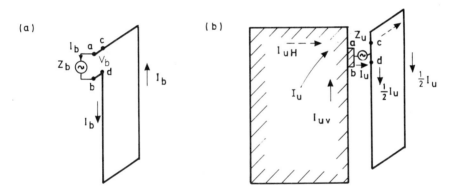

Fig.2.3.14.   Decomposion of pager antenna system; (a) balanced component and (b) unbalanced component.

(b)   Input impedance

The input impedance of the built-in antenna system is a combination of the balanced impedance Z_b, the impedance of the loop (shown in Fig. 2.3.14 (a)), and the impedance of the unbalanced component Z_u (shown in Fig.2.3.14(b)). Z_b is equal to the reciprocal of Y_i, which is obtained by eqn.(2.3.7). Here Z_b and Z_u are expressed by

$$Z_b = V_b/I_b,$$

and

$$Z_u = V_u/I_u. \tag{2.3.15}$$

The antenna system impedance Z_T is V_0/I_0. At the antenna terminals, the following relations exist;

$$V_u - \frac{1}{2} V_b = 0,$$

$$V_u + \frac{1}{2} V_b = V_0, \tag{2.3.16}$$

$$I_b + \frac{1}{2} I_u = I_0.$$

From these, Z_T is derived:

$$Z_T = \frac{V_u + \frac{1}{2} V_b}{I_b + \frac{1}{2} I_u} = \frac{1}{\dfrac{I_b}{V_b} + \dfrac{I_u}{4V_u}}$$

$$= \frac{1}{\dfrac{1}{Z_b} + \dfrac{1}{4Z_u}} = \frac{4Z_b Z_u}{Z_b + 4Z_u} \quad . \tag{2.3.17}$$

This system can then be expressed by a parallel circuit of Z_b and $4Z_u$ as shown in Fig.2.3.15. Usually Z_u is much greater than Z_b and Z_T may be treated as approximately Z_b.

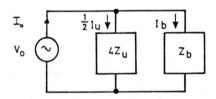

Fig.2.3.15.   Equivalent circuit expression of pager antenna system.

(c) Receiving pattern

The receiver sensitivity has directional characteristics that depend upon the performance of the antenna system. Here, the graphical representation of these directional characteristics on an appropriate coordinate system is called the receiving pattern. The receiving pattern is determined by the response to both the field of the loop (balanced component) (Fig.2.3.14 (a)) and that of the unbalanced component (Fig.2.3.14 (b)). Because of their reciprocal nature, the receiving pattern is the same as the radiation pattern. Hence the receiving pattern is found by the vector sum of the field produced by the loop and that produced by the unbalanced system. For the calculation of this pattern the antenna system located on the coordinate system shown in Fig.2.3.16 (a) is used, where the loop element is placed on the x-axis as Fig.2.3.16 (b) shows. The unbalanced system is composed of an equivalent rectangular conducting plate and a loop element with its terminals (c-d) shorted as shown in Fig.2.3.14 (b). The equivalent rectangular conducting plate has length ℓ_u and width w. The loop element with its terminals (c-d) closed is treated here as a thin plate having length ℓ_a, since the currents $(1/2)I_u$ on each line are equal in quantity and in direction and the width ℓ_a is very narrow. This system is then equivalently represented by two thin plates, which are at right-angles to each other and are placed on the coordinate system as Fig.2.3.16 (c) shows. The unbalanced system consisting of two plates may be considered as a dipole system having a very short length and a narrow width compared with the wavelength. The currents flowing on these two plates can be calculated by simulating the plates with a wire-grid model and by applying the method of moments to the model. The current distribution on the plates so obtained is illustrated in Fig.2.3.16 (d), where the absolute values of the currents are shown by the height of the oblique lines on each wire of the model. In the Figure the two plates are shown as if they were aligned on one plane, only for the sake of illustration. Now the receiving patterns can be calculated by using the loop current I_b for the balanced system and the currents on the equivalent two-plate system for the unbalanced system. The calculated pattern is illustrated in Fig.2.3.17 (a), where the electric field strength $E_{\theta T}$ on the x-y plane is shown. In this calculation, $\ell_b = \ell_u = 0.03 \lambda$, $\ell_a = 0.0075 \lambda$ and w = 0.015 λ are used. This is the combined pattern of that generated by the current I_b and that generated by the currents of the unbalanced system and is obtained by the following process.

The θ-component of the electric field $E_{\theta b}$ on the x-y plane produced

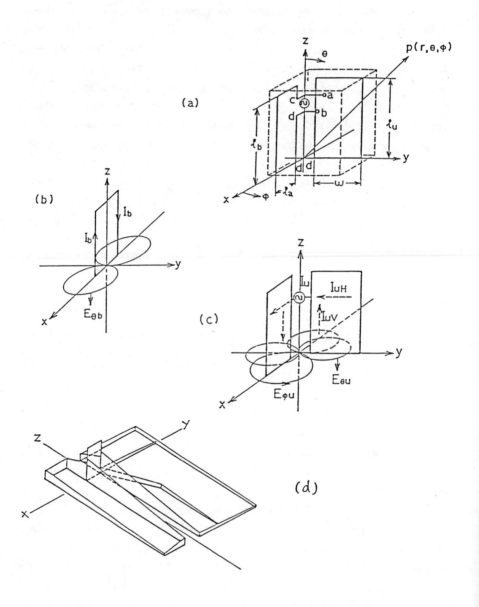

Fig.2.3.16. (a) Antenna and the coordinate system, (b) balanced (loop) system, (c) unbalanced system, and (d) current distribution of the unbalanced system.

by the balanced system current I_b can be obtained from

$$E_{\theta b} = 120\pi^2 \, [I_b] \, \frac{A}{\lambda^2} \, \frac{e^{-jkr}}{r} \, \cos\phi, \qquad (2.3.18)$$

where $[I_b] = |I_b| e^{j\theta_b}$. The pattern of $E_{\theta b}$ calculated from eqn.(2.3.18) is a well-known 'figure-eight' pattern as shown symbolically in Fig.2.3.16 (b). On the other hand, the θ-component of the electric field $E_{\theta u}$ is calculated from the unbalanced system currents shown in Fig.2.3.16 (d) by using the method of moments. The $E_{\theta u}$ pattern is found to be also a nearly 'figure-eight' pattern as shown in Fig.2.3.17 (b), where the same antenna dimensions used in Fig.2.3.17 (a) are used. The direction of the pattern maximum is seen tilted by about 30 degrees from the y-axis. This resulted from the right-angle arrangement of the two plates as shown in Fig.2.3.16 (c) and the angle ϕ_0 is evaluated approximately to be $\tan^{-1}(\ell_a/w)$.

In the process of combining $E_{\theta b}$ and $E_{\theta u}$ to obtain the total field $E_{\theta T}$, the phase difference $(\theta_u - \theta_b)$ must be taken into consideration. Here θ_u denotes the phase of the unbalanced system currents $[I_u]$ $(= |I_u| e^{j\theta_u})$. Since the unbalanced system is assumed here to be a short dipole it has a capacitive impedance and hence the phase θ_u is considered to be 90 degrees progressed from the phase θ_b, when the loop system is at the resonance condition.

The currents flowing on the plates shown in Fig.2.3.16 (d) may be divided essentially into two components: vertical and horizontal components I_{uV} and I_{uH}, as was shown in Fig.2.3.16 (c). Then it may be considered that the θ-component $E_{\theta u}$ is produced by I_{uV} and the ϕ- component $E_{\phi u}$, by I_{uH}.

The total field $E_{\theta T}$ on the x-y plane is now expressed as a function of ϕ by

$$E_{\theta T}(\phi) = E_{\theta b} + E_{\theta u}$$

$$\propto m_b \, |f_b(\phi)| + j \, n_u \, |g_{uV}(\phi)|, \qquad (2.3.19)$$

where m_b is a constant proportional to I_b, n_u a constant proportional to I_{uV}. and f_b and g_{uV}, respectively, are pattern functions corresponding to the balanced and unbalanced patterns produced by I_b and I_{uV}. By using these parameters the directional pattern $D(\phi)$ on the x-y plane is derived:

$$|D(\phi)| = \sqrt{|f_b(\phi)|^2 + (n_u/m_b)^2 |g_{uV}(\phi)|^2}. \qquad (2.3.20)$$

The ratio (n_u/m_b) can be calculated from the relationship between the balanced and unbalanced impedances and the input circuit parameters of the balanced system. This can also be found from the measurement of the pattern. The procedure will be described later. The value used for calculating the pattern in Fig.2.3.17 (a) was 16.5, which was evaluated for a practical model in the 150 MHz band.

There is a simple method to find $E_{\theta u}$. $E_{\theta u}$ is the field produced by the current I_{uV} on the equivalent two-plate system. Here these two plates are simulated by thin wires, each having a diameter which is equal to a quarter of the width of the corresponding plate (Kraus, 1950 b) and the two-plate system is considered as a two-element array, on which I_{uV} flows in opposite directions. Then $E_{\theta u}$ is given by

$$E_{\theta u} = j\ 120\pi[I_{uV}]\ \frac{\ell_b}{\lambda}\ \frac{e^{-jkr}}{r}\ \sin(\frac{k\ell}{2}\ \sin\ \phi'), \qquad (2.3.21)$$

where $\ell_b = \ell_u$ is assumed and ℓ is taken as the distance between the two plates approximately equal to $(1/2)(\ell_a^2 + w^2)^{1/2}$. To show the pattern calculated from eqn.(2.3.21), the new coordinate system $(x'-y')$ shown in Fig.2.3.17 (c) should be used.

The pattern obtained from eqn.(2.3.21) is compared with that obtained from the method of moments by the dotted line in Fig.2.3.17 (b).

The total field $E_{\theta T}$ and the pattern $|D(\phi)|$ on the x-y plane are then expressed by using eqns.(2.3.18), (2.3.20) and (2.3.21) to be

$$E_{\theta T} = m_b\ \cos\ \phi + j\ n_u\ \sin\ (\frac{k\ell}{2}\ \sin\ \phi), \qquad (2.3.22)$$

and

$$|D(\phi)| = \sqrt{(\cos\phi)^2 + (n_u/m_b)^2\ \sin^2(\frac{k\ell}{2}\ \sin\phi)}. \qquad (2.3.23)$$

The ratio (n_u/m_b) can be evaluated from the measurement of the pattern. At first, m_b can be found by the measurement of $E_{\theta T}(0)$ on the x-y plane, since for $\phi = 0$, $E_{\theta T}(0) = m_b$. By the same technique, n_u can be found from $E_{\theta T}(\frac{\pi}{2})$, since $E_{\theta T}(\frac{\pi}{2}) = j\, n_u\, \sin(\frac{1}{2}\, k\ell)$; alternatively, n_u can be obtained by calculating the ratio of $E_{\theta T}(\frac{\pi}{2})$ and $E_{\theta T}(0)$, which are easily measured.

The measured pattern of a practical model in the 150 MHz band is shown in Fig.2.3.17 (d). From this pattern the ratio (n_u/m_b) is found to be 15. The dotted line in the Figure is the pattern calculated from eqn.(2.3.23), to which $(n_u/m_b) = 15$ is applied. As can be seen in the Figure, there is a fairly good agreement between the calculated and the measured patterns. It can also be said that these patterns agree closely with the pattern shown in Fig.2.3.17 (a), which was calculated by using the method of moments and $(n_u/m_b) = 16.5$.

In practical use, the equipment may be in various positions. The three cases considered are those where the equipment is placed on the coordinate system in the different orientations shown in Fig.2.3.18. The patterns produced are also shown for each case. In the Figure, the pattern of $E_{\phi u'}$ is that which is produced by I_{uH} and is calculated from the following equation, when a model shown in Fig.2.3.16 (b) is assumed:

$$E_{\phi u'} = j\, 60\pi\, [I_{uH}]\, \frac{\ell}{\lambda}\, \frac{e^{-jkr}}{r}\, \sin \phi, \qquad (2.3.24)$$

where $[I_{uH}] = |I_{uH}|e^{j\theta_H}$.

Since these situations will often be encountered in practical use, the patterns shown here are very helpful in designing the antenna system. In this respect, the field components contributing to the patterns for the positions A, B, and C are also given in Table 2.3.1 where 'omni' and 'eight', respectively, denote the shape of the directive patterns, omnidirectional and figure-eight, and the subscripts u and u' correspond to I_{uV} and I_{uH}. Response to more than two field components is desirable for operation in an urban environment and this will be discussed later.

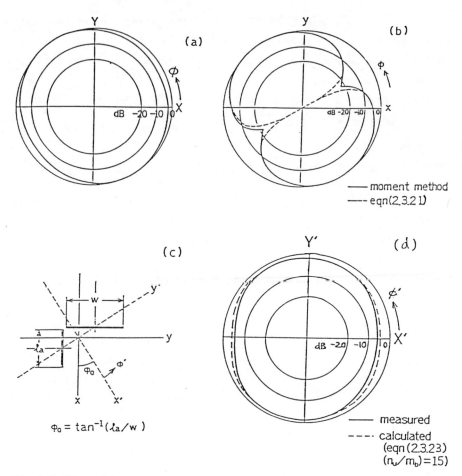

Fig.2.3.17.   (a) $E_{\theta T}$ pattern,   (b) $E_{\theta u}$ pattern,   (c) the   coordinate
system, and (d) $E_{\theta T}$ patterns measured and calculated.

Table.2.3.1   Field components for different equipment positions.

Type	θ component		ϕ component	
A	$E_{\theta b} + E_{\theta u}$	omni	$E_{\phi u'}$	eight
B	$E_{\theta b}$	eight	$E_{\phi u} + E_{\phi u'}$	omni
C	$E_{\theta u'}$	omni	$E_{\phi b}$	omni

The experimental results are shown in Fig.2.3.19, where A, B, and C correspond to the three positions shown in Fig.2.3.18. It is seen in the Figure that pattern A is nearly omnidirectional as a result of combination of $E_{\theta b}$ and $E_{\theta u}$ as is expected. Without including the unbalanced mode in the antenna system, the pattern produced by a loop

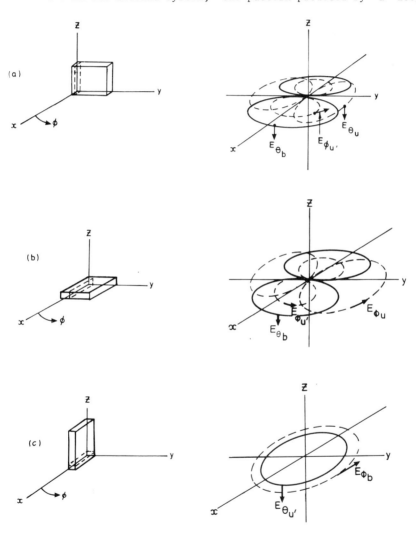

Fig.2.3.18   Receiving patterns depending upon position of the equipment box.

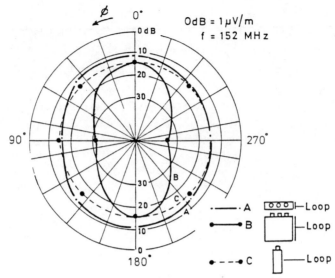

Fig.2.3.19.   Measured receiving patterns for different equipment placement.

element would become nearly a figure-eight shape. In the position B, the pattern becomes a figure-eight shape; this has been proved experimentally and is given in Fig.2.3.19. In the position C, there should be no response by the loop element alone, but the pattern C as shown in Fig.2.3.19 is nearly omnidirectional, although the response is about 5 dB lower than that obtained in position A. This omnidirectional pattern is attributed to I_{uH}. This pattern corresponds to that of $E_{\theta u}$, in Fig.2.3.18 (c). In the position B, the pattern becomes a figure-eight shape, which was also proved experimentally by pattern B in Fig.2.3.19.

2.3.3 Body effect and gain

(a) Body effect

As a pocket-size pager is usually carried most of the time in the bearer's pocket, special care in the design is needed to avoid sensitivity degradation due to the body effect.

It was found (Ito, Haruki, Fujimoto 1973) that the magnetic field

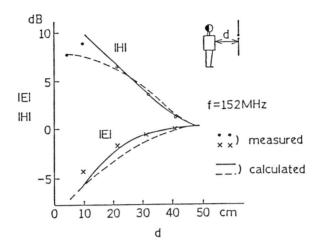

Fig.2.3.20.   Field intensity E and H in front of a human body at
    152 MHz.

intensity H was higher than the electric field intensity E in close
proximity to the human body. Measured values of E and H with respect
to the distance from a human body at 152 MHz are shown in Fig.2.3.20.
It can be seen in the Figure that at 2.5 to 10 cm from a human body,
the difference between E and H reaches as much as 12 dB. In Fig.2.3.
20, the full line expresses values calculated with an assumption that
the human body is an infinitely-long lossy dielectric elliptic cylind-
er with the complex permittivity $\varepsilon_b = \varepsilon' - j\varepsilon''$, where ε'' is related
with the conductivity $\sigma_b = \omega\varepsilon''\varepsilon_o$; ($\varepsilon_o = 8.8 \times 10^{-14}$ F/cm), and the
relative permeability μ_b. The field intensity in front of the diele-
ctric elliptic cylinder is calculated as the sum of the incident field
E_i and the scattered field E_s by the elliptic cylinder. The coordinate system is shown in Fig.2.3.21, where the elliptic cylinder is
placed on the x-axis, and the field intensity $\underline{E}$ generated by a current
source $\underline{I}$ at a far distant place is calculated as a function of d, the
distance from the elliptic cylinder. The parameters used are a = 10
cm, b = 16 cm, $\varepsilon_b = 47-j87$, and $\mu_b = 1$. The value of ε_b is determined
by referring to Schwan's data (Schwan 1980). Here, 0 dB is taken for
the intensity at d = 50 cm. A 925 MHz case is shown in Fig.2.3.22,
where both measured and calculated results are shown and $\varepsilon_b = 37.0 -$

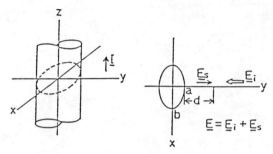

Fig.2.3.21.   Elliptic cylinder simulating a human body and the coordinate system used for the field calculation.

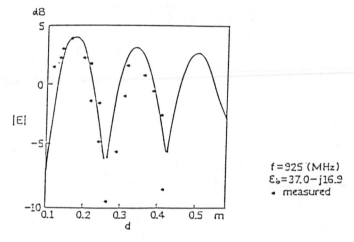

Fig.2.3.22.   Electric field intensity in front of a human body.

j16.9 is used for the calculation.

The calculation of the field can be made in another way by assuming a human body as a semi-infinite plane solid reflector with a reflection factor Γ (refer to Appendix A.2.2(p186)). It may be said that this is a very simple way to treat the problem, but it gives a fairly good result, especially for lower frequency regions. A model shown in Fig.2.3.23 (a) illustrates the principle of the calculation; the field intensity in front of the human body is calculated by taking the antenna image into consideration. An example of the calculated result (Ito, et al. (1973)) obtained by using this method is shown by the dotted line in Fig.2.3.20 and compared with the measured result and an-

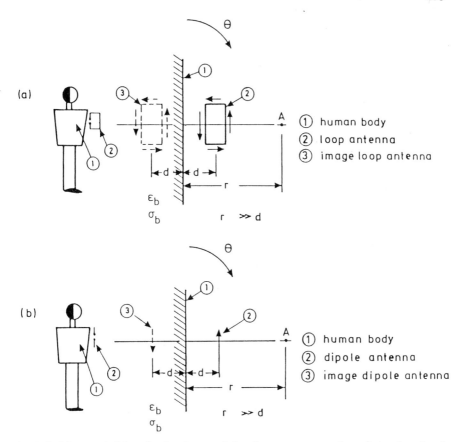

Fig.2.3.23.   Field calculation models for antennas placed in front of
a human body: (a) for loop antenna (b) for dipole antenna.

other calculation. It is assumed in the calculation that the   current
on the loop element is uniform and the human body has the   reflection
factor of 40 % at 152 MHz.   The value of Γ taken here was   greater
than that given by Schwan (1980);   however, it was found in practice
rather reasonable to predict experimental results more   closely.   The
difference between the electric and the magnetic field intensities   in
the vicinity of a human body can be explained by using the model shown
in Fig.2.3.23, where the image effect of the   antenna   is   taken   into
consideration.

As can be seen in the Figure, the loop antenna has   its   image   with the current flowing in the same direction as that of the original loop. Values of H with respect to the distance d from the human body can be calculated by

$$H = K [1 + \Gamma e^{-j2kd}] \frac{e^{-jkr}}{r} , \qquad (2.3.25)$$

where K is a constant, Γ the reflection factor, $K = 2\pi/\lambda$, and other symbols are as defined in the Figure.

In contrast, the dipole antenna's image has current flow in the opposite direction to that of the actual dipole and E is obtained by

$$E = K' [1 - \Gamma e^{-j2kd}] \frac{e^{-jkr}}{r} . \qquad (2.3.26)$$

The field produced by the image loop is additive to that produced by the actual loop; the field generated by the image dipole should be subtracted from the field generated by the actual dipole. This is the reason for the great difference between E and H in front of a human body. Although the calculation was done rather approximately by using the simple models shown above, it agrees fairly well with the measurements.

It should be noted that the loop antenna must be placed with its surface perpendicular to the reflector surface as shown in Fig.2.3.23 (a) for positive utilization of image effect due to a human body. If, however, the loop surface is parallel to the reflector surface, as shown in Fig.2.3.24, the current flow on the image loop element is in the opposite direction to that of the original loop element, so that the contribution of the image loop must be subtracted from the field produced by the actual loop in the vicinity of the reflector.

When a pager is put into its bearer's pocket, it is natural for the wider side of the equipment to face the bearer's body. It might be expected that a loop antenna should be placed along the wider side of the equipment so as to have a larger loop area and higher gain, since the gain of the loop antenna is proportional to its area. However, when the equipment is placed inside a pocket, the gain reduces tremendously because of the body effect; the image of the loop in the human

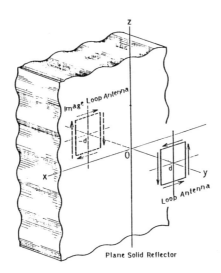

Fig.2.3.24.   A loop antenna facing reflector surface in parallel   and
    its image antenna; arrows indicate direction of current flow.

body has a negative effect on the field produced by the   actual   loop.
In order to utilize the image effect positively,   the   antenna   is installed along the narrower side of the equipment as shown in   Fig.2.3.
25.   On doing this the antenna gain in free space would be   sacrificed
by the reduction of the loop area,   but this is offset   by   the   image
effect and the total gain can exceed that of a loop installed   on   the
wider side of the equipment when the pager is   used   in   the   bearer's
pocket.

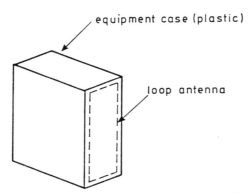

Fig.2.3.25.   Installation of loop inside pager equipment.

(b) Antenna system gain under the body effect

The antenna system gain in terms of the field intensity is given (refer to Appendix A 2.2(p186)) by

$$G_{body} = \sqrt{\frac{R_r + R_{loss}}{R_r + R_{loss} + R_m}} \cdot 2 \cos \left(\frac{2\pi}{\lambda} d \cos \theta\right), \qquad (2.3.27)$$

when the effect of the image produced by the body on the gain is taken into account. R_m is the mutual resistance between the actual loop and the image loop. For a small loop $R_{loss} \gg R_r$, R_m and the gain G_{body} on the horizontal plane ($\theta = \frac{\pi}{2}$) may be approximated by

$$G_{body} = 2 \cos \left(\frac{2\pi}{\lambda} d\right) . \qquad (2.3.28)$$

Unlike a loop, a dipole has an image element whose phase is negative and the gain G'_{body} is

$$G'_{body} = 2 \sin \left(\frac{2\pi}{\lambda} d\right) . \qquad (2.3.29)$$

It should be noted that the above approximations cannot be applied to the case where d is extremely small and $R_{loss} > R_m$.

An example of the values of G_{body} of an antenna system, both calculated and measured, is shown in Fig.2.3.26, where a loop antenna of ℓ_b

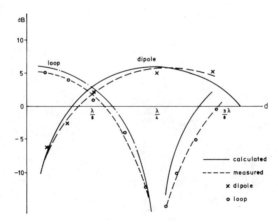

Fig.2.3.26. G_{body} of an antenna system evaluated from the field intensity.

= 66 mm and ℓ_a = 13 mm, and a short dipole of 120 mm are used. The gains are plotted against the distance of the antenna from the body. The frequency used is 470 MHz. The increase in the gain from the human body effect is 6 dB at most.

2.3.4 Field performance with two-polarization response

A pager is used not only in a pocket, but also in various other locations, in a carrying bag, on a desk, in an operator's hand, for example, and it would be ideal if the pager performance did not change under these conditions. In practice, however, no image effect can be expected when a pager is operated outside a pocket, and some gain reduction is unavoidable. This problem can be partly overcome by the unbalanced component, which can supplement the loop antenna performance. Because of the unbalanced component, the antenna system can respond to a field to which the loop in isolation cannot respond. Fig.2.3.16 (b) and (c) showed that the loop element (balanced component) can respond to a vertically polarized wave, while the unbalanced component will respond to a horizontally polarized wave. The unbalanced component reduces the risk of the null response that would result from using the loop element only. Response in two polarizations is attractive in urban area operations where a field may have a random distribution in terms of amplitude, phase, and polarization, and the capability of receiving waves in both polarizations may provide an increased response by summing up fluctuating field distributions. This effect has not been analyzed quantitatively, but some improvement in performance has been experienced in experimental operations. (Tanaka, 1985). (cf.Section 2.4.2).

2.3.5. Design data

Design data and experimental results for VHF and UHF models are given here as examples; firstly a model for a VHF pager in the 150 MHz band and secondly models for UHF pagers in the 470 MHz and 920 MHz bands are given in 2.3.4(g).

(1) VHF model

(a) Antenna structure

The loop element can be composed of a thin wire, a thin plate, printed wire or other materials. A thin-wire small loop antenna is used here for the model. Antenna dimensions and other design parameters are given in Table 2.3.2.

(b) Impedance parameters and quality factor

By using the values given in Table 2.3.2, impedance parameters are calculated and given in Table 2.3.3.

Table 2.3.2.
Antenna dimensions
and design parame-
ters

ℓ_b	65	mm
ℓ_a	13.8	mm
a	1.2	mm
σ	1.1×10^7	S/m
f_0	152	MHz

Table 2.3.3.
Calculated impedance
parameters

R_r	0.0017	Ω
R_{loss}	0.3	Ω
L_T	958×10^{-10}	H
ωL_T	91.4	Ω
Q	304.7	

(c) Gain

The gain of the loop antenna is found by using eqn.(2.3.6) combined with eqn.(2.3.5):

$$G_L \doteqdot 10 \log_{10}(\frac{0.0017}{0.3}) - 0.39 \text{ [dB]} \qquad (2.3.30)$$

$$= -22.8 \qquad \text{[dB]} .$$

The capacitor necessary for resonance is calculated as 11 pF. With the circuit structure shown in Fig.2.3.9, the value of t is calculated to be 8 mm for obtaining $Y_i|_{res}$ = 20 mS. With these conditions the measured gain G_{Lm} is −23 dB, which agrees well with the calculated G_L from eqn.(2.3.30).

(d) Built-in antenna

When the loop antenna is built into the pager circuit, the Q and gain of the loop antenna will be changed by the effect of adjacent materials. The gain G_L' in this case is calculated by using η' of eqn. (2.3.14):

$$G_L' = 10 \log_{10}(2R_r \frac{Q_L'}{\omega L_T}) - 0.39 \ [dB] \qquad (2.3.31)$$

$$= 10 \log_{10}Q_L' - 47.6 \ . \qquad [dB] \qquad (2.3.32)$$

G_L' as a function of Q_L' is plotted in Fig.2.3.27. If Q_L' of the antenna can be determined, G_L' can be calculated with the aid of eqn.(2.3.32).

The antenna impedance is also varied by the adjacent material effect and the tapping point t shifted from that determined in a free space

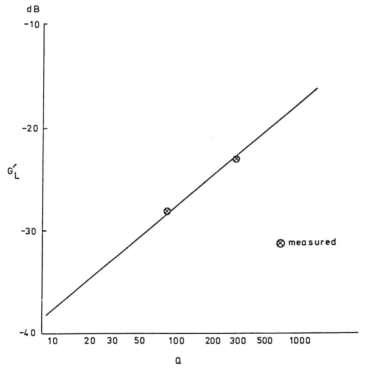

Fig.2.3.27.   Gain vs. Q_L'

condition. For example, the tapping point t shifted from 8 mm to 14 mm when the antenna was built into the pager model with dimensions of 120 × 60 × 20 [mm]. Measured gain was -28 dB, about a 5 dB drop from that obtained in the free space condition. Measured Q_L' was 83. The gain G_L' evaluated by eqn.(2.3.32) was -28.4 dB, which agrees with that measured.

The bandwidth W of this antenna is calculated to be

$$W = \frac{f_0}{Q_L} = \frac{152}{\frac{1}{2}(83)} = 3.7 \ . \qquad [\text{MHz}] \qquad (2.3.33)$$

It is interesting to compare this value with the bandwidth W_f in a free space condition, which is

$$W_f = \frac{f_0}{\frac{1}{2}Q} = \frac{152}{\frac{1}{2}(304.7)} \approx 1.0 \ . \qquad [\text{MHz}] \qquad (2.3.34)$$

When the pager model was put into the operator's pocket, a gain increase of about 5 dB was observed.

(e) Comparison with other types of antenna

A small dipole and a ferrite antenna were compared with a small loop antenna. Models used for the comparison are shown in Fig.2.3.28. The size of the pager model is 120 × 50 × 20 [mm]. The dipole model

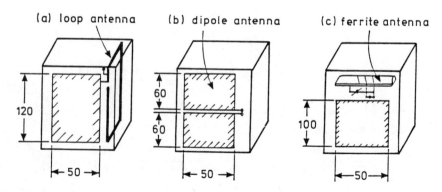

(a) loop antenna   (b) dipole antenna   (c) ferrite antenna

Fig.2.3.28. Models used for comparison. (a) a small loop antenna (b) a small dipole antenna (c) a ferrite antenna

(b) is composed of two thin conducting plates of 50 × 60 [mm], as shown in Fig.2.3.28(b). The model (c) consists of a small ferrite antenna and a thin conducting plate which simulates a pager circuit having a size of 50 × 100 [mm].

The relative sensitivity of these model pagers was measured in the field in both free space and in-pocket conditions. Table 2.3.4 shows the results. In free space, the small loop model showed the highest sensitivity and the ferrite antenna model was worst with 5 dB lower sensitivity than that of the loop. When the model was placed inside of an operator's chest pocket (left-hand side), a sensitivity increase of 5 to 7 dB was observed as expected, for the pagers with loop and ferrite antennas, while the sensitivity of the dipole model decreased by as much as 7 dB. This implies that the sensitivity of the loop model is superior to the dipole model by 13.5 dB.

Table 2.3.4. Sensitivity comparison of built-in small antennas

	free space [dB]	in-pocket [dB]	sensitivity relative[dB]	dimensions [mm]
dipole antenna	−21	−21 − 7 = −28	0	50 × 120
ferrite antenna	−24.5	−24.5 + 7 = −17.5	+10.5	10 × 50 × 4 $\mu Q = 40$
loop antenna	−19.5	−19.5 + 5 = −14.5	+13.5	19 × 120

(f) Receiving patterns

Receiving patterns in the horizontal plane were compared for the loop and dipole models and are shown in Fig.2.3.29. The measurement was made for the case where the pager model was put into an operator's pocket and the receiving pattern is shown against the position of human body. For most orientations of the human body the sensitivity obtained by the loop model exceeded that obtained by the dipole model by about 3 to 7 dB. The dipole model shows higher sensitivity for a range of angles several tens of degrees in the opposite direction to the position of the model with respect to the human body.

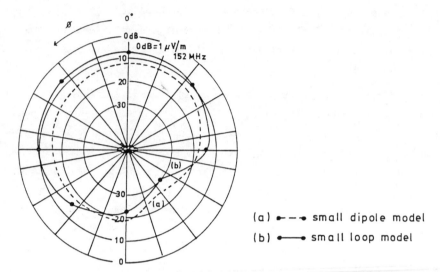

Fig.2.3.29. Receiving patterns of the loop model (a) and dipole model
(b) shown in Fig.2.3.28.

(g) Practical models

Pagers presently used employ either thin-wire or a thin plate loop
antenna and two examples are shown in Fig.2.3.30 for an operating frequency of 250 MHz.

(2) UHF models

There is no essential difference between VHF and UHF pager design
concepts. The major difference between them may be found in the tuning circuit. As the operating frequency becomes high, the inductive
impedance of the loop increases and the tuning capacitance will not be
small enough to satisfy the resonance condition, because of its residual stray capacitance. To avoid this difficulty another capacitor $C_{\ell 2}$
is placed in series with the loop inductance, as was shown in Fig.2.3.
11. An example of the impedance variation of a loop having dimensions
of ℓ_a = 15 mm and ℓ_b = 65.5 mm is shown in Fig.2.3.31, where the operating frequency used is 470 MHz. In the Figure, $C_{\ell 2}$ is placed in series with $C_{\ell 1}$ and by varying the value of $C_{\ell 2}$ the antenna impedance is
varied as shown in the Figure; it can be arranged to have a value
which can match the load impedance (50 Ω). Various other ways for

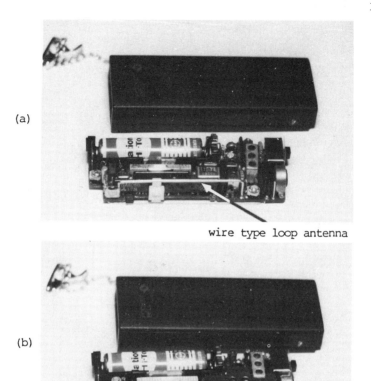

(a)

wire type loop antenna

(b)

plate type loop antenna

Fig.2.3.30. Small loop antennas used for pagers; (a) thin wire type and (b) thin flat plate type.

tuning were tested and one example is shown in Fig.2.3.32.

In a loop shown in Fig.2.3.32, an additional fixed capacitor $C_{\ell 3}$ is placed on a corner of the loop element. The variation of the input impedance Z_i against the value of $C_{\ell 2}$ (maximum 10 pF) is shown in the Figure.   Using $C_{\ell 3}$ is another effective way to realize the reso- nance.

Measured receiving patterns in both free space and in-pocket condi- tions are shown in Fig.2.3.33. The pattern is essentially the same as in the VHF case, but the attenuation behind the human body is greater

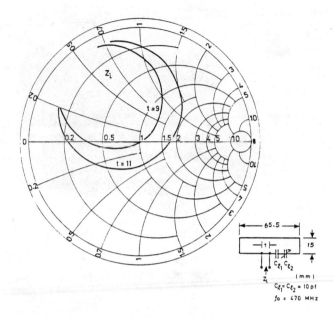

Fig.2.3.31. Impedance Z_i against series capacitor $C_{\ell 2}$ and tapping point t.

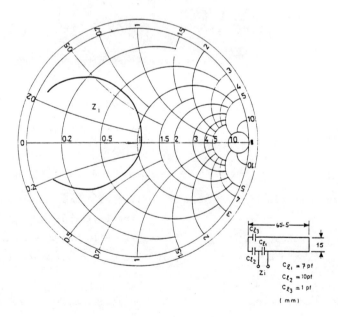

Fig.2.3.32. Impedance Z_i against $C_{\ell 2}$ with an additional fixed capacitor $C_{\ell 3}$ in the loop.

than that in the VHF model. Both measured and calculated patterns in 920 MHz band are shown in Fig.2.3.34, where the model shown in Fig.2.

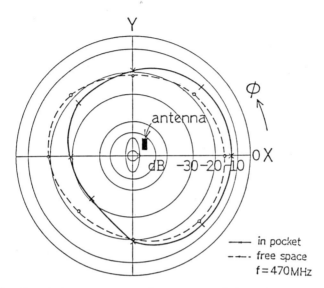

Fig.2.3.33. Receiving patterns of a pager model in free space and in-operation.

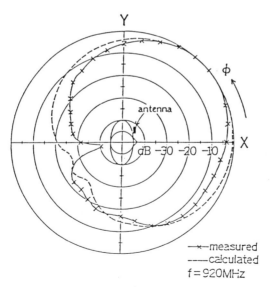

Fig.2.3.34. Receiving patterns (in-pocket condition) measured and calculated.

3.21 is used for the calculation. A larger gain decrease in the UHF region as compared with that in the VHF region comes from the effect of the proximity of the loop to the body. This is because the absorption of the electromagnetic energy by the human body increases and the antenna efficiency decreases due to the impedance variation caused by the adjacent material effect, as the frequency increases.

2.4. Inverted-L Antennas

An antenna which has the structure shown in Fig.2.4.1 is called an Inverted-L antenna (ILA) and consists of a short monopole as a vertical element and a wire horizontal element attached at the end of the monopole.

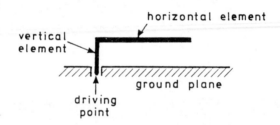

Fig.2.4.1.   Fundamental structure of inverted -L antenna (ILA).

The I L A is basically a low-profile structure, because the height of the vertical element is usually constrained to a fraction of the wavelength. The horizontal element is not necessarily very short, and usually has a length of about a quarter wavelength.

As the structure is essentially low profile, the ILA may be categorized as a physically constrained small antenna. In practical applications, various modified structures have been developed; some examples are shown in Fig.2.4.2 - Fig.2.4.4.

A simple and typical modification of ILA is an inverted-F antenna (IFA) shown in Fig.2.4.2. A small I-L element is attached at the end of the vertical element of an ILA and the appearance is that of a letter F facing the ground plane - thus its name.

The ILA has an inherently low impedance, since the antenna is essen-

Fig.2.4.2. Inverted-F antenna (IFA) (ILA with another inverted-L element attached to the vertical element).

tially a vertical short monopole loaded with a long horizontal wire at the end of the monopole. The input impedance is nearly equal to that of the short monopole plus the reactance of the horizontal wire closely placed to the ground plane. To increase the radiation impedance, another inverted-L-shaped element is attached at the end of the vertical element and this is why the ILA is modified to have the IFA form.

This modification is very important because the input impedance of an IFA can be arranged to have an appropriate value to match the load impedance, without using any additional circuit between the antenna and the load.

By utilizing this feature the IFA, rather than the ILA, has been used in practice and applied often to moving bodies such as rockets and aircraft, because of its low-profile structure.

One drawback of an ILA consisting of thin wires is the narrow bandwidth, typically only one per cent, or less of the centre frequency. To widen the bandwidth, a modification can be made by replacing the wire element by a plate, as shown in Fig.2.4.3. This type of ILA has been applied on portable equipment, and a brief discussion appears in Section 2.4.3.

Another possibility for widening the bandwidth is to use an integration technique. Two examples are shown in Fig.2.4.4 (a) and (b), where (a) shows an ILA with an impedance element Z_ℓ placed at the end

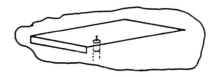

Fig.2.4.3. IFA with wire element replaced by plate element.

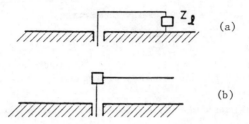

Fig.2.4.4.   (a) ILA with an impedance Z_ℓ placed at the end of the
horizontal element.   (b) ILA with a device or a circuit (black box)
placed between the vertical and horizontal elements.

of the horizontal element and (b) shows an ILA loaded with a device or
a circuit between the vertical and horizontal elements.

The integration technique aims not only at increasing bandwidth, but
also at the modification of the current distributions on both the vertical and horizontal elements.

Variations in the current distributions will change the antenna
characteristics such as gain, impedance, and radiation pattern. In
this Section, two practical examples are shown: an IFA with a form
shown in Fig.2.4.4 (a) using a parasitic I-L element as Z_L, and another IFA using the type shown in Fig.2.4.4 (b) for increasing system
gain by integrating a transistor circuit. The latter IFA consists of
very short horizontal and vertical elements, so that it can be classified as an electrically small antenna.

One more important property of the ILA is its performance with both
vertical and horizontal polarizations, because the antenna has both
vertical and horizontal elements. In an urban environment, for example, where the electromagnetic field may have random fluctuating distributions, compounding of the vertical polarization and the horizontal polarization can provide an averaging effect and improve the reception. The usefulness of an ILA utilized in a randomly fluctuating
field has been demonstrated in Tokyo in an experiment by using model
antennas for mobile phone systems (Tanaka et al., 1985).

The most attractive feature of the ILA, a low-profile structure, is
that the antenna element can be flushmounted onto the surface of the

equipment. This ensures safety in handling and provides resistance to breakage in practical field use (Itoh et al., 1969). One example of a flushmounted antenna is considered in Section 2.4.3 where an ILA element is attached onto the top of a rectangular equipment box. This equipment is assumed to be portable, with dimensions comparable to or smaller than the wavelength. The equipment box is simulated by a rectangular conducting box and is treated as a radiating element. The radiation patterns are calculated for various sizes of the box and the results provide useful design parameters for portable applications.

An IFA is a very useful antenna provided design features such as its low profile and impedance matching capabilities can be fully utilized. In addition to these features, its performance with two-polarization would be useful for the urban environmental use. Taking these facts into account it can be said that IFA is an especially attractive antenna for mobile communications.

2.4.1 Treatment of the ILA

An ILA consisting of a very thin wire element can be treated by the method of moments mentioned in Section 2.1, and the antenna characteristics such as input impedance, current distributions, and radiation patterns, can be calculated. Variations of the input impedances with the dimensions of the antenna will be given later in this Section based mainly on calculations using the method of moments.

For calculating the radiation patterns of the ILA, however, the analysis here will be made simpler by assuming zeroth-order (sinusoidal) current distributions on the antenna elements; this is a rough approximation, but the method is useful in practice (Nagai, 1969). By this means, radiation from each element can be found individually and it is easy to identify which element contributes to a given polarization. This concept can be applied even when an antenna is modified in structure.

(1) Input impedance characteristics

The input impedance of the ILA has been previously analysed for some parameters by King (1969) and Guertler (1977). These have shown that the ILA is not really practical unless its configuration is modified to have a high enough input impedance to match the load impedance. The IFA is the simplest way of modifying the ILA structure and so this Section discusses impedance characteristics of both ILA and IFA, with emphasis on practical design considerations.

The input impedances of typical ILA structures, shown in Fig.2.4.5 (a), are given as a function of the height h in Fig.2.4.5 (b), where the length ℓ_h of the horizontal element is taken as the parameter. As the vertical part of the antenna is a short monopole, the values of the input impedance are normally very low, and impedance will increase with antenna height. For the IFA shown in Fig.2.4.6 (a), the input impedance as a function of frequency is given in Fig.2.4.6 (b), where values are provided for the parameter of the length ℓ_s of the attached elements, while $(\ell_h + \ell_s)$ and h are fixed. When the height h of the antenna is varied, the input impedances vary with frequency as shown in Fig.2.4.6 (c) and (d), where in (c) h is taken as 30, 40 and 50 mm, $\ell_s = 7$ mm, and in (d) 10, 12 and 14 mm.

As can be seen from the Figures, the length ℓ_s of the attached element plays an important role in increasing the input impedance. By comparing data shown in Fig.2.4.5 (b) and Fig.2.4.6 (b)-(d), the effectiveness of an attached element for modifying an I-L shape into an I-F shape can be clearly understood.

(2) Radiation patterns

Radiation pattern of the IFA is essentially the same as that of the ILA when the length ℓ_s is very short. Hence only the case for the ILA is considered here, and, as noted earlier, a rather simple way of finding the radiation pattern is used instead of the moment method. By this means, one can analytically understand the contribution made by each element to the pattern.

An ILA is assumed to be located on the ground plane, as shown in Fig.2.4.7 (a), and by taking the image into consideration, the antenna is treated as equivalent to a short dipole antenna driven at the centre and a pair of parallel wires connected at each end of the dipole, as shown in Fig.2.4.7 (b). Fig.2.4.7 (c) illustrates the coordinate

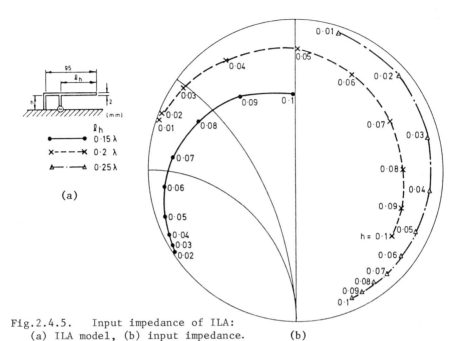

Fig.2.4.5.   Input impedance of ILA:
   (a) ILA model, (b) input impedance.   (b)

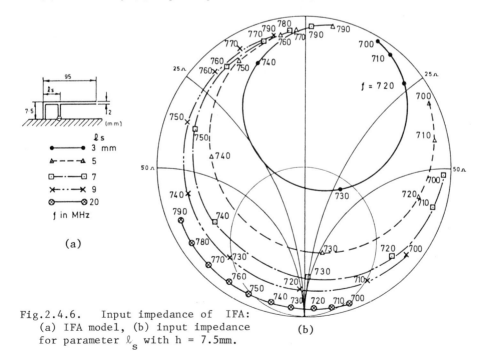

Fig.2.4.6.   Input impedance of IFA:
   (a) IFA model, (b) input impedance
for parameter ℓ_s with h = 7.5mm.   (b)

122

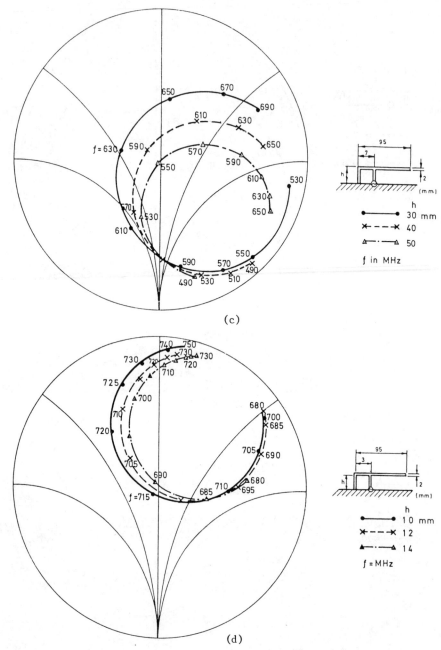

Fig.2.4.6.   Input impedance of IFA: (c) for parameter h with ℓ_s = 7mm
and (d) with ℓ_s = 3mm.

123

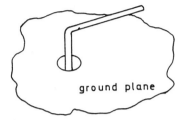

Fig.2.4.7.(a)   I L A on the ground plane.

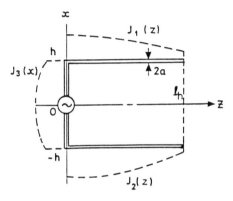

Fig.2.4.7.(b)   Antenna geometry and current distributions assumed.

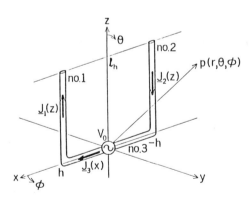

Fig.2.4.7.(c)   Coordinate system.

system, where the vertical element, here a dipole element, is placed
on the x-axis, and the driving-point is located at the origin, while
the horizontal element and its image are aligned parallel to the z-
axis.

The currents flowing on each element are assumed to be $\underline{J}_1$, $\underline{J}_2$, and $\underline{J}_3$ (as in Fig.2.4.7 (c)), and are expressed by

$$\underline{J}_1(z) = \hat{\underline{z}} \, J_z \, \sin\{k(\ell_h - z')\}\cos(kh),$$

$$\underline{J}_2(z) = -\hat{\underline{z}} \, J_z \, \sin\{k(\ell_h - z')\}\cos(kh), \qquad (2.4.1)$$

$$\underline{J}_3(x) = \hat{\underline{x}} \, J_x \, \cos(k\,x')\sin(k\ell_h),$$

where $\hat{\underline{x}}$ and $\hat{\underline{z}}$ are unit vectors.

By calculating vector potentials for each of the elements and performing integrations with respect to the radiation vectors, the fields produced by each element can be found as follows:

(a) E fields produced by the no. 1 and the no. 2 elements are

$$E_\theta = -60J_z \, \frac{e^{-jkr}}{r} \, \cos(kh)\frac{SIN}{\sin\theta} [e^{jk\ell_h\cos\theta} - j\{\cos\theta\cdot\sin(k\ell_h) - \cos(k\ell_h)\}],$$

$$(2.4.2)$$

and

$$E_\phi = 0, \qquad (2.4.3)$$

where

$$SIN \triangleq \sin(kh\cdot\sin\theta\cdot\cos\phi), \qquad (2.4.4)$$

and

$$r = \sqrt{x^2 + y^2 + z^2}, \qquad (2.4.5)$$

(b) E fields produced by the no. 3 element are

$$E_\theta = -j60J_x \, \frac{e^{-jkr}}{r} \, \sin(k\ell_h)\cdot\cos\theta\cdot\cos\phi\cdot f(\theta, \phi, h), \qquad (2.4.6)$$

and

$$E_\phi = j60J_x \, \frac{e^{-jkr}}{r} \, \sin(k\ell_h)\cdot\sin\phi\cdot f(\theta, \phi, h), \qquad (2.4.7)$$

where

$$f(\theta, \phi, h) \triangleq \frac{\sin(kh)\cdot COS - \sin\theta\cdot\cos\phi\cdot\cos(kh) \; SIN}{1 - \sin^2\theta\cdot\cos^2\phi} \qquad (2.4.8)$$

and

$$\text{COS} \triangleq \cos(kh \cdot \sin\theta \cdot \cos\phi) \quad . \tag{2.4.9}$$

Now, if it is assumed that $J_x = J_z = I_0$, $\ell_h = \frac{\lambda}{4}$, and $h \ll \lambda$, the E fields obtained above can be expressed by simplified forms as follows:

(c) E fields produced by the no. 1 and the no. 2 elements

$$E_\theta = -60I_0 \frac{e^{-jkr}}{r} kh \cos\phi [\cos(\frac{\pi}{2}\cos\theta) + j\{\sin(\frac{\pi}{2}\cos\theta) - \cos\theta\}] ,$$

$$\tag{2.4.10}$$

and

$$E_\phi = 0, \tag{2.4.11}$$

and

(d) by the no. 3 element,

$$E_\theta = -j60I_0 \frac{e^{-jkr}}{r} kh \cos\theta \cdot \cos\phi , \tag{2.4.12}$$

and

$$E_\phi = j60I_0 \frac{e^{-jkr}}{r} kh \sin\phi . \tag{2.4.13}$$

Let us consider the radiation patterns in the x-y, y-z, and x-z planes for the sake of simplicity. These are as follows:

(e) On the x-y plane ($\theta = \frac{\pi}{2}$), the E fields become

$$E_\theta = -60I_0 \frac{e^{-jkr}}{r} kh \cos\phi , \tag{2.4.14}$$

which is produced by the no. 1 and no. 2 elements, and

$$E_\phi = j60I_0 \frac{e^{-jkr}}{r} kh \sin\phi , \tag{2.4.15}$$

which is produced by the no. 3 element.

Those patterns are illustrated in Fig.2.4.8 (a). As can be seen from eqns.(2.4.14) and (2.4.15) and Fig.2.4.8 (a), E_θ and E_ϕ have the same pattern and if both vertically and horizontally-polarised components are combined appropriately, omnidirectional characteristics may be obtained.

(f) On the x-z plane ($\phi = 0$), the E fields become

$$E_{\theta_{1-2}} = -60I_0 \frac{e^{-jkr}}{r} kh[\cos(\frac{\pi}{2}\cos\theta) + j\{\sin(\frac{\pi}{2}\cos\theta) - \cos\theta\}],$$

$$(2.4.16)$$

which is produced by the no. 1 and the no. 2 elements, and

$$E_{\theta_3} = -j60I_0 \frac{e^{-jkr}}{r} kh\cos\theta \, , \qquad (2.4.17)$$

which is produced by the no. 3 element.

Fig.2.4.8 (b) illustrates the patterns drawn from eqns. (2.4.16) and (2.4.17). There is no E_ϕ component, but two E_θ components are generated, differing both in phase and in the direction of the maximum radiation. This implies that the omnidirectional pattern can also be obtained easily in the x-z plane by arranging the phase of each element appropriately.

(g) On the y-z plane, no field will be produced by the no. 1 and the no. 2 elements; i.e.,

$$E_\theta = 0, \qquad (2.4.18)$$

but by the no. 3 element,

$$E_\phi = j60I_0 \frac{e^{-jkr}}{r} kh \qquad (2.4.19)$$

will be generated. The pattern in this case is a circle as shown in Fig.2.4.8 (c).

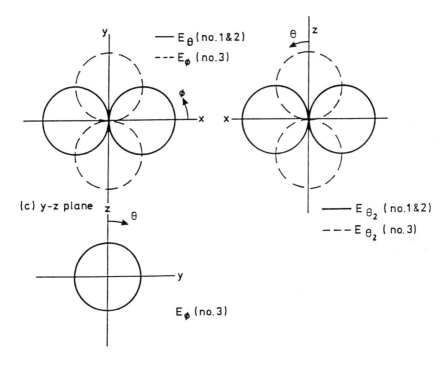

(a) x-y plane   (b) x-z plane

E_θ (no.1&2)
E_ϕ (no.3)

(c) y-z plane

E_{θ_2} (no.1&2)
E_{θ_2} (no.3)

E_ϕ (no.3)

Fig.2.4.8.   Radiation patterns.

2.4.2 Modification of ILA and IFA structure

Two examples of modified ILA structures are discussed. One is an IFA that achieves wide bandwidth by using a plate element and is useful for the application to either vehicular or portable equipment. Some examples used for experiments in the practical trials will be shown. The other example is an ILA where a normal mode helix is used as the horizontal element and a transistor is placed between the horizontal and vertical elements. The latter antenna has been practically applied to a portable receiver-amplifier and improved S/N performance was obtained.

(a) IFA with plate element

To get broad bandwidth characteristics, the horizontal element is

128

changed from a wire to a plate. An experimental antenna is illustrated in Fig.2.4.9, where the lengths P_x and P_y are varied as parameters. The frequency characteristics, measured for several sizes of
antenna, are shown in Fig.2.4.10. For the case (d) in the Figure, the
bandwidth for VSWR < 2 can be read as about 2.5%, but with a wire element, the bandwidth is about 0.8% (see Fig.2.4.6). Thus, the replacement of the horizontal element from a wire to a plate can be seen to
be effective in making bandwidth broader.

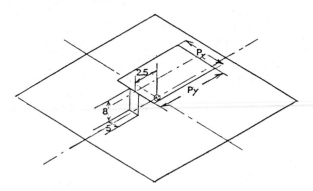

Fig.2.4.9   IFA with a wire horizontal element replaced by a plate.

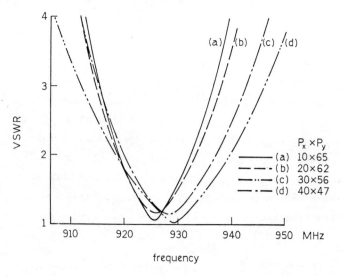

Fig.2.4.10.   Frequency characteristics of the antenna shown in Fig.2.
  4.9.   The size of ground plane used is 320 × 320 (mm).

The bandwidth is affected very much by the size of the ground plane, on which the antenna is mounted. By reducing the ground plane size, the bandwidth of an IFA system can be broadened.

Another example of an IFA, fabricated with a printed circuit board, is shown in Fig.2.4.11 (a). This antenna has another parasitic ele-

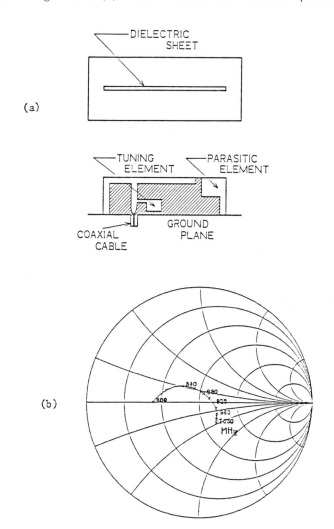

Fig.2.4.11. IFA fabricated with a printed circuit board and its frequency characteristics: (a) antenna structure and (b) frequency characteristics.

ment near the end of the horizontal element to broaden the frequency characteristic and also a tuning element in the middle. The antenna element is placed on a conducting plate of size 120×50 (mm). The frequency characteristic in the 900 MHz band is fairly broad as Fig.2. 4.11 (b) shows. The broad bandwidth in this case may also be attributable to the use of a small ground plane which lowered the Q of the antenna system.

In practical experiments, various modified types of IFA have been developed and tested. Some models used in the field test of mobile phone system in Tokyo are mentioned in Section 2.4.4.

(b) ILA integrated with active device

Here an ILA is integrated with a transistor circuit between vertical and horizontal elements, as shown in Fig.2.4.12. In general, the objectives of integration of a three-terminal device, such as transistor, are (1) to obtain variation of the current distribution on the antenna element and (2) to transform the impedance at some intermediate position on the antenna element. By varying the phase of the current on the antenna element, radiation patterns can be varied; for instance, the direction of maximum radiation may be shifted from one side to the other. The impedance transformation will serve as a means of optimizing the antenna impedance to match the load impedance, even when the antenna is very short and would normally have a very low radiation impedance.

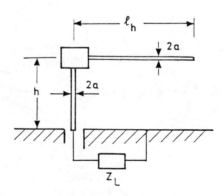

Fig.2.4.12.   ILA integrated with a device or devices.

On optimizing antenna impedance, impedance matching becomes feasible and appreciable antenna gain may be obtained, even though the size of the antenna is very small compared with the wavelength.

The model considered here is a small built-in ILA developed for a portable receiver-amplifier to replace a quarter-wavelength monopole in 40 MHz band. A transistor circuit is integrated into the ILA element for the purpose of impedance transformation and amplification of current flowing on the horizontal element. The antenna performance was compared with the quarter-wavelength monopole previously used for the equipment. As will be shown later, about 10 dB improvement in terms of S/N at the receiver output was observed, although the size of the antenna is electrically small.

The method of analysis of this type of antenna is shown first and the results obtained for this example are destribed. Fig.2.4.13 illustrates a model of this type of antenna. The size of the circuit to be integrated with the antenna should be as small as possible so as not to interfere significantly with radiation.

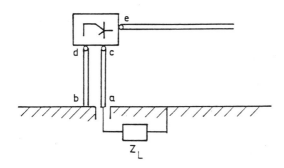

Fig.2.4.13.   ILA integrated with a transistor circuit.

An ILA integrated or loaded with a transistor circuit may be equivalently expressed by using the image of the antenna system as shown in Fig.2.4.14. This has a symmetrical structure with respect to the y-axis and an induced voltage $2V_0$ at the driving point. This antenna system is further decomposed into two parts, one pertaining to a balanced component and the other to an unbalanced component, as shown in Fig.2.4.15 (a) and (b), respectively, based on the model of the cur-

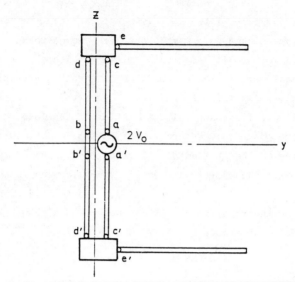

Fig.2.4.14.   Equivalent expression of the antenna system shown in Fig.2.4.13.

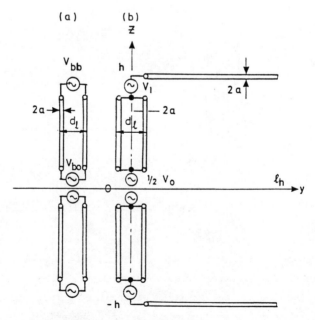

Fig.2.4.15.   Decomposition of the antenna system shown in Fig.2.3.14.
(a) part pertaining to the balanced component.
(b) part pertaining to the unbalanced component.

133

rents flowing on the antenna element.

The part pertaining to the balanced mode is equivalently expressed by a two-thin-wire transmission line with length h and distance d_ℓ between the wires. The terminal voltages are here designated as V_{bo} and V_{bb}, as shown in Fig.2.4.15 (a).

The part related to the unbalanced mode which contributes directly to radiation is equivalently expressed by a type of ILA shown in Fig. 2.4.15 (b), where the vertical element consists of two thin wires shorted at both ends. On the antenna element, two voltages V_1 and V_0, derived from induced voltages at the circuit terminals and the driving point, respectively, are located as shown in Fig.2.4.15 (b). The vertical elements consisting of two thin wires are replaced by a thin wire of equivalent diameter 2a' where a' is approximately given by $\sqrt{ad}$ (Uda, Mushiake, 1954), so that the equivalent expression of the unbalanced mode part can be redrawn as shown in Fig.2.4.16. In Fig.2.4.16 the antenna system is represented by an ILA with voltages V_1 at the intermediate position and V_0 at the driving point of the antenna and with the vertical element having the diameter 2a'.

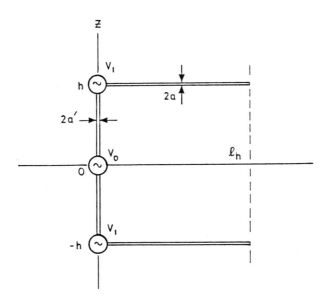

Fig.2.4.16.   Equivalent expression of the unbalanced mode part.

The analysis of this antenna system can be made by first treating it as two separate parts, one relating to a balanced component and the other to an unbalanced component, and then combining them. The experimental structure of the antenna (Fujimoto, Hiroi, 1969) is as shown in Fig.2.4.17, where (a) illustrates the antenna structure, (b) details of the circuitry, and (c) antenna installation in the receiver box. A (normal-mode) helix is used for the horizontal element and a

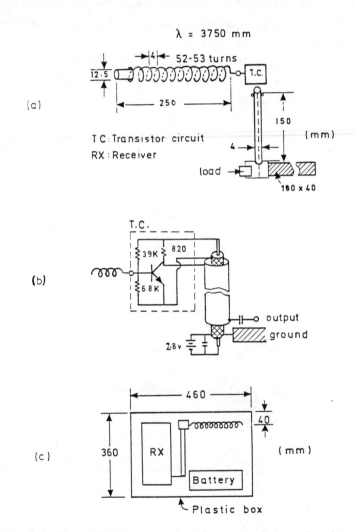

Fig.2.4.17.   ILA integrated with a transistor circuit.

coaxial line is used as the vertical element where the outer conductor functions as the radiation element and the inner conductor serves
as the D.C. path to the transistor circuit. The length of the vertical element is 0.04 λ and that of the horizontal element is 0.067 λ as
shown in Fig.2.4.17 (a). This antenna system was intended to be
built into the box and replaces a conventional monopole element, which
has a length of 115 cm (0.03 λ) for a receiver in the 40 MHz band.
The output S/N characteristics of the receiver seen in Fig.2.4.18 show
a remarkable improvement of about 7 dB at and over a 55 dB input level, compared with the output of the monopole antenna. Note that in
the Figure, the coordinate represents the output S/N. Since the active device generates noise, it is not sufficient to consider only
gain in amplification; S/N must be used for the evaluation of the performance of an antenna system incorporating an active device.

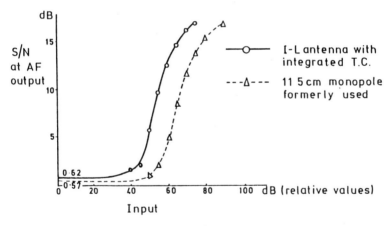

Fig.2.4.18.   S/N performance.

2.4.3. I L A placed on the top side of a rectangular conducting box

One of the applications of ILAs to portable equipment involves
the placement of an antenna element on the top side of a rectangular
conducting box. The antenna system is shown in Fig.2.4.19. When the
conducting box is small compared with the wavelength, the box should
be included in the antenna system, since radiation currents will flow

on the surface of the box and the radiation from the box should not be ignored. This sort of problem is treated in detail in Chapter 4, where loop, monopole and dipole elements are examined. The ILA is, however, excluded from Chapter 4 and considered here instead because it is highly relevant to this Chapter. The method of analysis is the same as that used in Chapter 4.

The coordinate system for the analysis is shown in Fig.2.4.19. In the analysis, the conducting box is represented by a group of thin wires as shown in Fig.2.4.20, which forms an approximate electrical representation of the surface of the box (Hirasawa, Fujimoto, 1982 a,

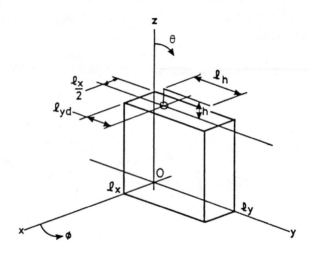

Fig.2.4.19. ILA placed on the top side of a conducting box, with the coordinate system used.

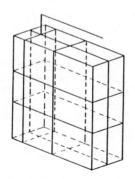

Fig.2.4.20. Wire-grid model of an ILA placed on a conducting box.

1982 b). The shape of the box in practice may not be exactly rectangular and it is usually not made from a conducting material but, for this
simple treatment, the assumptions are made that the equipment has a
rectangular shape and is highly conductive. In practice metal frames,
printed circuit boards and various other interior metallic parts and
components tend to act electrically as a block of a conductor which
has roughly the profile of a rectangular box.

The method of moments described in Section 2.1 is used to find the
current distributions on the surfaces of the box, and thus the radiation patterns.

Fig.2.4.21 (a) shows the current distributions (absolute values)
with hatched parts when the length ℓ_z of the box is 150 cm and the
frequency is 800 MHz, with other dimensions as given in the Figure.
When the box is lengthened to 200 mm, the current distributions become
as shown in Fig.2.4.21 (b). Based on the current distributions obtained above, radiation patterns are calculated and shown in Fig.2.4.
22 (a) to (i), where the length ℓ_z of the box is taken as ranging from
50 mm to 250 mm, in intervals of 25 mm. On comparing these patterns
with those shown in Fig.2.4.8 for the ILA in isolation, it is evident that the radiation patterns of an ILA placed on a conducting

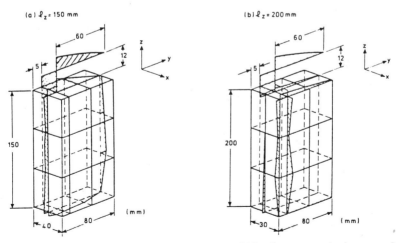

Fig.2.4.21. Current distributions on an ILA element and the surface
of a conducting box.

138

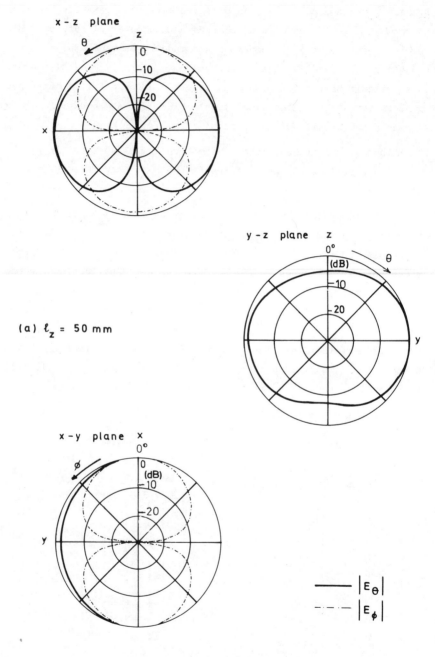

Fig.2.4.22. (a)   Radiation patterns of an ILA on a conducting box.

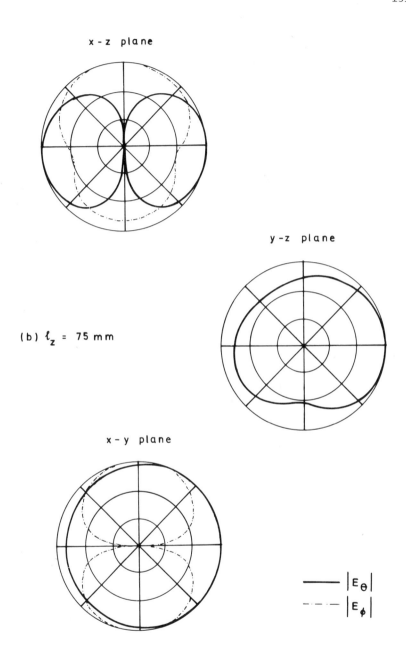

x - z plane

y - z plane

(b) ℓ_z = 75 mm

x - y plane

——— $|E_\theta|$

— · — · — $|E_\phi|$

Fig.2.4.22. (b)   Radiation patterns of an ILA on a conducting box.

140

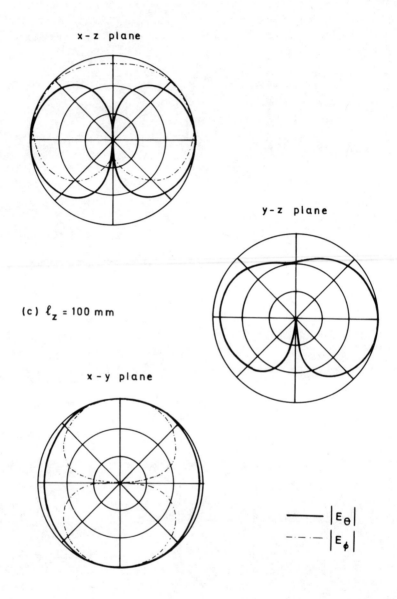

Fig.2.4.22. (c)   Radiation patterns of an ILA on a conducting box.

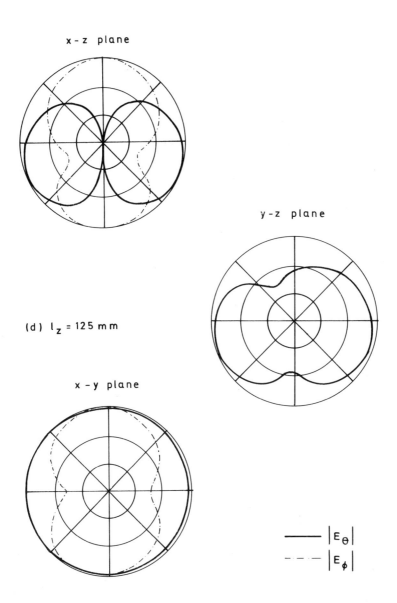

x - z plane

y - z plane

(d) l_z = 125 mm

x - y plane

——— $|E_\theta|$

— - — $|E_\phi|$

Fig.2.4.22. (d)   Radiation patterns of an ILA on a conducting box.

142

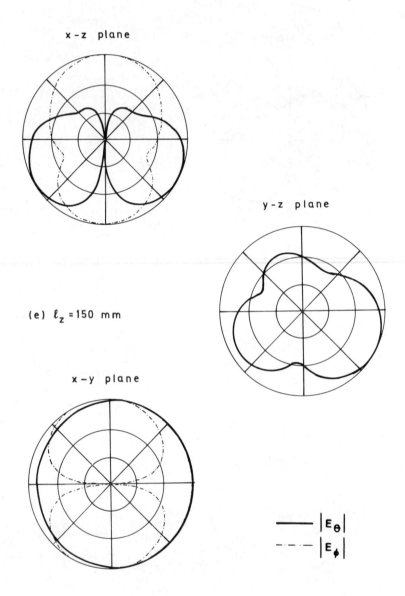

Fig.2.4.22. (e)   Radiation patterns of an ILA on a conducting box.

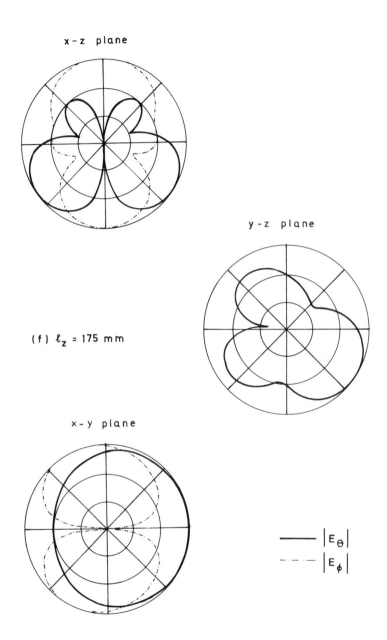

x - z plane

y - z plane

(f) ℓ_z = 175 mm

x - y plane

——— $\left|E_\theta\right|$

– – – $\left|E_\phi\right|$

Fig.2.4.22. (f)   Radiation patterns of an ILA on a conducting box.

144

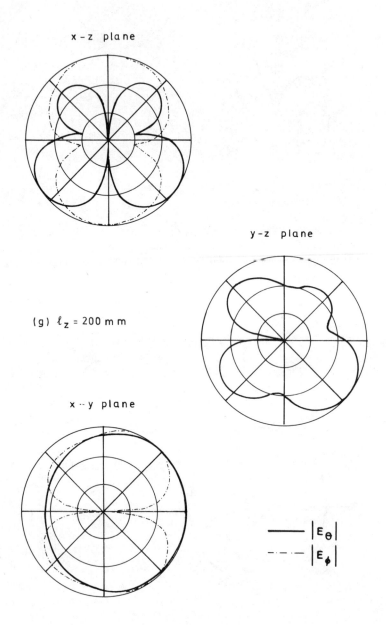

x - z plane

y - z plane

(g) ℓ_z = 200 m m

x -- y plane

——— $|E_\Theta|$

—·—·— $|E_\phi|$

Fig.2.4.22. (g)   Radiation patterns of an ILA on a conducting box.

145

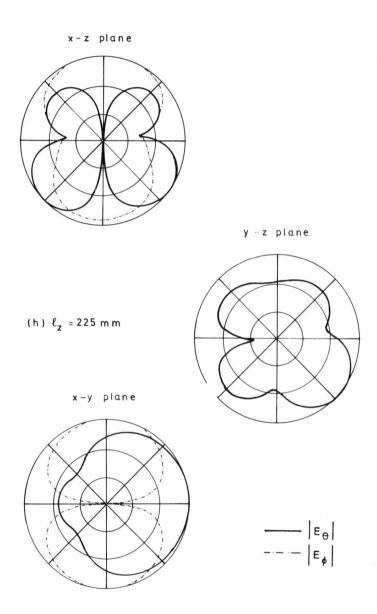

x – z plane

y – z plane

(h) $\ell_z = 225\,mm$

x – y plane

$\overline{}$ $|E_\theta|$

$- \cdot - \cdot -$ $|E_\phi|$

Fig.2.4.22. (h)   Radiation patterns of an ILA on a conducting box.

146

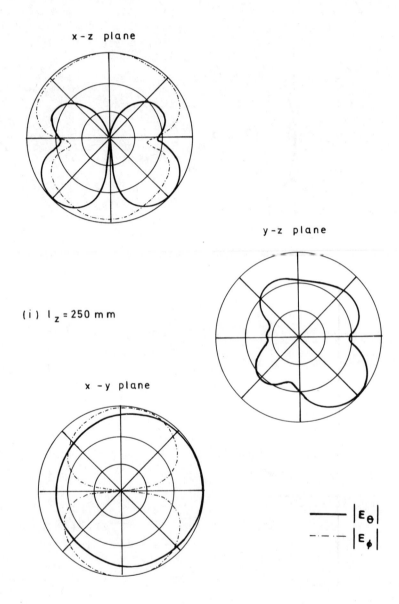

Fig.2.4.22. (i)   Radiation patterns of an ILA on a conducting box.

box are modified considerably by the contribution of the currents
flowing on the surfaces of the box.

A more convenient form of IFA with a plate horizontal element as
shown in Fig.2.4.23 (a) has been developed as a testing model for the
portable-phone systems (Haruki, 1982, and Taga, 1983). Fig.2.4.23 (b)
shows the detail of the antenna structure used for an experiment.
The driving-point is placed at a location that
is appropriate in terms of both the impedance and the feed from the
circuit inside the box. The circumference of the plate may be set to
about a half-wavelength, and then the antenna system may be treated as
a magnetic current loop having the length of a half-wavelength. Measured radiation patterns are shown, using the coordinate system of
Fig.2.4.23, in Fig.2.4.24 (a) to (c), where the length ℓ_z of the box
is 160 mm. These patterns correspond closest to those shown in Fig.2.
4.22 (f), although the length of the box is not exactly the same in
those two cases. Fairly good agreement can be observed between the
theoretical calculations and the experimental results.

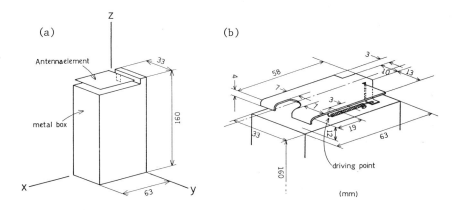

Fig.2.4.23. IFA with a plate horizontal element on a rectangular
metal box: (a) antenna element on a top side of the box and (b)
detail of the antenna element (courtesy of NTT)

148

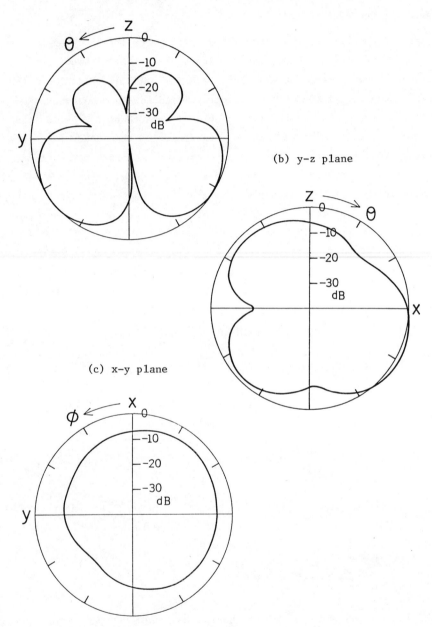

(a) x-z plane

(b) y-z plane

(c) x-y plane

Fig.2.4.24.   Radiation patterns of the antenna model shown in   Fig.2.
4.23.

2.4.4 IFA performance in practical fields

In a city area, where the field may have a randomly fluctuating
structure, it is expected that an antenna like an IFA can give some
improved output by the combined reception of both vertical and horizontal elements. To verify the field performance of an IFA, model antennas shown in Fig.2.4.25 were produced and tested on trial in the
Tokyo metropolitan area by receiving the mobile phone test signal in
900 MHz bands. The antenna was installed on the roof of a car and the
received signal output was recorded while the car was running around
the city area. The data were analysed statistically. The report
(Tanaka et al., 1985) said that as far as the average level was concerned, some increase in the signal output was obtained as compared
with the output received by the halfwave dipole antenna installed on
the roof-top of the car. These results would suggest a very interesting and important facet of the antenna performance in an urban environment and indicate the usefulness of an antenna having a two-polarization function in such randomly fluctuating field applications.

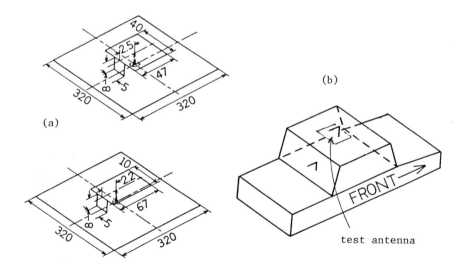

Fig.2.4.25. IFA with a plate element used for field test: (a) antenna models and (b) antenna mounted on a roof-top of a car.

150

The same thing can be said for the IFA placed on a box whose size is comparable to or smaller than the wavelength. A similar experiment was performed in the Tokyo area by using the model antennas shown in Fig.2.4.26 (a) and (b) where the box simulates a portable equipment. In this case, the antenna performance was compared with the performance of a monopole system shown in Fig.2.4.26 (c).

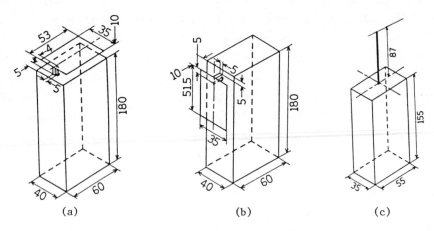

(a)   (b)   (c)

Fig.2.4.26.   Antenna systems mounted on a small metal box: (a) IFA
    mounted on a top side of the box,   (b) IFA placed on a side of the
    box, and (c) a monopole antenna system used for the comparison.

Almost similar results were obtained as in the case of antennas mounted on a car. Although some quantitative differences were observed, the average output signal of the IFA system was greater than that of the monopole antenna system in the Tokyo metropolitan area.   The model (b) in the Figure was better than the model (a) with about 2 to 3 dB difference in the output signal performance.   The measured radiation patterns of each model are shown in Fig.2.4.27.

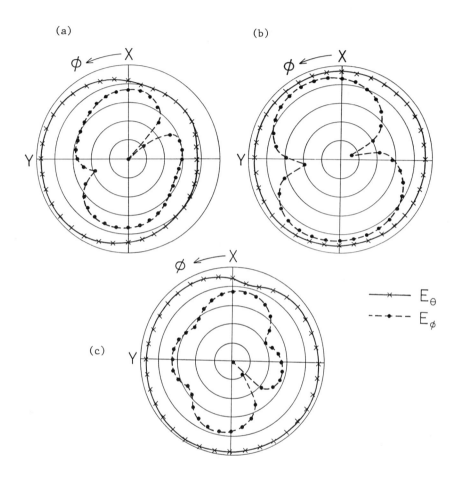

Fig.2.4.27. Radiation patterns of antennas mounted on a small metal box shown in Fig.2.4.26: (a) for the antenna placed on a top side, (b) on a side of a metal box, and (c) for the monopole placed on a top side of the box.

152

2.5 Dipole Antennas

Dipole antennas having functions of either beam shift or pattern
control performed without any movement of the element will be described here.

Since the dimensions of this type of antenna are not necessarily

small as compared with the wavelength, the antenna system cannot be
classified as an electrically small antenna. Because the antenna
functions are augmented without any appreciable change in its dimensions, the antenna system may be categorized as a functionally small
antenna. In other words, it can be said that the antenna dimension
is reduced effectively when a certain function is added to the antenna,
a function that could not otherwise be realized by an antenna of the
same dimension.

This type of antenna has a variety of uses in array pattern shaping,
beam scanning, beam shifting, and additional control of sidelobe and
bandwidth. Applications will be found where either control or shaping
of the radiation pattern is required and yet the antenna is desired to
be smaller than ordinary antennas. Here, however, the emphasis is on
its potential application to mobile communications, where small antenna size is essential and there is a demand for pattern control during
movement.

In principle, the radiation pattern of an antenna can be modified by
variation of the current distribution on the antenna element. The
variation in the current distribution can be achieved by applying the
integration technique to an antenna; in practice this is performed by
the loading of one or more components or devices onto the antenna element.

Either beam shift or pattern control of a dipole antenna can be carried out by making its current distribution asymmetric using loadings
of either a reactance component or an active device. In this Section,
a dipole of length 0.8 λ is used to show this technique. To control beam direction, at least two elements are needed in principle;
however, a single element dipole of length 0.8 λ loaded with a reac-

tance or an active device can have beam control capabilities.

One possible application of this type of antenna is to vehicles. When, for instance, an automobile runs in a city area, the direction of the incoming wave varies as it moves. If the direction of the pattern maximum could be made to follow the direction of the incoming wave, better signal reception would be expected. In some cases, the reception may be improved further by applying the diversity technique. This type of antenna may be used for achieving either pattern control or diversity reception.

In choosing a loading element, a reactance component is preferable to a resistance component, since it does not degrade antenna efficiency seriously. To achieve variable control performance, the reactance component should be a device whose value can be varied electronically. Active devices can be utilized in various other ways by making use of functions such as amplification, phase shifting, and frequency conversion. Control performance can be done by either analogue or digital means and satisfactory performance is more likely if the equipment employs a micro-computer.

Two types of dipole antennas, one loaded with a reactance component and the other with a transistor circuit, devised for beam shifting or pattern controlling, are introduced in Sections 2.5.1 and 2.5.2. It is interesting to note that array thinning can be expected if loaded dipole elements are used, since by arraying two electronic-component-loaded vertical dipoles in parallel, the pattern can be controlled three-dimensionally. With the usual phased array, at least three elements may be necessary to achieve about the same degree of three-dimensional pattern control. This problem is briefly discussed in Section 2.5.1.

2.5.1 Dipole antennas with reactance component loading

Antenna structures considered here are of two types (Hirasawa, Fujimoto, 1980). The first one has a symmetric structure with two reactance components loaded at points symmetrical with respect to the centre of the dipole element, where the driving point is located. This type, shown in Fig.2.5.1, will be referred to as TRDA, for "Two-

154

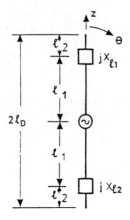

Fig.2.5.1.   Dipole antenna loaded
with two   reactance   components
(TRDA).

Reactance-component-loaded-Dipole Antenna". Values of the two reactances $X_{\ell 1}$ and $X_{\ell 2}$ will be independently chosen to achieve asymmetric
current distribution on the dipole element. The second type is devised to realize asymmetric current distribution by loading one reactance
component at a location symmetric with respect to the driving point,
which is located off the centre of the dipole element, as shown in
Fig.2.5.2. By varying the value of the reactance X_{ℓ}, the direction of
the maximum radiation can be shifted. This type of dipole antenna is
called an ORDA, "One-Reactance-component-loaded-Dipole Antenna".

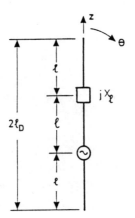

Fig.2.5.2.   Dipole antenna loaded
with one   reactance   component
(ORDA).

(1) Method of solution

Dipole elements are assumed very thin (radius a $\ll \lambda_0$) and the sizes
of components to be loaded are considered so small that no significant
effect on radiation needs to be considered. The currents flowing on
dipole elements loaded with reactance components can be calculated by
the method of moments in Section 2.1, where piecewise sinusoidal current expansion functions as shown in eqn.(2.1.4) are used, with the
assumption that each function is non-zero only over a small portion of
a wire. Piecewise sinusoidal functions are also used for weighting
functions. Driving voltage and loading reactance are applied at wire
positions corresponding to the peaks of the sinusoidal expansion functions.

For a TRDA, values of loading reactances $X_{\ell 1}$ and $X_{\ell 2}$ are varied independently and the radiation pattern is computed for various combinations of $X_{\ell 1}$ and $X_{\ell 2}$. The optimum values of the reactances are then
found, in consideration of maximum beam shift and minimum variation in
the input impedance.

The coordinate system is shown in Fig.2.5.3. The TRDA and ORDA are
aligned along the z-axis. For the ORDA case, the centre of the dipole
element is located at the origin and for the TRDA case, the driving
point is at the origin. An array arrangement with two elements is
also discussed.

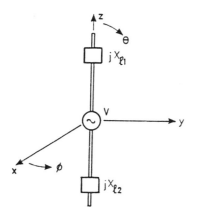

Fig.2.5.3.   Coordinate system.

(2)   TRDA performance

The length $2\ell_D$ chosen for a TRDA is 0.8 λ, since the length with which maximum beam shift may be obtained is between 0.5 λ and 1.0 λ, and a value 0.8 λ appears to be near optimum. Reactance components are then loaded on each side of the dipole element at a distance of ℓ_2 from the centre. In this example, the distance ℓ_2 between the loading point and the centre is taken as three-quarters of the half-length of the dipole, so that $\ell_1 = 0.3 \lambda$ and $\ell_2 = 0.1 \lambda$.

The calculated current distribution on a TRDA is shown in Fig.2.5.4. Both amplitude and phase distribution show distinct asymmetry. Values of reactances $X_{\ell 1}$ and $X_{\ell 2}$ are taken as 200 Ω and 300 Ω, respectively. As expected, peak amplitudes are observed close to the location of $X_{\ell 1}$ and $X_{\ell 2}$ but each peak has different values, and a phase reversal is seen near the driving point. These will contribute to shifting the beam direction of the dipole.

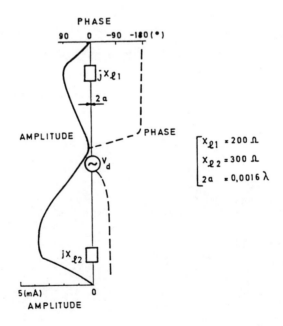

Fig.2.5.4.   Current distribution on a TRDA element.

The radiation pattern of this TRDA is shown in Fig.2.5.5, where two patterns are provided; one is with $X_{\ell 1}$ = 200 Ω and $X_{\ell 2}$ = 300 Ω, and another with $X_{\ell 2}$ = 660 Ω and $X_{\ell 1}$ unchanged. As can be seen from the Figure, the direction of the maximum radiation is shifted about 28 degrees in total. The beam can be scanned if the value of $X_{\ell 2}$ is varied continuously from 300 Ω to 600 Ω by an electronic method.

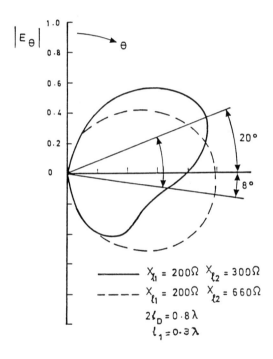

Fig.2.5.5. Radiation patterns of TRDA.

The input impedance Z_i is calculated and shown in Fig.2.5.6, where the value of reactance $X_{\ell 2}$ is varied, while that of $X_{\ell 1}$ is fixed at 200 Ω. The imaginary part of the impedance does not vary significantly as $X_{\ell 2}$ increases beyond 350 Ω, while the real part of the impedance shows a gradual increase with the increase of $X_{\ell 2}$.

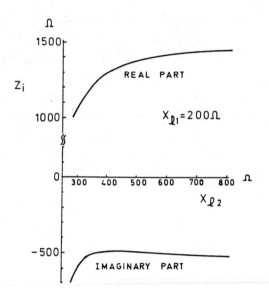

Fig.2.5.6.   Input impedance Z_i of TRDA.

(3)   ORDA performance

Radiation patterns for three values of reactance loading X_ℓ are
shown in Fig.2.5.7, where chosen values of X_ℓ are -600 Ω, 0 Ω, and 200
Ω.   The Figure shows that the beam direction is shifted by about 32
degrees from $\theta = 54°$ to $\theta = 86°$.   Since the pattern is split into two
when $X_\ell = 200$ Ω,   the maximum shift achievable should be considered to
be less than 32 degrees.   In the ORDA example introduced here, the
length $2\ell_D$ is taken to be 0.8 λ and $\ell = \frac{2}{3}\ell_D$.

The input impedance is shown against the variation of X_ℓ in Fig.2.5.
8.   The imaginary part is seen to be nearly flat for X_ℓ less than -300
Ω and shows a gradual decrease for X_ℓ greater than -300 Ω.   The real
part increases with increasing X_ℓ up to the resonance point, where the
imaginary part becomes zero, and starts decreasing after the resonance
point.   In any case the variation in the impedance of an ORDA is greater than that of TRDA, and hence the TRDA seems to be more useful than
the ORDA in practical use.

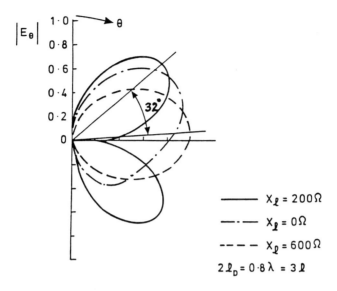

Fig.2.5.7.   Radiation patterns of ORDA.

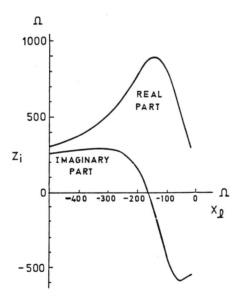

Fig.2.5.8.   Input impedance Z_i of ORDA.

160

(4) Array of two TRDAs or two ORDAs

An array arrangement of two antennas as shown in Fig.2.5.9 will be discussed here. Two similar elements, $2\ell_D = 0.8 \lambda$ and $\ell_1 = 0.3 \lambda$, each driven with the same voltage V_D with two reactance components $X_{\ell 1}$ and $X_{\ell 2}$ loaded, are arrayed separated by a distance d_a, and values of $X_{\ell 1}$ and $X_{\ell 2}$ are varied in a similar fashion on each element. The coordinate system is also illustrated in Fig.2.5.9.

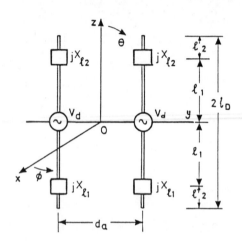

Fig.2.5.9. Array arrangement of two TRDA's with the coordinate system.

The current distribution on one of the two TRDA-array elements is illustrated in Fig.2.5.10. The distance d_a is taken as a half-wavelength and values of $X_{\ell 1}$ and $X_{\ell 2}$ are chosen to be 200 Ω and 300 Ω, respectively. As can be observed in the Figure, the distribution has not changed significantly from that on the single TRDA element (Fig.2. 5.4). Only a slight difference is observed in the amplitude, that is, a small increase in the peak value at the place where $X_{\ell 2}$ is loaded. This is mainly attributed to mutual coupling existing between the two elements.

Radiation patterns of the two-element TRDA array are shown in Fig.2. 5.11 with two different combinations of loaded reactances: (a) $X_{\ell 1}$ = 200 Ω and $X_{\ell 2}$ = 300 Ω, and (b) $X_{\ell 1}$= 200 Ω and $X_{\ell 2}$ = 600 Ω. The slight variation in the current distribution causes only a slight modification of the radiation pattern, as seen by comparing Figs.2.5.5 and 2.5.11. The maximum beam deflection attained is nearly the same as that for the single TRDA.

For the input impedance Z_i, shown in Fig.2.5.12, only the values of the imaginary part show great change from those for the single TRDA (Fig.2.5.6) as X_ℓ is varied, although the tendency of variation in both cases is almost the same. The slope of the increase in the real part is slightly greater in the TRDA array than in the single TRDA. In any case, the input impedance Z_i shows not very much change for the variation of $X_{\ell 2}$ starting from about 450 Ω up to about 800 Ω.

The radiation pattern of the two-element ORDA array is similar to that of the single ORDA and the maximum beam shift Θ_m obtained can be as much as 32 degrees. For maximum beam shift the ORDA, either in a single element or in an array arrangement, seems superior to the TRDA,

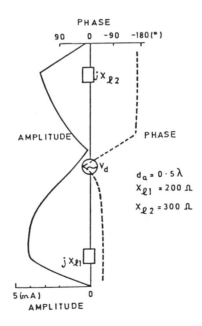

Fig.2.5.10.   Current distribution on one TRDA element.

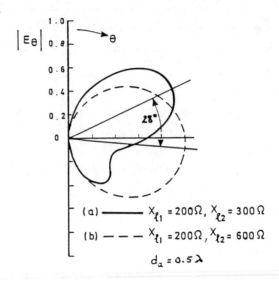

Fig.2.5.11.   Radiation patterns of two-element TRDA array.

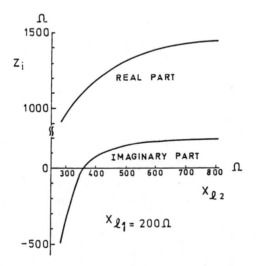

Fig.2.5.12.   Input impedance Z_i of two-element TRDA array.

with a difference of several degrees (about 32 degrees on the ORDA and about 28 degrees by the TRDA). • However, by taking advantage of two-component loading, a TRDA may yield a wider beam shift than an ORDA. When values of $X_{\ell 1}$ and $X_{\ell 2}$ are interchanged at the point where the beam is directed normal to the dipole axis, i.e., $\theta = 90°$, and by continuing to change $X_{\ell 1}$ and $X_{\ell 2}$, the same amount of beam deflection can be obtained on the opposite side of the normal direction, which will double the deflection in the beam shifts.

For instance when $X_{\ell 1}$ is fixed at 200 Ω and $X_{\ell 2}$ varies from 300 Ω to 580 Ω the beam shifts from 65° to 90°. If the loadings are interchanged and the 580 Ω reduced to 300 Ω, the beam swings to 115°, thus creating a total sweep θ_T of 50° as shown in Fig.2.5.13.

One more important point is that the variation in the input impedance of TRDA is flat over a wider range of variation in loaded reactance values than in the case for ORDA. From this point of view, TRDA may have greater potential for practical application than ORDA.

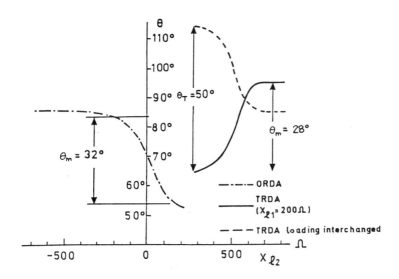

Fig.2.5.13. Comparison of the maximum beam-shift θ_m achieved by TRDA and ORDA, and the total beam shift θ_T by TRDA with loading interchanged.

If two reactances on each element of a two-element TRDA can be varied independently, beam shifting on the horizontal plane(x-y plane) will also become possible. Hence by combining beam deflection on the horizontal plane with that on the vertical plane, three-dimensional pattern control may become feasible. On using the conventional centre -driven dipole array, at least three elements may be necessary to achieve three-dimensional pattern control; with the TRDA, on the other hand, only two elements are required. This implies the possibility of array thinning by utilizing TRDA elements (Fujimoto, Hirasawa, 1985).

2.5.2 Dipole antennas with active device loading

An asymmetrically-driven dipole antenna loaded with a transistor circuit for the purpose of beam shift or control will be discussed in this Section (Hiroi, Fujimoto, 1971, 1972). The antenna system has the same structure as that of the reactance-component-loaded dipole antenna, ORDA, introduced in Section 2.5.1.The reactance component of the ORDA is replaced by a transistor circuit to form an active-device-integrated dipole antenna, which will be called TCDA, for "Transistor-Circuit-loaded Dipole Antenna".

The current distribution on a TCDA element can be varied by varying parameters of the transistor circuit. In practice, the transistor circuit loaded on the antenna performs functions of both a phase shifter and an amplifier. The phase and amplitude of the current distribution on the dipole element can be flexibly controlled by varying the parameters of the transistor circuit, using the bias voltage or current supplied to the transistor.

Figure 2.5.14 schematically illustrates a model of a TCDA of length $2\ell_D$. The place where the transistor circuit is loaded and the driving point are symmetrical with respect to the centre of the antenna element. The antenna element is placed on the z-axis, and the centre of the element is located at the coordinate-system origin. The antenna element is treated as if it were divided into three parts by the loading location ($z = -\ell_1$) and the driving point ($z = \ell_1$). The middle part of the element (between $z = -\ell_1$ and $z = \ell_1$) consists in practice of a coaxial line. Its outer conductor acts as a radiation element

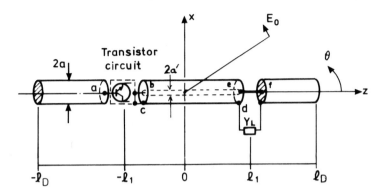

Fig.2.5.14.   Schematic structure of TCDA.

and the inner part serves as a bias supply line to the transistor circuit. The diameter of the dipole element is assumed to be   very   thin
($2a \ll \lambda$), and the size of the loading circuit is also considered very
small, so that no effects of the circuit upon the radiation   need   to
be considered.   The antenna system is treated only as a receiving   device, since the transistor is non-reciprocal, and   hereafter   only   the
receiving pattern performance of the TCDA will be considered.

(1)   Analysis and design of TCDA

The model of TCDA is illustrated   in Fig.2.5.15 (a),   where induced
voltages V_1 and V_2 and current $I(z)$ are assumed on the antenna element
and the load Y_L is connected to the antenna terminals. This antenna
model may be divided into two parts: a part related with radiation and
a part not related with radiation. Fig.2.5.15 (b) expresses the radiation part where   the   terminals   (b-c) and (d-e),   respectively,   are
shorted as b and c, and d and e, respectively, have same potential,
and the induced voltages V_{1a} and V_{2a} are found as the function of the
incident field strength E_0 later. Fig.2.5.15 (c) shows the non-radiation part which is a coaxial line, having the length $2\ell_1$, the radius
of the outer conductor a, and that of inner conductor a'. The   termi-
nal voltages V_{1b} and V_{2b} are derived by using V_{1a} and V_{2a} later. Z_0
and β are the characteristic impedance and the propagation constant
of the coaxial line.

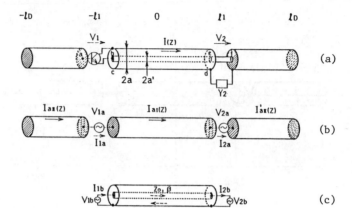

Fig.2.5.15.   Equivalent decomposition of TCDA: (a) antenna   system,
(b) radiation part, and (c) non-radiation part.

The analysis of a TCDA can be made by treating the radiation part
first   and then by combining it with the non-radiation part plus a
transistor circuitry; the characteristics of the TCDA as a whole can
then be determined.

(i) The radiation part

The radiation part of a TCDA may be modelled as a dipole antenna
driven at two points, where V_{1a} and V_{2a} are produced, as shown in Fig.
2.5.15(b).   Those points are considered as delta gaps and voltages ap-
pearing there are those produced by the current $I(z)$ induced on the
antenna element due to the incident field E_0, incident at an angle θ
to the antenna.

The current $I(z)$ on the antenna element can be obtained by solving
the integral equation that follows:

$$\frac{1}{4\pi j\omega\varepsilon} \left(\frac{\partial^2}{\partial z^2} + k^2\right) \int_{-\ell_D}^{\ell_D} \frac{I(z')}{r} e^{-jkr} \, dz'$$

$$= V_{1a}\delta(z-\ell_1) + V_{2a}\delta(z+\ell_1) + E_0 \sin\theta \, e^{-jkz} \cos\theta, \qquad (2.5.1)$$

where $r = \sqrt{(z-z')^2 + a^2}$.   (2.5.2)

By combining the solutions of eqn.(2.5.1) with the parameters used in Fig.2.5.15(b), the currents $I_a(z)$ on the antenna elements are expressed by

$$I_{aI}(z) = y_{11}(z)V_{1a} + y_{12}(z)V_{2a} + y_{13}(z,\theta)\frac{E_0}{k}, \qquad (2.5.3)$$

for $\ell_1 \leq z \leq \ell_1$, and

$$I_{aII}(z) = y_{21}(z)V_{1a} + y_{22}(z)V_{2a} + y_{23}(z,\theta)\frac{E_0}{k}, \qquad (2.5.4)$$

for $-\ell_D \leq z \leq -\ell_1$ and $\ell_1 \leq z \leq \ell_D$,

where y_{ij} ($i = 1, 2,$ and $j = 1, 2, 3$) are admittance parameters determined by the antenna dimensions. These are written as follows;

$$y_{11}(z) = \frac{j}{60} \frac{\sin k(\ell_D-\ell_1)}{\Omega} (\frac{\cos kz}{\cos k\ell_D} - \frac{\sin kz}{\sin k\ell_D}) , \qquad (2.5.5)$$

$$y_{12}(z) = \frac{j}{60} \frac{\sin k(\ell_D-\ell_1)}{\Omega} (\frac{\cos kz}{\cos k\ell_D} + \frac{\sin kz}{\sin k\ell_D}) , \qquad (2.5.6)$$

$$y_{13}(z,\theta) = \frac{j}{30\Omega\sin\theta} \{ (\cos qz - \frac{\cos q\ell_D}{\cos k\ell_D} \cos kz)$$

$$+ j(\sin qz - \frac{\sin q\ell_D}{\sin k\ell_D} \sin kz) \} , \qquad (2.5.7)$$

for $-\ell_1 \leq z \leq -\ell_D$,

and

$$y_{12}(z) = \frac{j}{60} \frac{\sin k(\ell_D-|z|)}{\Omega} (\frac{\cos k\ell_1}{\cos k\ell_D} + \frac{z}{|z|}\frac{\sin k\ell_1}{\sin k\ell_D}) , \qquad (2.5.8)$$

$$y_{22}(z) = \frac{j}{60} \frac{\sin k(\ell_D-|z|)}{\Omega} (\frac{\cos k\ell_1}{\cos k\ell_D} - \frac{z}{|z|}\frac{\sin k\ell_1}{\sin k\ell_D}) , \qquad (2.5.9)$$

168

$$y_{23}(z,\theta) = \frac{j}{30 \sin\theta} \{(\cos qz - \frac{\cos q\ell_1}{\cos k\ell_D} \cos kz)$$

$$+ j(\sin qz - \frac{\sin q\ell_D}{\sin k\ell_D} \sin kz)\} \quad , \tag{2.5.10}$$

for $\ell_1 \leq z \leq \ell_D$ and $-\ell_1 \leq z \leq -\ell_D$,

where $\Omega = 2\ell n(\frac{2\ell_D}{a})$ and $q = k\cos\theta$. $\tag{2.5.11}$

$y_{13}\frac{E_0}{k}$ and $y_{23}\frac{E_0}{k}$ are understood to be equivalent current sources generated by the incident field E_0.

(ii) Combination of radiation and non-radiation parts

The antenna system is conceptually treated as two parts connected in parallel as shown in Fig.2.5.16. One part, the radiation part, is represented by a dipole with two induced voltages V_{1a} and V_{2a} on the intermediate points of the elements. The non-radiation part, enclosed by a dotted line in the Figure, consists of a transistor circuit TC and a transmission line TL. These two parts are represented by a network structure as shown in Fig.2.5.17; the radiation part with the parameters y_{ij} of eqn.(2.5.3) and the non-radiation part with the parameters $Y_{A\cup D}$, in which parameters Y_{ij} of TC are combined with those of TL. The antenna system then can be treated with an equivalent circuit shown in Fig.2.5.18.

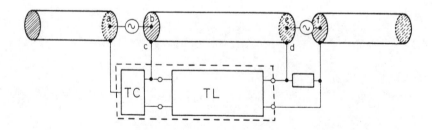

Fig.2.5.16. Decomposition of antenna system.

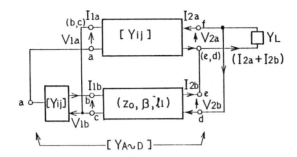

Fig.2.5.17.   Equivalent expression with two networks.

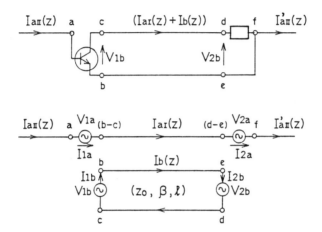

Fig.2.5.18.   Equivalent expression with circuit parameter.

To find the system performance, pattern control being of particular interest here, the power P_L at the load Y_L will be found as a function of the incident field E_0. The analysis starts with a combining procedure of the radiative and the non-radiative parts.

At the terminals, where V_{1a} and V_{2a} are generated, the radiative and non-radiative parts are interrelated by conditions existing at the terminals shown in Fig.2.5.18, and the following relationships hold:

$$I_{1a} = -Y_{11}(V_{1a} - V_{1b}) + Y_{12}V_{1b} \qquad (2.5.12)$$

$$-(I_{1a} + I_{1b}) = -Y_{21}(V_{1a} - V_{1b}) + Y_{22}V_{1b} \qquad (2.5.13)$$

170

for the TC and

$$V_{1b} = V_{2b}\cos(2\beta\ell_1) + jI_{2b}Z_0\sin(2\beta\ell_1) \qquad (2.5.14)$$

$$I_{1b} = I_{2b}\cos(2\beta\ell_1) + jV_{2b}Y_0\sin(2\beta\ell_1) \quad , \qquad (2.5.15)$$

for the TL, where $Y_0 = 1/Z_0$.

At the terminals (e-f), the following are satisfied:

$$V_{2a} + V_{2b} = 0 \qquad (2.5.16)$$

$$I_{2a} + I_{2b} = -V_{2a}Y_L. \qquad (2.5.17)$$

By using eqns.(2.5.12)-(2.5.17), I_{1a} and I_{2a} can be expressed by using parameters $Y_{A \cup D}$, where both radiation and non-radiation parameters are involved:

$$I_{1a} = -Y_A V_{1a} - Y_B V_{2a} \quad , \qquad (2.5.18)$$

$$I_{2a} = -Y_C V_{1a} - Y_D V_{2a} \quad , \qquad (2.5.19)$$

where

$$Y_A = \frac{Y_{11}\cos(2\beta\ell_1) + jZ_0\Delta\sin(2\beta\ell_1)}{\square} \quad , \qquad (2.5.20)$$

$$Y_B = \frac{Y_{11} + Y_{12}}{\square} \quad , \qquad (2.5.21)$$

$$Y_C = \frac{Y_{11} + Y_{21}}{\square} \quad , \qquad (2.5.22)$$

$$Y_D = \frac{(Y_L+Y_T)\cos(2\beta\ell_1) + j(Y_0+Y_T Y_L Z_0)\sin(2\beta\ell_1)}{\square} \quad , \qquad (2.5.23)$$

$$Y_T = Y_{11} + Y_{12} + Y_{21} + Y_{22} \quad , \qquad (2.5.24)$$

$$\Delta = Y_{11}Y_{22} - Y_{12}Y_{21} \quad , \qquad (2.5.25)$$

and

$$\square = \cos(2\beta\ell_1) + jY_T Z_0\sin(2\beta\ell_1) \quad . \qquad (2.5.26)$$

Since $I_{1a} = I_{aI}(-\ell_1)$ and $I_{2a} = I_{aI}(\ell_1)$, eqns.(2.5.18) and (2.5.19) can be combined with eqn.(2.5.3), after inserting $-\ell_1$ and ℓ_1 into z, to obtain V_{1a} and V_{2a} as the function of the incident field E_0 as follows:

$$V_{1a} = -\frac{E_0}{k}\frac{y_{13}(-\ell_1,\theta)(Y_D+y_{12}(\ell_1)) - y_{13}(\ell_1,\theta)(Y_B+y_{12}(-\ell_1))}{\Delta Y}$$

(2.5.27)

$$V_{2a} = -\frac{E_0}{k}\frac{y_{13}(\ell_1,\theta)(Y_A+y_{11}(-\ell_1)) - y_{13}(-\ell_1,\theta)(Y_C+y_{11}(\ell_1))}{\Delta Y}$$

(2.5.28)

where

$$\Delta Y = \{Y_A+y_{11}(-\ell_1)\}\{Y_D+y_{12}(\ell_1)\}-\{Y_B+y_{12}(-\ell_1)\}\{Y_C+y_{11}(\ell_1)\}.$$

(2.5.29)

Now, the currents I_{1a} and I_{2a} can be expressed as the function of the incident field strength E_0 by substituting V_{1a} and V_{2a} obtained above into eqns.(2.5.18) and (2.5.19).

By using the expressions of I_{1a}, I_{2a}, V_{1a}, and V_{2a}, the non-radiating parameters are expressed as

$$V_{2b} = -V_{2a} \tag{2.5.30}$$

$$I_{2b} = -I_{2a} - V_{2a}Y_L \tag{2.5.31}$$

$$V_{1b} = -V_{2a}\{\cos(2\beta\ell_1)+jY_LZ_0\sin(\beta\ell_1)\} - jI_{2a}Z_0\sin(\beta\ell_1) \tag{2.5.32}$$

and

$$I_{1b} = -I_{2a}\cos(2\beta\ell_1) - V_{2a}\{Y_L\cos(\beta\ell_1) + jY_0\sin(\beta\ell_1)\}. \tag{2.5.33}$$

(iii) Receiving pattern*

The power P_L consumed at the load Y_L is given by

$$P_L = R_e\{Y_L\}|V_{2a}|^2 , \tag{2.5.34}$$

where $R_e\{\ \}$ denotes the real part of a function.

---

* The word "receiving pattern" is defined in Section 2.3.2 (c)

By substituting V_{2a} in eqn.(2.5.28) into eqn.(2.5.34), P_L can be calculated and the receiving pattern in terms of the power can be found.

(iv) Design considerations

The receiving pattern of a TCDA can be calculated from eqn.(2.5.34) where the parameters $y_{13}(\ell_1, \theta)$ and $y_{13}(-\ell_1, \theta)$ in V_{2a} are expressed by

$$y_{13}(\ell_1, \theta) = jP(\theta) - Q(\theta) , \qquad (2.5.35)$$

$$y_{13}(-\ell_1, \theta) = jP(\theta) + Q(\theta) , \qquad (2.5.36)$$

where

$$P(\theta) = \frac{1}{30\Omega\sin\theta} \{\cos(k\ell_1\cos\theta) - \frac{\cos k\ell_1}{\cos k\ell_D} \cos(k\ell_D\cos\theta)\} \qquad (2.5.37)$$

and

$$Q(\theta) = \frac{1}{30\Omega\sin\theta} \{\sin(k\ell_1\cos\theta) - \frac{\sin k\ell_1}{\sin k\ell_D} \sin(k\ell_D\cos\theta)\}. \qquad (2.5.38)$$

Insertion of $P(\theta)$ and $Q(\theta)$ into eqn.(2.5.28) gives a simple form of eqn.(2.5.28) as

$$V_{2a} = - \frac{E_0}{k} T\{y_{13}(\ell_1, \theta) + U y_{13}(-\ell_1, \theta)\} \qquad (2.5.39)$$

$$= - \frac{E_0}{k} T\{jP(\theta)(U+1) + Q(\theta)(U-1)\}, \qquad (2.5.40)$$

where

$$T = \frac{1}{\Delta Y} \{y_{11}(-\ell_1) + Y_A\} \qquad (2.5.41)$$

and

$$U = - \frac{y_{11}(\ell_1) + Y_0}{y_{11}(-\ell_1) + Y_A} . \qquad (2.5.42)$$

The values of $P(\theta)$ and $Q(\theta)$ are essential for determining the receiving pattern, since they are related to the antenna dimensions ℓ_1 and ℓ_D and the angle θ. Variations of the receiving pattern are achieved by controlling the parameter U, since U can be varied according to the variation of the transistor parameters. When beam shifting or pattern control is to be designed, the parameter U should be chosen appropriately for the desired performance.

Calculation of the receiving pattern is not simple, since eqn.(2.5.28) involves such parameters as antenna dimensions, transistor parameters and transmission-line parameters. Accordingly, it would not be easy to find the condition under which the maximum beam shift could be obtained. One way to treat this problem practically is to simplify the parameters involved and to find some typical requirement for the maximum beam shift.

Now, as P_L is proportional to $(V_{2a} V_{2a}^*)$ (* stands for complex conjugate), the latter is interpreted by using (2.5.40) as

$$\left| jP(\theta)(U + 1) + Q(\theta)(U - 1) \right|^2 \qquad (2.5.43)$$

and is expressed by

$$P^2(\theta)\{(U_r+1)^2 + U_j^2\} + Q^2(\theta)\{(U_r-1)^2 + U_j^2\} + 4P(\theta)Q(\theta)U_j \qquad (2.5.44)$$

after substituting $U = U_r + jU_j$.

$P(\theta)$ is an even function of θ, and shows symmetrical variation with respect to $\theta = \frac{\pi}{2}$, as can be found by eqn.(2.5.37). On the other hand, $Q(\theta)$ is an odd function, which has a rotationally symmetric nature with respect to the point $\theta = \frac{\pi}{2}$. As an example, $P(\theta)$ and $Q(\theta)$ for $\ell_D = 0.4 \lambda$ are shown in Fig.2.5.19, where ℓ_1 is taken as the parameter.

When $U_r = 0$ and $U_j = \pm 1$ are chosen as an example of the simplest case, eqn.(2.5.44) simplifies to

$$\left| V_{2a} \right|^2 = 2\{P(\theta) \pm Q(\theta)\}^2 . \qquad (2.5.45)$$

The receiving pattern thus will be given by algebraic summation of $P(\theta)$ and $Q(\theta)$ as shown in Fig.2.5.20. From this Figure, it is seen that $Q(\theta)$ contributes to produce an asymmetric receiving pattern with

174

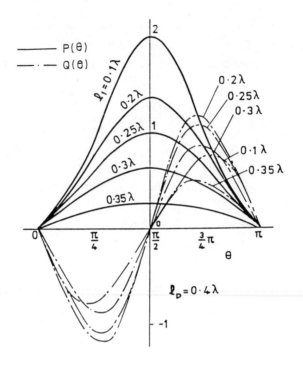

Fig.2.5.19. $P(\theta)$ and $\Omega(\theta)$ when $\ell_D = 0.4\lambda$.

respect to $\theta = \frac{\pi}{2}$, and the asymmetry is reversed by the sign of $Q(\theta)$;
that is, the beam direction in the region $(\frac{\pi}{2} \leq \theta \leq \pi)$ will move to the
other region $(0 \leq \theta \leq \frac{\pi}{2})$ by the change in the sign of $Q(\theta)$ as shown in
Fig.2.5.21. This means that by varying U_j from +1 to −1 the beam can
be scanned through a total of $2(\frac{\pi}{2} - \theta)$ degrees, about the normal
direction.

The function $(P(\theta) + Q(\theta))$ is shown with $P(\theta)$ and $Q(\theta)$ in Figs.(2.5.
22) − (2.5.26), for ℓ_1 = 0.1 λ, 0.2 λ, 0.25 λ, 0.3 λ, and 0.35 λ,
while ℓ_D is fixed at 0.4 λ. The beam shift angle read from the Fig-
ures is shown against ℓ_1 in Fig.2.5.27, where the shift angle Θ is
taken from the normal direction $(\theta = \frac{\pi}{2})$ to the antenna axis. Thus,
when the antenna length ℓ_D = 0.4 λ the maximum beam deflection may be
obtained by choosing ℓ_1 near to 0.3λ and the deflection angle Θ may be
about 35 degrees. On alternating U between +j and −j, the beam will
deflect about ±35 degrees from the direction normal to the antenna.

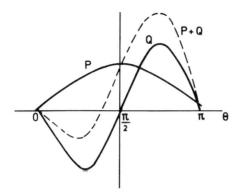

Fig.2.5.20.   Composition of receiving pattern by $P(\theta)$ and $\Omega(\theta)$.

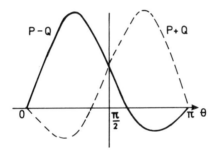

Fig.2.5.21.   Reversal of beam deflection due to the sign of $\Omega(\theta)$.

To realize this condition, Y_A and Y_C should be varied to satisfy U = $\pm j$ as U is given by eqn.(2.5.40).

It should be noted that a sidelobe will appear for the range where $Q > P$. If P is greater than Q for all the range, there will be no sidelobe. With $\ell_D = 0.4\,\lambda$, sidelobe level is not very low in most cases and is of the order of -10 dB.

When the antenna length ℓ_D is $\frac{3}{8}\,\lambda$, slightly shorter than $0.4\,\lambda$, side-lobes are found to be lower than in the case of $\ell_D = 0.4\,\lambda$, as shown in Figs.2.5.28 - 2.5.32, where U is taken as +j and ℓ_1's are chosen as $\frac{1}{8}\,\lambda$, $\frac{3}{16}\,\lambda$, $\frac{1}{4}\,\lambda$, and $\frac{5}{16}\,\lambda$, yet the beam deflects about 30 degrees. The beam shift angle Θ from the normal direction is shown with respect to ℓ_1 in Fig.2.5.33.

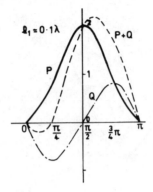

Fig.2.5.22.   Receiving pattern (P+Q) for ℓ_1 = 0.1λ and ℓ_D = 0.4λ.

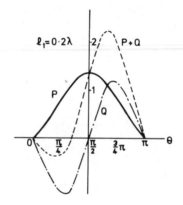

Fig.2.5.23.   Receiving pattern (P+Q) for ℓ_1 =0.2λ and ℓ_D = 0.4λ.

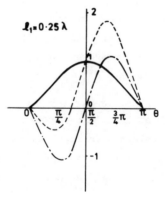

Fig.2.5.24.   Receiving pattern (P+Q) for ℓ_1 = 0.25λ and ℓ_D 0.4λ.

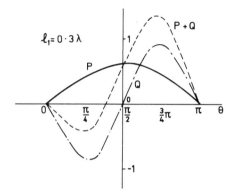

Fig.2.5.25.   Receiving pattern (P+Q) for ℓ_1 = 0.3λ and ℓ_D = 0.4λ.

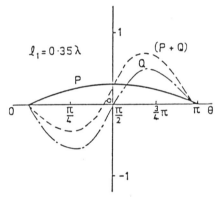

Fig.2.5.26.   Receiving pattern (P+Q) for ℓ_1 = 0.35λ and ℓ_D = 0.4λ.

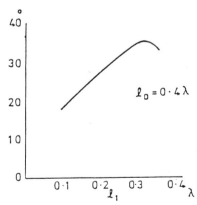

Fig.2.5.27.   Beam shift angle Θ vs. ℓ_1 when ℓ_D = 0.4λ.

178

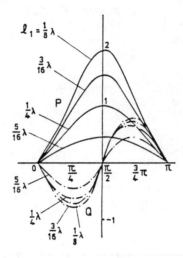

Fig.2.5.28.   Receiving pattern composition $P(\theta)$ when $\ell_D = \frac{3}{8}\lambda$.

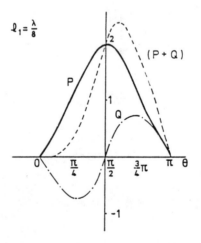

Fig.2.5.29.   Receiving pattern P+Q for $\ell_1 = \frac{\lambda}{8}$ and $\ell_D = \frac{3}{8}\lambda$.

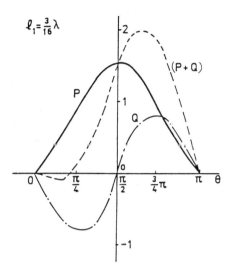

Fig.2.5.30.   Receiving pattern (P+Q) for $\ell_1 = \dfrac{3}{16}\lambda$ and $\ell_D = \dfrac{3}{8}\lambda$.

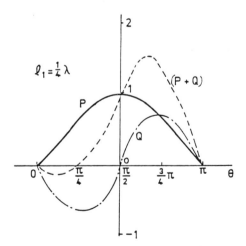

Fig.2.5.31.   Receiving pattern (P+Q) for $\ell_1 = \dfrac{1}{4}\lambda$ and $\ell_D = \dfrac{3}{8}\lambda$.

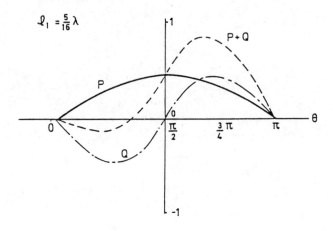

Fig.2.5.32. Receiving pattern (P+Q) for $\ell_1 = \frac{5}{16}\lambda$ and $\ell_D = \frac{3}{8}\lambda$.

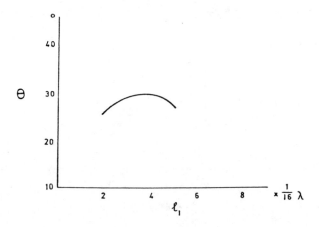

Fig.2.5.33. Beam shift angle Θ vs. ℓ_1 when $\ell_D = \frac{3}{8}\lambda$.

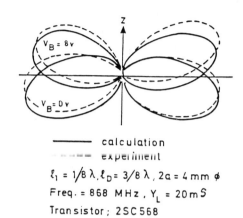

—————— calculation
- - - - - experiment
$\ell_1 = 1/8\,\lambda, \ell_D = 3/8\,\lambda, 2a = 4\,mm\,\phi$
Freq. = 868 MHz , Y_L = 20 mS
Transistor ; 2SC568

Fig.2.5.34.   Beam deflection with a TCDA.

An experimental result is illustrated in Fig.2.5.34. It has been observed that on varying the bias voltage to the transistor circuit from 0 V to 4.6 V, the beam has deflected from about 60 degrees to about 120 degrees, which is about ±30 degrees deflection from θ = 90°, as the theory has predicted.

In the above analysis, the parameter U is taken only as ±j for simplicity. In a more general treatment, the value of U would be chosen to optimize pattern synthesis, including beam shaping and sidelobe reduction.

Conclusion

This chapter has described the analysis and design of four types of small antennas. The theoretical treatment shown in Section 2.1 may be applied also to other types of small antennas. Another simple way of analysis using zeroth-order approximation has been given for the treatment of the ILA, small loop and active dipoles, which offers an easy way to understand those antenna functions analytically in the process of treatment.

The practical importance of the antennas introduced in this chapter is as follows:

The NMHA and the rectangular small loop were discussed initially as typical examples of electrically small antennas. These two types of small antennas are made practically useful, even though they are very small in dimension, by attaining self-resonance with their elements. As a result of self-resonance, a conjugate circuit between the antenna and the load can be avoided and a worthwhile gain is obtained. These antennas are now in use for VHF and UHF mobile communications.

Next, the ILA and the IFA (Inverted-F Antennas) are introduced as examples of physically constrained small antennas. These antennas have two advantages in mobile communications: (1) their low profile is useful to vehicles such as automobiles, planes and trains, and to portable equipment in land mobile systems, and (2) their two-polarization function is important for VHF and UHF mobile applications, especially in an urban environment. In urban areas where wave reflection, diffraction, and scattering may often be experienced, the electromagnetic field may have a randomly variable structure and the signals received at a vehicle would fluctuate randomly as the vehicle moved. An antenna which has two-polarization function may smooth the fluctuations of the signals to some extent by averaging random variations in terms of amplitude, phase, and polarization of the field. Thus improved signal reception may be expected.

The small rectangular loop antenna built-in pager equipment has shown increased sensitivity when operated in the bearer's pocket. This was achieved by arrangement of the antenna so as to utilize the image effect produced by the operator's body. An omnidirectional pattern was obtained by a single loop antenna combined with unbalanced mode currents. These currents are deliberately devised to flow on materials other than the antenna element.

With an active circuit integrated into an ILA, the maximum direction of the antenna pattern was shifted by means of electronic control of the circuit parameters. Other such techniques to achieve pattern control and shaping were applied to dipoles. Either passive components or active components were integrated into dipoles and, for example, a beam shift to a maximum of 35 degrees was obtained by varying the integrated transistor circuit parameters. These antennas were introduced as examples of functionally small antennas. The possibility of three-dimensional pattern control with at least two dipole elements which may lead to array thinning was discussed.

Each of these types of antennas has its own individual features. The discussion in this chapter has concentrated on applications of antennas to land mobile communications. Their use, however, is, of course, not constrained to these applications, and they can be employed in a wide range of other systems whenever small antennas are required.

184

Appendix A 2.1 Two-line circuit system

A two-line circuit, consisting of two lines of radius a with distance d between them, is here assumed to have different potential V_1 and V_2 with respect to the ground and the currents I_1 and I_2 flowing on each line, as shown in Fig.A 2.1.1. This system can be decomposed

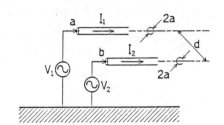

Fig.A 2.1.1

into two components, balanced and unbalanced systems, as shown in Fig. A 2.1.2. Current flows and potential are in opposite direction on the two lines of the balanced system; current flow on each line is I_b and potential on each line is $V_b/2$. In the unbalanced system, current flows and potentials are in the same direction, respectively $I_u/2$ and V_u on each line.

Relations among those potentials and currents are given as follows;

$$
\left.
\begin{aligned}
V_1 &= V_u + \frac{1}{2} V_b \\
V_2 &= V_u - \frac{1}{2} V_b \\
I_1 &= \frac{1}{2} I_u + I_b \\
I_2 &= \frac{1}{2} I_u - I_b
\end{aligned}
\right\}
\qquad \text{(A 2.1.1)}
$$

From these, the following are derived:

$$
\left.
\begin{aligned}
V_u &= \frac{1}{2} (V_1 + V_2) \\
V_b &= V_1 - V_2 \\
I_u &= I_1 + I_2 \\
I_b &= \frac{1}{2} (I_1 - I_2)
\end{aligned}
\right\}
\qquad \text{(A 2.1.2)}
$$

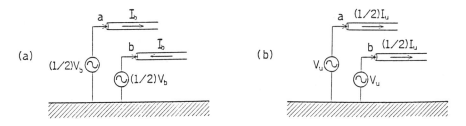

Fig.A 2.1.2. Decomposition of two-line system shown in Fig.A 2.1.1.:
(a) balanced system and (b) unbalanced system.

Now the two-line circuit can equivalently be expressed by the circuits shown in Fig.A 2.1.3, where (a) expresses the balanced system
and (b) the unbalanced system. The unbalanced system is finally represented by a system shown in Fig.A 2.1.3 (c), where the two-line
system is represented by an equivalent line with radius $a' = \sqrt{ad}$ for a
$\ll d \ll \lambda$. Eqn.(2.3.13) in the text is derived by setting $V_i = V_0$, $V_2 =$
0, $V_a = V_u$, and $I_a = I_u$, in eqns.(A 2.1.1) and (A 2.1.2).

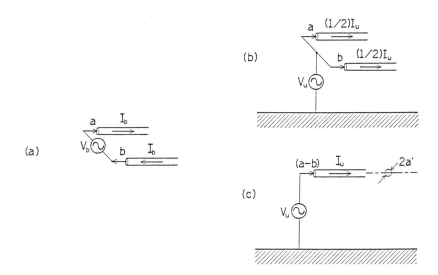

Fig.A 2.1.3. Equivalent expressions of the system shown in Fig.A 2.
1.2: (a) balanced two lines, (b) unbalanced system, and (c) equivalent expression of the unbalanced system (b).

186

Appendix A 2.2   A simplified treatment of an antenna system   with   the
proximity effect to the human body

When an antenna is located very near to a human body, the energy radiated from the antenna is reflected by, absorbed by, and transmitted
through the human body. A human body may be considered as a dielectric material with finite conductivity and the field outside the body
may be calculated as the sum of two fields: that of the direct wave
and that of the wave scattered by this dielectric material. The exact
treatment of this problem is not easy, because the human body has a
very complicated structure, not only in its shape, but also in its
electromagnetic properties. The complexity of its structure increases
as the frequency becomes high, since the body is not homogeneous.
Discussion of this problem is beyond the scope here; the human body is
assumed to be simply a semi-infinite plane solid having the dielectric
constant ε_b and the finite conductivity σ_b as shown in Fig.2.3.21.
With this model, although it is considered very approximate, the field
calculated in front of the body in the VHF and UHF regions does not
differ very much from the measured results. Analysis by this model
was found to be adequate for application to the design of an antenna
system placed near a human body, with a fairly high degree of approximation in the VHF and UHF regions.

The field reflected on the surface of the human body can be replaced
by that produced by an image antenna, as shown in Fig.2.3.21, where d
denotes the distance between the antenna and the surface of the human
body. The field $E_T(\theta)$ is the sum of that produced by the actual antenna and that produced by the image antenna, and is given by

$$E_T(\theta) = K \ (I_1 \frac{e^{-jkr_1}}{r_1} + I_2 \frac{e^{-jkr_2}}{r_2}) \ f(\theta) \ . \qquad (A\ 2.2.1)$$

K is a constant related to the radiation of the antenna on which the
current I_1 flows, I_2 is the current flowing on the image antenna, $f(\theta)$
is the pattern function of the antenna, and r_1 and r_2 are the dis-
tances to the observation point from the actual antenna and image antenna, respectively. By assuming the reflection factor Γ_b on the sur-

face of the human body, the value of $E_T(\theta)$ is given by

$$E_T(\theta) = K I_1 F [1 + \Gamma_b e^{-jk(r_2 - r_1)}] f(\theta), \qquad (A\ 2.2.2)$$

where $F = \dfrac{e^{-jkr_1}}{r_1}$, $r_1 \doteq r_2$ is assumed for the far distant point in the amplitude term and I_2 is taken to be $\Gamma_b I_1$, since the field produced by I_2 corresponds to the field reflected on the surface of the body which is modified by the reflection factor Γ_b. Here Γ_b is a complex value, given by

$$\Gamma_b = |\Gamma_b| e^{-j\theta_\Gamma} = \Gamma_{br} + j\Gamma_{bj} . \qquad (A\ 2.2.3)$$

The antenna input terminal voltage V_1 and the current I_1 are expressed as

$$
\left.
\begin{aligned}
V_1 &= I_1 Z_r + I_2 Z_m \\
V_2 &= I_1 Z_m + I_2 Z_r ,
\end{aligned}
\right\} \qquad (A\ 2.2.4)
$$

where V_2 and I_2 are the voltage and current assumed at the terminals of the image antenna, Z_r ($=R_r + jX_r$) is the self-impedance of the antenna and is the same for both the actual antenna and the image antenna, and Z_m is the mutual impedance between the actual and image antennas. By using eqn. (A 2.2.4), the input impedance Z_i of the antenna is expressed by

$$Z_i = \frac{V_1}{I_1} = Z_r + |\Gamma_b| |Z_m| e^{-j(\theta_m + \theta_\Gamma)} , \qquad (A\ 2.2.5)$$

where $Z_m = R_m + j X_m = |Z_m| e^{-jk\theta_m} . \qquad (A\ 2.2.6)$

Now the power P_A at the actual antenna is found to be

$$
\begin{aligned}
P_A &= |I_1|^2 R_i \\
&= |I_1|^2 [R_r + \Gamma_{br} R_m - \Gamma_{bj} X_m], \qquad (A\ 2.2.7)
\end{aligned}
$$

where R_i is the real part of Z_i.
From eqn. (A 2.2.7) I_1 can be obtained as

$$I_1 = \sqrt{\frac{P_A}{R_r + \Gamma_{br} R_m - \Gamma_{bj} X_m}} \cdot \qquad (A\ 2.2.8)$$

To compare with the standard antenna, consider a halfwave dipole antenna into which the current flow is I_d and the power supplied is P $= P_A$. The field $E_d(\theta)$ produced by the standard dipole antenna is given by

$$E_d(\theta) = K\ I_d\ F\ f(\theta)$$

$$= K \sqrt{\frac{P}{R_d}}\ F\ f(\theta), \qquad (A\ 2.2.9)$$

where R_d is the resistive component of the standard dipole antenna impedance.

The gain G_A of the antenna system with respect to the standard dipole antenna in terms of the field intensity is then obtained as

$$G_A = \left| \frac{E_T(\theta)}{E_d(\theta)} \right|$$

$$= \sqrt{\frac{R_d}{R_{Ar} + \Gamma_{br} R_m - \Gamma_{bj} X_m}} \cdot \left| 1 + \Gamma_b\ e^{-j2kd\cos\theta} \right| \cdot \qquad (A\ 2.2.10)$$

(1) The short dipole antenna case

When a short dipole is placed in front of a human body with the dipole axis parallel to the surface of the body, as shown in Fig.2.3. 23 (b) and if the human body can be assumed to be a perfect electric conductor, $\Gamma_b = -1$, or $\Gamma_{br} = -1$ and $\Gamma_{bj} = 0$, or $\theta_{\Gamma b} = \pi$. Then the antenna system gain G_{AS} becomes

$$G_{As} = \sqrt{\frac{R_d}{R_r - R_m}} \cdot 2\ \sin\ (kd\ \cos\theta). \qquad (A\ 2.2.11)$$

(2) The magnetic dipole antenna case

When an electric dipole antenna is replaced by a magnetic dipole, as in the case where a loop antenna is used as shown in Fig.2.3.23 (a), and if the human body is again assumed to be a perfect electric conductor, then $\Gamma_b = 1$, i.e., $\Gamma_{br} = 1$, and $\Gamma_{bj} = 0$ or $\theta_{\Gamma b} = 0$, and the system gain G_{Am} can be expressed by

$$G_{Am} = \sqrt{\frac{R_d}{R_r + R_m}} \cdot 2 \cos(kd \cos\theta). \qquad (A\ 2.2.12)$$

When the standard halfwave dipole is replaced by the same antenna in free space as the one to be tested, R_d should be replaced by R_r.

If an antenna loss resistance R_{loss} could not be omitted, as in a very small antenna system, $(R_r + R_{loss})$ should be used in place of R_r.

REFERENCES

Fujimoto, K. (1968). A loaded antenna system applied to VHF portable communication equipment.
IEEE Trans., VT-17, 6-12

Fujimoto, K. (1970). A treatment of integrated antenna systems.
IEEE AP-S International Symposium 120-123.

Fujimoto, K. and Hiroi, Y. (1969). Active inverted-L antenna.
Paper of Technical Group, IECE Japan, AP68-70, 1-16.
(in Japanese)

Fujimoto, K. and Hiroi, Y. (1970). Active inverted-L antenna.
Paper of Technical Group, IECE Japan, AP70-29, 1-12.
(in Japanese)

Fujimoto, K. and Hirasawa, K. (1985). Applications of reactance-integrated dipole antennas to array synthesis and thinning.
IEEE 14th Convention of Electrical and Electronics Engineers in Israel, Proceedings, 2.3.1.

Guertler, R.J.F. (1977). Isotropic transmission-line antenna and its toroid-pattern modification.
IEEE Trans., AP-25, 386-392.

Hansen, R.C. (1975). Optimum inductive loading of short whip antennas
IEEE Trans., VT-24, 21-29.

Harrington, R.F. (1968). Field computation by moment method.
Macmillan Co., New York.

Harrington, R.F. (1978). Reactively controlled directive arrays.
IEEE Trans., AP-26, 390-395.

Harrison, C.W. (1963). Monopole with inductive loading.
IEEE Trans., AP-11, 394-400.

Haruki, H. et al. (1974). A small loop antenna for pocket-size VHF, UHF radio equipment.

Paper of Technical Group, IECE Japan, AP73-29, 7-12.
(in Japanese).

Haruki, H. and Kobayashi, T. (1982). F-type antenna for UHF portable
equipment. National Convention Records, IECE Japan, 3, 613
(in Japanese).

Hirasawa, K. and Strait, B.J. (1971). Analysis and design of arrays
of loaded thin wires by matrix methods.
Cambridge Research Laboratories, AFCRL-71-0296.

Hirasawa, K. (1978 a). Study of a reactively loaded grid-type corner
reflector antenna.
Electronics and Communications in Japan, 61-B, 45-53.

Hirasawa, K. (1978 b). Design of arbitrarily shaped thin wire antennas
by passive impedance loadings.
Electronics and Communications in Japan, 61-B, 55-63.

Hirasawa, K. (1979). Control of plane-wave scattering by a thin wire
with impedance loads.
Electronics and Communications in Japan, 62-B, 56-64.

Hirasawa, K. (1980). Optimum gain of reactively loaded Yagi antennas.
Trans. IECE Japan, J63-B, 121-127.
(in Japanese).

Hirasawa, K. and Fujimoto, K. (1980). On electronically-beam-controllable dipole antenna.
IEEE AP-S International Symposium, 692-695.

Hirasawa, K. and Fujimoto, K. (1981). On wire-grid method for analysis of wire antennas near/on conducting bodies.
Proc. IEE International Conference on Antennas and Propagation, 531-
534.

Hirasawa, H. and Fujimoto, K. (1982 a). Characteristics of wire antennas on a rectangular conducting body.
Trans. IECE Japan, J65-B, 1133-1139.
(in Japanese).

Hirasawa, K. and Fujimoto, K. (1982 b). On wire-grid method for analy-

192

sis of wire antennas near/on a rectangular conducting body.
Trans. IECE Japan, J65-B, 382-389.
(in Japanese).

Hiroi, Y. and Fujimoto, K. (1971). Receiving pattern of a transistor-
loaded active antenna.
1971 Internaitonal Symposium on Antennas and Propagation Japan, 69-70.

Hiroi, Y. and Fujimoto, K. (1972). Analysis and design of the electronically-beam-controllable antenna.
IEEE AP-S International Symposium, 241-244.

Hiroi, Y. and Fujimoto, K. (1974). A normal mode helical antenna.
Paper of Technical Group IECE Japan, AP74-92, 17-22.
(in Japanese).

Hiroi, Y. and Fujimoto, K. (1976 a). Normal mode helical antenna.
Paper of Technical Group IECE Japan, AP76-24, 7-12.
(in Japanese).

Hiroi, Y. and Fujimoto, K. (1976 b). Practical usefulness of normal
mode helical antenna.
IEEE AP-S International Symposium, 238-241.

Inagaki, N., Tamura. K, and Fujimoto, K.(1971). Theoretical investigation on the resonance length of normal mode helical antennas.
Technical Report of Nagoya Institute of Technology, 23, 335-341.
(in Japanese).

Itoh, H. et al. (1969). 915 MHz telemetry antenna for M-4S rocket.
National Technical Report 15, 347-353. (published by Matsushita Electric Ind. Co., Osaka, Japan)
(in Japanese).

Itoh, H., Haruki, H. and Fujimoto, K. (1973). A small-loop antenna
for pocket-size VHF radio equipment.
National Tech. Report, 19, 145-154.
(in Japanese).

Jordan, E.C. and Balmain, K.G. (1968). Electromagnetic waves and radiating systems.

Prentice-Hall, Inc., New Jersey.

Kagoshima, K. and Sekiguchi, T. (1973). Design of impedance-loaded circular loop antenna.
Trans. IECE Japan, J56-B, 303-310.
(in Japanese).

King R.W.P. (1950). The theory of linear antennas.
p.190. Harvard University Press, Cambridge, Massachusets.

King, R.W.P., Mack, R.B., and Sandlor, S.S. (1968). Arrayo of cylindri cal dipoles.
Cambridge University Press, New York.

Kraus, J.D. (1950 a). Antennas.
p.177. McGraw-Hill, New York.

Lin, C.J., Nyquist, D.P. and Chen, K.M. (1970). Short cylindrical antennas with enhanced radiation or high directivity.
IEEE Trans., AP-18, 576-580.

Mishima, H. and Taga, T. (1980). Mobile antennas and duplexer for 800 MHz band mobile telephone system.
IEEE AP-S International Symposium, 508-511.

Nagai, K. and Sato, T. (1967). Radiation characteristics of parallel-fed inverted-L antenna.
National Convention Records, IECE Japan, 3, 395.
(in Japanese).

Popovic, B.D., Dragovic, M.B. and Djordjevic, A.R. (1982). Analysis and synthesis of wire antennas.
Chapters 8 and 9. Research Studies Press, England

Richmond, J. and Geary, N.H. (1970). Mutual impedance between coplanar -skew dipoles.
IEEE Trans., AP-18, 414-416.

Schwan H.P. and Foster K.R. (1980). RF-field interactions with biological systems: electrical properties and biophysical mechanisms.
Proc. IEEE, 68, 104-113.

Strait, B.J. and Hirasawa, K. (1970). On long wire antennas with multiple excitations and loadings.
IEEE Trans., $\underline{AP-18}$, 669-670.

Taga, T. et al. (1983). Detachable F-type antenna for portable-phone.
National Convention Records, IECE Japan, $\underline{3}$, 2170.
(in Japanese).

Tanaka Y. et al., (1985). Performance of antenna systems having cross polarization in mobile communications, National Convention Record, IECE Japan, Part 3, S5-6. (in Japanese).

Uda, S. and Mushiake, Y. (1954). Yagi-Uda antenna.
p.20. Maruzen, Inc., Tokyo, Japan.

Weeks, W.L. (1968). Antenna engineering.
p.58. McGraw-Hill, New York.

CHAPTER 3

Material Loaded Antennas

INTRODUCTION

Wire antennas were the first forms of practical radiators in use and it was found by the early experimentalists that wire monopoles could be bent into various shapes to conserve height. It was appreciated that a shortened antenna had a capacitive input term and that this could be tuned out by various exterior circuits or more conveniently by wire loadings attached to the antenna, generally located at the top. Several examples are given in the glossary of antenna types. These techniques remain in use today and are very useful particularly for HF transmission where a full height monopole may require supporting towers that are higher than can be tolerated on cost or other considerations (Smith and Johnson, 1957).

At higher frequencies one might expect that it is easier to design and build short efficient antennas but this is seldom the case where portability is a key requirement. Commonly it is required at VHF and, to some extent, at the top of the HF band, to have a shortened wire monopole that is mechanically self-supporting but not much thicker than a wire, for example on a portable radio set. This chapter is concerned with using dielectric and ferrite materials to make antennas physically smaller by exploiting their wave trapping properties. A precedent has been set for using this technique with the ferrite-loaded inductive winding, shown below, used for many years inside medium-and long-wave radio receivers. The signal received by the winding is increased many times due to the high permeability of the ferrite rod which intensifies the magnetic flux passing through it (Blok et al., 1955; Van Suchtelen, 1952).

Medium-and long-wave ferrite 'antenna rod'

At these low frequencies, the extremely low efficiency of the antenna can be tolerated from a systems standpoint due to the relatively high signal strengths involved. This is not the case at VHF, where a reasonably efficient antenna is required and with the recent advances in low-loss material technology, there has been a renewed interest in using material loading techniques for antenna size reduction. The configuration chosen most frequently for experimentation has been the coated monopole antenna and a full evaluation of this antenna will be given here.

The coated wire antenna has received some attention in the past but not only as a height-reduced antenna. King and Smith (1981) have, for a number of years, studied the behaviour of insulated coatings for probes placed into conductive media, such as water or earth. Here the coating is not only used as an insulation to conductive paths but to isolate the probe parameters from small changes in the properties of the medium by creating an 'impedance buffer zone' around the probe. The findings are not readily applied to height-reduced antennas in air principally because it is the antenna parameters, such as bandwidth and efficiency, that are of importance to the designer. For large height reductions, coated antennas in air exhibit very pronounced resonant behaviour, mainly due to trapped surface-wave action, and although they are basically slow-wave structures their properties are determined by a strong cavity action unlike the probes of King and Smith (1981).

In addition to the short coated monopole, this chapter discusses the design of reduced-size conformal antennas and concludes with a description of a variety of specialised applications of the material-coating technique.

3.1 The concept of coated wire antennas and early investigations

When electromagnetic waves flow through material with a relative permittivity ε_r and permeability μ_r, the wavelength is reduced by a factor $(\varepsilon_r \mu_r)^{1/2}$. Since the physical size of antennas relates to the wavelength in the medium, it is evident that immersed antennas can function with smaller dimensions than in the free-space situation. This is illustrated in Fig.3.1.1 for a monopole on a ground-plane, where the length of the wire antenna is reduced by a factor $F = (\varepsilon_r \mu_r)^{1/2}$; the input impedance r_o at resonance is essentially reduced by the ratio $(\varepsilon_r / \mu_r)^{1/2}$.

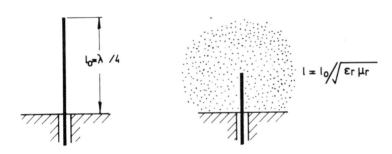

Fig.3.1.1   Resonant length monopoles in free-space and medium. λ is the free-space wavelength.

For height-reduced antennas, Fig.3.1.2, the coating will not be infinite in extent and intuitively one expects that the height-reduction factor F will not be as great as $(\varepsilon_r \mu_r)^{1/2}$. Clearly the F factor is a function of the shape, size and electrical characteristics of the

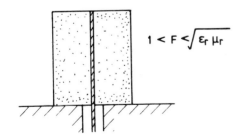

Fig.3.1.2   Height-reduced antenna.

198

coating and for a large F factor the coating would need to be as thick as possible. Obviously from practical weight considerations, the thickness of the coating is limited and the question then arises as to the amount of height reduction that can be achieved under these conditions.

Besides weight constraints there are other factors to be considered. As shown in Fig.3.1.1, the input impedance of an antenna immersed in a medium can be reduced appreciably and one has to consider the system implications. For example, will the antenna have such a low impedance that it cannot be efficiently matched into and how will the losses in the coating affect the antenna efficiency and bandwidth? All these questions will be addressed in the later Sections and suitable design curves are given which will enable the designer to make the optimum choice for a particular requirement.

It is instructive here to review early practical contributions to the topic to illustrate the usefulness of the coating technique. The earlier investigations were confined to the use of purely dielectric coatings and this was no doubt brought about by the wide range of low-loss dielectric materials available in the UHF/VHF band where the principal applications lie.

Firstly James and Burrows (1973) used coatings of powdered dielectric material, Fig.3.1.3, to demonstrate the change in monopole bandwidth and input impedance with height reduction. The air spaces in the powdered coatings reduced the effective permittivity of the mate-

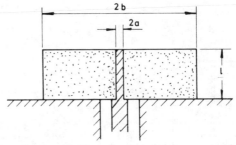

Fig.3.1.3   Cross-sectional sketch of coaxially driven monopole coated by a cylindrical sleeve of powdered dielectric material of relative permittivity ε_r.

rials and thus limited the F factors possible. The details of the experiments and materials used are given in Table 3.1.1 together with the F factors. Radiation patterns are shown in Fig.3.1.4. In order

Table 3.1.1.   Dimensions, materials and summary of results for coated monopole, Fig.3.1.3.

Case	A	B	C	D
a, cm	0.3	0.3	0.3	0.3
ℓ, cm	7.6	3.85	2.15	1.63
Dielectric material	None	Titanium dioxide	Barium titanate	Barium titanate
ε_r	–	18	90	90
b, cm	–	5.1	5.1	10.0
Resonant frequency, MHz	900	900	910	900
Bandwidth, MHz Δf	236	145	104	144
Resistance at resonance r_o,Ω	38.8	12.5	5.5	5.4
F = height reduction factor	1.0	1.98	3.53	4.61

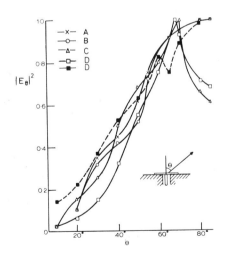

Fig.3.1.4   Measured radiation patterns in the elevation plane for coated monopole, Fig.3.1.3. All cases were measured at 900MHz, except —■— D, which was measured at 1200MHz. © IEE.

to achieve an F factor of 4.6, it was found necessary to have a 20cm wide coating at 900 MHz and this highlighted the need to use high-permittivity ceramics to reduce the size of the coating or to increase the height reduction achievable. The input resistance at resonance reduced to 5 ohms and the bandwidth by a factor of nearly 2.

It was also observed in these experiments that some azimuth directivity could be obtained by placing the wire monopole off the axis of the cylindrical coating and this property was further investigated to height reduce directional antennas by James et al. (1974). A Yagi antenna on a ground-plane was immersed in a box-like coating of barium titanate powder, Fig.3.1.5, giving an estimated permittivity of about 20. Full details of the dimensions of the antennas are given in Table 3.1.2 along with a summary of the results. The large number of varia-

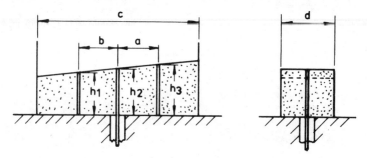

Fig.3.1.5   Coated Yagi antenna ⓒ IEE.

Table 3.1.2   Dimensions and summary of results

Case	a	b	c	d	h_1	h_2	h_3	f_o	r_o	Δf	w	s
	cm	cm	cm	cm	cm	cm	cm	MHz	Ω	%	deg	dB
A	7.5	9.6	–	–	6.45	7.5	7.65	870	24	18.8	78	–10
B	7.5	9.6	28.0	10.0	2.18	2.55	2.61	1000	11	10.5	56	–4.4
C	2.55	3.26	19.0	10.0	2.18	2.55	2.61	1000	15	15.5	54	–10
D	–	3.26	16.5	10.0	2.18	2.55	–	1000	17.5	26.5	42	–20

f_o = resonant frequency, w = beamwidth main lobe of radiation pattern and s = sidelobe level relative to main beam. The element diameter was 0.6cm in every case. Case A is the unloaded antenna.

bles in this experiment constrained the investigation to a purely trial and error optimisation process. Smith Chart plots of the input impedance of the coated antenna are given in Fig.3.1.6 showing that both
the bandwidth and impedance are decreased, except for case D, where
the bandwidth is increased slightly.

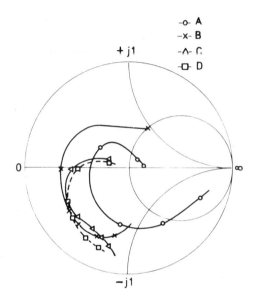

Fig.3.1.6   Smith Chart plot of Yagi-antenna input impedance normali-
    sed to 50 ohms. Cases A-D were measured between 600 and 1100 MHz
    in 100 MHz increments. (C) IEE.

In general though, certain combinations of wire element spacing can
bring about improvements in both bandwidth and directive characteristics, compared to the uncoated case. This can be seen in Fig.3.1.7
where the measured radiation patterns are presented.

The authors are not aware of any further attempts to make use of
this interesting concept but this may be due to the lower efficiency
of the coated Yagi which somewhat negates any improvements in bandwidth and directivity. Further work on directivity effects has been
done by Lytle and Laine (1978) and Buettner (1980) with cylindrical
dielectric coatings on monopoles, for use as geophysical probes, and
this will be described later on in Section 3.5.3.

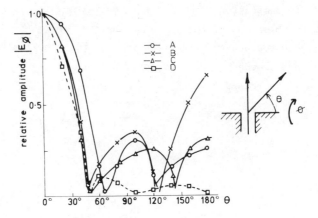

Fig.3.1.7   Coated Yagi relative radiation patterns in the horizontal
  ground-plane measured at resonant frequency, f_0.
  Case A: f_0=870MHz   Case B-D: f_0=1000MHz.   © IEE.

These early experiments pinpointed the loss of efficiency in the
coated structures as an important parameter caused by a combination of
the power dissipated in the coating and the low value of the input
resistance.   It was apparent however that for very large F factors,
dielectric-coated monopoles would have a very poor efficiency, typically 10% for F=6.   The reason for this low antenna   efficiency   was   not
understood earlier on and it was not until the work of James and
Henderson (1978) emmerged at a later date that the excessive losses in
antennas with large F factors could be accounted for.

In the meantime, industrial research and the work of Woodman (1977)
established that wideband communications antennas   could   be   usefully
reduced in volume using dielectric-coated wire cages.   Fig.3.1.8 shows
a discone antenna made in this way, consisting in its final form, of
five ceramic monopoles and five polythene cylinders filled with water
strapped across the base to improve the low-frequency end of the band.
The antenna has a functional bandwidth of 250-1100 MHz for an input
VSWR of less than 2 and is 30% smaller in length than its uncoated
counterpart.   This size reduction is obtained for an efficiency of 45
%.   The antenna was designed from empirical formulas from coated monopole experiments and the following relationship for the loss of effi-

Fig.3.1.8   Photograph of discone antenna by Woodman (1977). © IEE.

ciency was found

$$\eta = \eta_o \ (1 - 1.75 \ \tan \delta_\varepsilon \ \ln V)$$

where η is the overall antenna efficiency, η_o is the unclad efficiency, $\tan \delta_\varepsilon$ is the loss tangent of the coating and V is the volume in
cm^3. Several ceramic materials and water were used for coatings. The
empirical relationship above is shown in Fig.3.1.9 while the relationship between the height-reduction factor and the permittivity of each

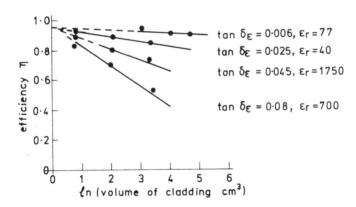

Fig.3.1.9   Experimental antenna efficiencies and empirical curves for
    various dielectric coatings. In all cases, the antenna length ℓ
    was 10cm except for ε_r=77, where ℓ=15cm.   © IEE.

coated monopole is shown in Fig.3.1.10. Woodman concluded that,with a commercially available material having $\varepsilon_r \sim 900$ and $\tan \delta_\varepsilon \sim 0.002$, an efficiency approaching 95% would be possible for the discone but no further reports have been published.

At this stage it was apparent that the physical action of the coated antenna needed to be understood if any further improvements were to follow and the limitations in the performance evaluated. The rest of this Section is devoted to the analysis of the coated antenna and the results that have been deduced from it.

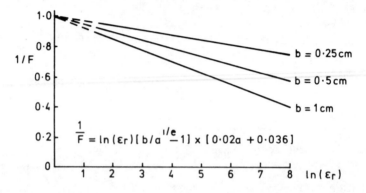

Fig.3.1.10   1/F against permittivity for various coating thicknesses, b.'a' is the wire radius in cm, ℓ=10cm in all cases.   © IEE.

3.2 Early analytical approaches to coated antennas

Previous to the cavity approach of James and Henderson (1978) which will be described in Section 3.3. the coated monopole antenna had not been analysed. Various other configurations and analysis have been considered in the past but in general, losses and efficiency factors were not modelled and the feed systems were unrealistic (Towaij and Hamid (1972); Tai (1948); Polk (1959); Stovall and Mei (1975); Vasil'ev (1974); Richmond and Newman (1976); Ting (1969); Madani et al. (1972)). A different approach by Richmond and Newman (1976) used the moments method (Harrington, 1967) to analyse the thinly coated dipole and although the coating was modelled in an approximate manner, it did give some interesting results, as shown in Fig.3.2.1.

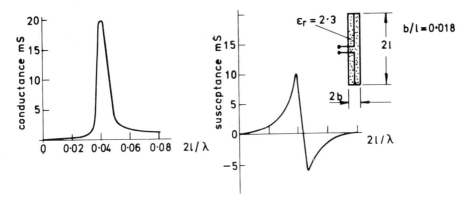

Fig.3.2.1   Input conductance and susceptance of the thinly coated di-
         pole antenna by Richmond and Newman (1976).   © IEEE.

This work could only be applied to very thin coatings and it was
conjectured by the present authors that the moments method could be
applied to very short monopoles with thick coatings to solve for the
input impedance. For a short squat antenna with a large F factor, the
radiation will have only a small perturbation effect on the basic resonance properties of the structure. This enabled some approximation
to be made in order to formulate a moments method solution. It was
assumed that a perfect magnetic wall boundary condition existed on the
cylindrical dielectric surface and was replaced in the formulation by
a surface of equivalent magnetic current density $\underline{J}^M$. The wire had an
electric current density $\underline{J}^E$ as shown in Fig.3.2.2 (a).

The fields at a general observation point P within the coating are
given in terms of $\underline{J}^M$ and $\underline{J}^E$ as

$$\underline{E}(P) = -\underline{\nabla}\Lambda^E - j\omega\underline{\xi}^E - \underline{\nabla} \times \underline{\xi}^M/\varepsilon_o\varepsilon_r$$

$$\underline{H}(P) = -\underline{\nabla}\Lambda^M - j\omega\underline{\xi}^M + \underline{\nabla} \times \underline{\xi}^E/\mu_o$$

where Λ^E, Λ^M are the electric and magnetic scalar potentials
       $\underline{\xi}^E$, $\underline{\xi}^M$ are the electric and magnetic vector potentials

ε_o and μ_o are the absolute permittivity and permeability of free-
space, respectively

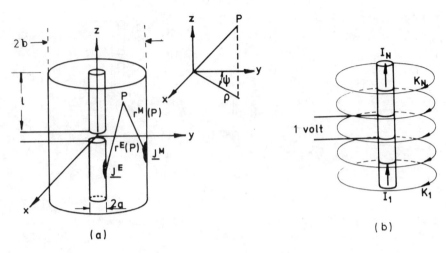

Fig.3.2.2 (a)   Current sources used in moments method   solution   for
the coated dipole with large F factor.   (b) Discretised version of
(a).

$$\omega = k\sqrt{\varepsilon_o \mu_o}$$

$$k = 2\pi/\lambda$$

$$\Lambda^E = \int_{-\ell}^{\ell} \int_o^{2\pi} \sigma^E(z) \ f^E(P) \ a \ d\psi dz$$

$$\Lambda^M = \int_{-\ell}^{\ell} \int_o^{2\pi} \sigma^M(z) \ f^M(P) \ a \ d\psi dz$$

$$\underline{\xi}^E = \int_{-\ell}^{\ell} \int_o^{2\pi} \mu_o \ \underline{J}^E(z) \ f^E(P) \ a \ d\psi dz$$

$$\underline{\xi}^M = \int_{-\ell}^{\ell} \int_o^{2\pi} \varepsilon_o \varepsilon_r \ \underline{J}^M(z) \ f^M(P) \ b \ d\psi dz$$

where $f^E(P) = \exp(-jk\sqrt{\varepsilon_r} \ r^E(P))/4\pi r^E(P)$

$f^M(P) = \exp(-jk\sqrt{\varepsilon_r} \ r^M(P))/4\pi r^M(P)$

σ^E, σ^M are surface charge densities located on the surface $\rho = a$ and
$\rho = b$, respectively.

To solve for the input impedance, certain discretisations and approximations are necessary shown pictorially in Fig.3.2.2 (b) as follows.

(a) $\underline{J}^E$ is approximated by a current $I(z)$ along the wire axis and is then replaced by N segments of current of constant value $I[i]$ and of length $\Delta\ell$ ($i = 1,2,3....N$).

(b) Charge densities are approximated by finite differences.

(c) $\underline{J}^M$ is approximated by a sheet of magnetic current $K(z)$ flowing in the ψ direction. $K(z)$ is then discretized by N magnetic current rings of radius b, $K[i]$ ($i = 1,2,3....N$).

The boundary conditions are applied by enforcing that $E_z(P) = 0$ at each segment on the wire and at $z = +\ell$ and also that $H_{\psi}(P) = 0$ at $x = b + \delta_b$, where δ_b is a small incremental distance from b to avoid field singularities. The application of the boundary conditions at the match points on each segment results in set of linear equations for the unknown current elements, which are computed by matrix inversion, assuming a simple 1 volt delta generator at the central wire segment. Under these conditions, the input impedance of the antenna is given by the inverse of the current on the central segment.

Fig.3.2.3 shows the measured input impedance of a coated monopole antenna fed by a coaxial line in a ground-plane. The dashed curve is

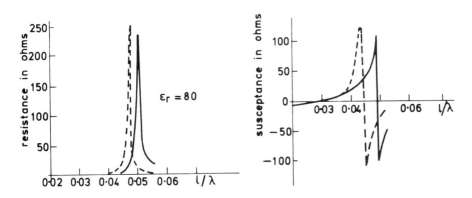

Fig.3.2.3. Input impedance of coated dipole, $\varepsilon_r=80$, $b/\ell=1$, $F\gg1$.
----- computed   ——— measured

the computed values for the coated dipole structure but divided by a factor of 2 to account for the monopole/ground-plane configuration. The computation was found to be insensitive to the choice of δ_b, provided $\delta_b \ll b$, and to the value of N provided that N > 17.

The model gave a very low input resistance at resonance as found in practice and good agreement with the first resonance condition but the solution gradually diverged from the experimental values as the electrical length increased, assumably due to the increase in the effect of radiation. It thus became apparent that although this model could predict the resonance condition for short antennas, it had several deficiencies and a more accurate analysis was required which could be used to model a wide variety of antenna coatings and F factors. This led to the cavity approach which will now be described.

3.3   Resonant cavity analysis of the coated monopole

From the findings of the early experiments, it is seen that the use of dielectric coatings for height reduction can be accompanied by a substantial reduction in antenna efficiency, input impedance and generally, bandwidth. The analytical work on these structures was inadequate in describing these effects and for this reason, a new analysis based on modal properties was chosen which modelled the coated monopole as a resonant cavity. This technique is capable of giving an accurate picture of all the important antenna parameters and in particular the input impedance can be calculated for a realistic coaxial line launcher, as shown in Fig.3.3.1. As far as the authors are aware, this is the first analysis that accounts for both the feed launcher and antenna effects.

Physically the action of the coated monopole is easily visualised although difficult to analyse. The annular slot in the ground-plane excites a Goubau-type surface-wave mode (Hersch, 1960) in the coating region which is tightly bound to the wire and decays rapidly outside the coating. The wave travels along the length of the wire and is reflected at the end-face back towards the slot with some of the power radiated off into free-space. The wave is reflected back towards the

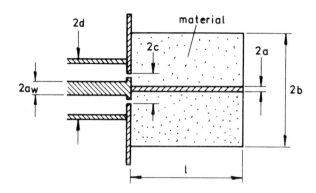

Fig.3.3.1   Sectional view of antenna showing coaxial feed,   coaxial
feed launcher and material coating.   Metal conductors are denoted
by hatched regions.

end-face from the ground-plane and this process   repeats   indefinitely
until   all the power is either radiated off at the discontinuity or is
dissipated in the coating.   If the material was   loss-free,   then   all
the power would be radiated off and the antenna itself would   be   100%
efficient.   It can therefore be clearly seen that   the   ratio   of   the
power radiated to that dissipated in the coating   determines   the   antenna efficiency and bandwidth.   The model   analysis   bears   out   this
physical action and the process of calculating all the antenna parameters can be broken down into four stages.

(i) the   computation   of   the   wavelength   in the coating (λ_g) gives a
close estimate of the resonant length of the monopole and   the   height-
reduction factor F.   The coated monopole is resonant when   the   length
$\ell \sim \lambda_g/4$ and the F factor is given by

$$F = \lambda/\lambda_g \qquad (3.3.1)$$

(ii) An estimation is required for the amount of power radiated off at
the end-face, denoted from now on by T where

$$T = 1 - |\Gamma_e|^2 \qquad (3.3.2)$$

and $\Gamma_e = |\Gamma_e| \exp(j\phi)$ is the reflection coefficient of   the   reflected
surface   wave mode at the end-face. $|\Gamma_e|$ will be close to unity and ϕ
gives the capacitive end-effect, which reduces the length of the monopole for resonance from $\lambda_g/4$ slightly, but is a second-order effect.

(iii) the input impedance can be calculated once Γ_e is known.

(iv) power loss estimations are then made giving the Q factor and efficiency values for the antenna, using T, computed from (ii). This will be dealt with in Section 3.3.4.

3.3.1 Computation of the coated guide wavelength and the F factor

The trapped surface wave fields that can be supported by the coaxial structure are expressed in cylindrical coordinates (ρ, ψ, z) as

$$E_{\rho\nu s} = - \frac{j\beta}{k_{\nu s}^2} \frac{dE_{z\nu s}}{d\rho} \tag{3.3.3}$$

$$H_{\psi\nu s} = - \frac{j\omega\varepsilon_o \varepsilon_\nu}{k_{\nu s}^2} \frac{dE_{z\nu s}}{d\rho}$$

where $\nu=2$ for the coating region and $\nu=3$ for the air region, $z<\ell$.

$$E_{z2s} = \{a_2 J_o(k_{2s}\rho) + a_3 Y_o(k_{2s}\rho)\} \exp(-j\beta z)$$

$$E_{z3s} = a_4 H_o^{(1)}(k_{3s}\rho) \exp(-j\beta z) \tag{3.3.4}$$

The coordinate system used is shown in Fig.3.3.2. To compute these fields it is assumed that the material has very small losses and this has been found to be a reasonable approximation for the λ_g calculation. $J_o(x)$, $Y_o(x)$ and $H_o^{(1)}(x)$ are Bessel functions (McLachlan, 1934). β is the phase constant of the wave ($= 2\pi/\lambda_g$). The coefficients a_2, a_3, a_4 are determined from the application of the boundary

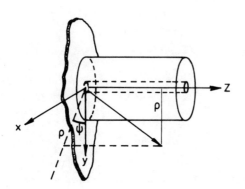

Fig.3.3.2 Coordinate system used for coated guide wavelength calculation.

conditions on the fields eqns. (3.3.3) and (3.3.4) at the surfaces $\rho=a$ and $\rho=b$, which also results in a transcendental equation (3.3.5) in terms of β. The lowest-order mode that can exist in the coating is the TM_{oo} mode which is the first solution of eqn. (3.3.5). This solution is ψ independent which is compatible with the symmetrical excitation of the slot.

$$\Delta_5 (\Delta_3 - \Delta_4) + \varepsilon_r (\Delta_2 \Delta_4 - \Delta_1 \Delta_3) = 0 \qquad (3.3.5)$$

where

$$\Delta_1 = \frac{Y_o'(k_{2s}b)}{k_{2s}bY_o(k_{2s}b)} \qquad \Delta_2 = \frac{J_o'(k_{2s}b)}{k_{2s}bJ_o(k_{2s}b)}$$

$$\Delta_3 = \frac{J_o(k_{2s}a)}{Y_o(k_{2s}a)} \qquad \Delta_4 = \frac{J_o(k_{2s}b)}{Y_o(k_{2s}b)}$$

$$\Delta_5 = \frac{H_o^{(1)'}(k_{3s}b)}{k_{3s}bH_o^{(1)}(k_{3s}b)}$$

$$Z_n'(x) = dZ_n(x)/dx \text{ where } Z_n = J_n(x), Y_n(x), H_n^{(1)}(x)$$

and for the TM_{oo} mode the modal coefficients are

$$a_3 = -\Delta_3 a_2$$

$$a_4 = \left\{ \frac{J_o(k_{2s}b)Y_o(k_{2s}a) - J_o(k_{2s}a)Y_o(k_{2s}b)}{H_o^{(1)}(k_{3s}b)Y_o(k_{2s}a)} \right\} \cdot a_2 \qquad (3.3.6)$$

Eqn. (3.3.5) can be approximated under certain conditions. When $\beta \to k$, the transcendental equation becomes

$$J_o(k_2a)Y_o(k_2b) - J_o(k_2b)Y_o(k_2a) = 0$$

whereas for $\beta \to k\sqrt{\varepsilon_r\mu_r}$ it becomes

$$J_1(k_2b)Y_o(k_2a) - Y_1(k_2b)J_o(k_2a) = 0$$

The F factors for this antenna given by eqns. (3.3.1) and (3.3.5) have been computed for several permittivities and permeabilities of

212

coating and the curves below are a good approximation for an initial design.

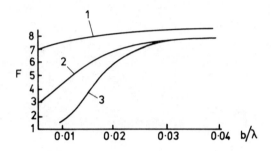

Fig.3.3.3   Computed values of F factor for a given coating thickness.
(1) $\varepsilon_r=1$, $\mu_r=81$ (2) $\varepsilon_r=9$, $\mu_r=9$ (3) $\varepsilon_r=81$, $\mu_r=1$.

It can be seen immediately that a much thinner material coating is required if magnetic materials are used. Take as an example $b = 0.01\lambda$, then with the purely magnetic material an F factor of 7.5 can be achieved but only 1.5 with the purely dielectric materials. This property of ferrite materials gives them a clear advantage over dielectric material for making small antennas and it will be shown later on how ferrite-coated antennas can be made at VHF and HF frequencies.

Using eqn.(3.3.5) it is now possible to predict approximately the resonant frequency of operation of a coated antenna and we can now move on to examining the end-reflection coefficient Γ_e so that the antenna system parameters can be estimated.

3.3.2   Estimation of end-face reflection coefficient

The end-face at $z=\ell$ is an abrupt discontinuity for the surface-wave mode, resulting in radiation into free-space but with the majority of the surface-wave power reflected back down the line. In order to make the calculations simpler, the coordinate system in Fig.3.3.2 is transformed along the z axis so that the origin now lies on the end-face as shown in Fig.3.3.4.

The technique used for analysing the end-effect is based on the variational method published by Angulo and Chang (1959) for a terminated dielectric rod. The fields $(\underline{E}_R, \underline{H}_R)$ in the radiation region $z>0$ are

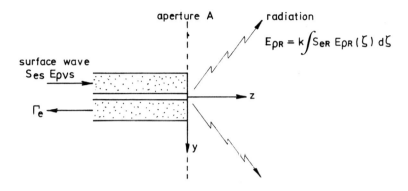

Fig.3.3.4   End-effect coordinates and field forms.

represented as an integral of a continuous spectral distribution of modes, as described by Shevchenko (1971) and shown in Fig.3.3.4 with

$$E_{\rho R}(\zeta) = \frac{j\gamma}{k\zeta} J_1(k\zeta\rho) \exp(-j\gamma z)$$

$$H_{\psi R}(\zeta) = \frac{j\omega\varepsilon_o}{k\zeta} J_1(k\zeta\rho) \exp(-j\gamma z) \qquad (3.3.7)$$

where $\gamma^2 = k^2(\zeta^2 - 1)$

In the integral for $(\underline{E}_R, \underline{H}_R)$, ζ ranges from 0 to ∞ and when $\zeta > 1$, γ is imaginary and the fields become evanescent along z. Therefore the fields can be written as

$$E_{\rho R} = k\int_0^1 S_{eR}(\zeta)E_{\rho R}(\zeta)d\zeta$$

$$+ k\int_1^\infty S_{eR}(\zeta)E_{\rho R}(\zeta)d\zeta \qquad (3.3.8)$$

The first term contributes to the radiation and the second term gives the near-field effect around the termination which results in the re-flection coefficient being a complex quantity. $S_{eR}(\zeta)$ is an excita-tion coefficient which depends on the fields existing on the end-face aperture A which extends over the plane z=0, and will be determined by applying orthogonality and boundary conditions on A.

The distribution fields $(\underline{E}_R(\zeta), \underline{H}_R(\zeta))$ obey the orthogonality rela-tionship at $z=0$

$$\int_0^{2\pi} \int_0^{\rho_A} E_{\rho R}(\zeta) \cdot H_{\psi R}(\zeta') \, \rho d\rho \, d\psi = N_R^2(\zeta) \, \delta \, (\zeta - \zeta') \text{ as } \rho_{\Delta L} \qquad (3.3.9)$$

δ is the Dirac delta function. After substituting for the fields in eqn.(3.3.9) from eqn.(3.3.7) and implementing the asymptotic forms of the cylinder functions as

$$J_0(z) \sim (\frac{2}{\pi z})^{\frac{1}{2}} \cos(z - \pi/4) \qquad Y_0(z) = (\frac{2}{\pi z})^{\frac{1}{2}} \sin(z - \pi/4)$$

$$J_1(z) \sim (\frac{2}{\pi z})^{\frac{1}{2}} \cos(z - 3\pi/4) \qquad Y_1(z) = (\frac{2}{\pi z})^{\frac{1}{2}} \sin(z - 3\pi/4) \qquad (3.3.10)$$

the integral in eqn.(3.3.9) can be evaluated by noting that

$$\frac{\sin(k\rho_A(\zeta - \zeta'))}{\pi(\zeta - \zeta')} \to \delta(\zeta - \zeta') \text{ as } \rho_A \to \infty \qquad (3.3.11)$$

giving

$$N_R^2(\zeta) = - \frac{2\pi\omega\varepsilon_o\gamma}{k^4\zeta^3} \qquad (3.3.12)$$

The total surface wave fields flowing in the region $z<0$ may be writ-ten as

$$E_{\rho\nu s}^T = E_{\rho\nu s} \, (e^{-j\beta z} + \Gamma_e \, e^{j\beta z})$$

$$H_{\psi\nu s}^T = H_{\psi\nu s} \, (e^{-j\beta z} - \Gamma_e \, e^{j\beta z}) \qquad (3.3.13)$$

where $E_{\rho\nu s}$ and $H_{\psi\nu s}$ are defined in eqn.(3.3.3). The surface wave fields are orthogonal to the radiation fields.

In the region $z<0$ there are also spectral fields radiated in the $-z$ direction but it was found that these gave a negligible contribution to the calculation of Γ_e for the trial aperture field chosen and are not given here.

The variational method for calculating Γ_e is now applied at the end-face as follows. It is assumed that a trial field $E_{\rho A}$ exists in the aperture A and this generates the modal and spectral fields in the regions z<0 and z>0. The surface wave and spectral transverse electric fields have to be continuous across the boundary at z=0 and are equated to the trial aperture field giving

$$E_{\rho A} = (1 + \Gamma_e) \, S_{es} E_{\rho vs} \qquad\qquad (3.3.14)$$

$$E_{\rho A} = k \int_o^\infty S_{oR}(\zeta) E_{\rho R}(\zeta) d\zeta \qquad\qquad (3.3.15)$$

The coefficients S_{es} and $S_{eR}(\zeta)$ are easily evaluated by applying the orthogonality conditions, eqn.(3.3.9). Eqn.(3.3.14) is multiplied by $H_{\psi vs}$ and integrated over the region $0 \le \rho < \infty$, $0 < \psi < 2\pi$ giving

$$S_{es} N_s^2 (1 + \Gamma_e) = \int_A E_{\rho A} H_{\psi vs} \, dA \qquad\qquad (3.3.16)$$

where

$$N_s^2 = -2\pi\beta\omega\varepsilon_o [\frac{\varepsilon_r I_1}{k_{2s}^2} + \frac{I_2}{k_{3s}^2}] \qquad\qquad (3.3.17)$$

and

$$I_1 = \int_a^b [a_2 \, J_o'(k_{2s}\rho) + a_3 \, Y_o'(k_{2s}\rho)]^2 \, \rho d\rho$$

$$I_2 = \int_b^\infty [a_4 \, H_o^{(1)'}(k_{3s}\rho)]^2 \, \rho d\rho$$

Also, multiplying eqn.(3.3.15) by $H_{\psi R}(\zeta)$ and integrating over $0 \le \rho < \infty$, $0 \le \psi < 2\pi$ gives

$$k \, S_{eR}(\zeta) \, N_R^2(\zeta) = \int_A E_{\rho A} \, H_{\psi R}(\zeta) \, dA \qquad\qquad (3.3.18)$$

$N_R^2(\zeta)$ is given by eqn.(3.3.15).

The continuity of the transverse magnetic field in the plane A is now enforced to give

$$S_{es}(1 + \Gamma_e) \, H_{\psi\nu s} = k \int_o^\infty S_{eR}(\zeta) \, H_{\psi R}(\zeta) \, d\zeta \qquad \text{for } \nu = 2,3 \qquad (3.3.19)$$

Now multiplying eqn. (3.3.19) above by $E_{\rho A}$ and then integrating over the aperture plane A gives the variational form of the relative end admittance

$$\frac{1 - \Gamma_e}{1 + \Gamma_e} \frac{(\int_A E_{\rho A} H_{\psi\nu s} \, dA)^2}{N_s^2} = \int_o^\infty \frac{(\int_A E_{\rho A} H_{\psi R}(\zeta) \, dA)^2}{N_R^2(\zeta)} \, d\xi$$

The term $(1-\Gamma_e)/(1+\Gamma_e)$ is the relative end admittance of the termination and being of a variational form means that any small errors in the choice of trial aperture field will result in second order errors in the end admittance. Note that the choice in aperture field need only convey the variation of the field in ρ and not the actual value.

For this particular problem, $E_{\rho A}$ was chosen as the incident field $E_{\rho\nu s}$ and the expression for the end admittance reduces to

$$\frac{1 - \Gamma_e}{1 + \Gamma_e} = \frac{1}{N_s^2} \int_o^\infty \left(\frac{2\pi\beta\omega\varepsilon_o}{k\zeta N_R(\zeta)}\right)^2 \left(\frac{I_3}{k_{2s}} + \frac{I_4}{k_{3s}}\right)^2 d\zeta = \int_o^\infty f(\zeta) \, d\zeta \qquad (3.3.20)$$

where

$$I_3(\zeta) = \int_a^b J_1(k\zeta\rho) \cdot [a_2 J_1(k_{2s}\rho) + a_3 Y_1(k_{2s}\rho)] \, \rho d\rho$$

$$I_4(\zeta) = \int_b^\infty a_4 J_1(k\zeta\rho) \, H_1^{(1)}(k_{3s}\rho) \, \rho d\rho$$

This expression can be split into real and imaginary parts, corresponding to the radiative and evanescent regions of the spectral integral. Thus

$$\frac{1 - \Gamma_e}{1 + \Gamma_e} = G_e + jB_e \qquad (3.3.21)$$

where G_e is the relative radiation conductance and B_e is the relative capacitance. From eqn. (3.3.20)

$$G_e = \int_0^1 f(\zeta)d\zeta \qquad jB_e = \int_1^\infty f(\zeta)d\zeta \qquad (3.3.22)$$

An examination of B_e shows that it is always capacitive.
From eqn.(3.3.21)

$$\Gamma_e = \frac{1 - G_e - jB_e}{1 + G_e + jB_e} = |\Gamma_e|e^{j\phi} \qquad (3.3.23)$$

Values of Γ_e computed by numerical integration of eqn.(3.3.20) are given in Fig.3.3.5 for a purely dielectric material with ε_r=81 and b/a=20. As anticipated, the value of $|\Gamma_e|$ is very close to unity for

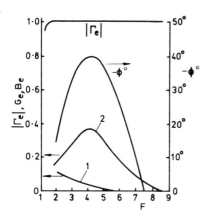

Fig.3.3.5 Computed values of $\Gamma_e = |\Gamma_e|\exp(j\phi)$ as a function of F. (1) is the relative conductance G_e. (2) is the relative susceptance B_e.

a high F factor, indicating that only a small proportion of the incident power is radiated in one wave reflection. Under these conditions, the dissipation in the material would have to be very small to achieve an acceptable efficiency. As F reduces, the radiated power increases but the numerical solution becomes unreliable and a much improved trial field would be necessary to accurately model this region of the curve. Experimental results presented later on show that the values of Γ_e computed here are of the correct order and are sufficiently accurate for a good antenna design.

It is interesting to examine a material with the same $\varepsilon_r\mu_r$ product as the above dielectric material but with $\varepsilon_r=\mu_r$=9. This material has similar properties to a commercially available low-loss VHF ferrite.

G_e, B_e, $|\Gamma_e|$ and ϕ are plotted in Fig.3.3.6. The value of $|\Gamma_e|$ is much lower than for a purely dielectric material with the same F factor, indicating that a ferrite material will be more efficient for the same dissipative losses and this is another clear advantage of ferrites over dielectrics. Table 3.3.1 shows the maximum radiation occurs if $\varepsilon_r = \mu_r$ which is consistent with Fresnel's laws (Stratton, 1941).

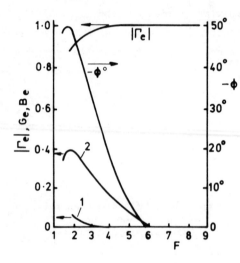

Fig.3.3.6 Computed values of Γ_e for $\varepsilon_r = \mu_r = 9$, b/a=20. Curve (1) is G_e. Curve (2) is B_e.

ε_r	μ_r	$|\Gamma_e|$
81	1	0.9973
20	4	0.9928
9	9	0.9918
4	20	0.9950
1	81	0.9988

Table 3.3.1 Typical values of Γ_e for $\varepsilon_r \mu_r$=81, b/a =20.

Now that Γ_e has been evaluated it is possible to calculate the input impedance for the monopole structure. The phase correction factor ϕ is required to calculate an accurate length for resonance in the coated monopole and this process will now be explained.

3.3.3 Calculation of the input impedance

A TEM mode is the principal mode in a standard air-filled coaxial line and this is reflected from the antenna/ground-plane junction, with a reflection coefficient Γ. Ideally for a perfectly matched antenna, Γ should be zero. The transverse field components of this mode are

$$E^T_{\rho w} = (e^{-j\beta_w z} + \Gamma e^{j\beta_w z})/\rho$$

$$H^T_{\psi w} = (e^{-j\beta_w z} - \Gamma e^{j\beta_w z})/(120\pi\rho) \qquad (3.3.24)$$

The other fields involved in this calculation are shown in Fig.3.3.7.

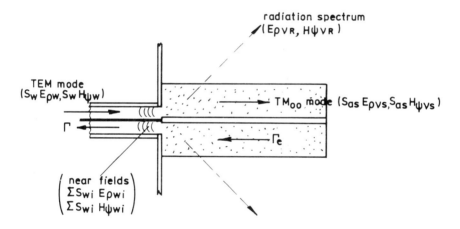

Fig.3.3.7   Slot fields and physical action.

On reflection at the slot discontinuity, the fields generated in the slot excite a series of evanescent coaxial line modes and these give the near-field effect in the region of the slot for $z<0$. These are TM modes below cut-off and are given by

$$E_{\rho wi} = -\frac{\alpha_i}{x_i} [J_1(x_i\rho)Y_0(x_i a_w) - J_0(x_i a_w)Y_1(x_i\rho)] e^{\alpha_i z}$$

$$H_{\psi wi} = -\frac{j\omega\varepsilon_o}{\alpha_i} E_{\rho wi} \qquad (3.3.25)$$

where x_i is a root of

$$J_o(x_i a_w) Y_o(x_i d) - J_o(x_j d) Y_o(x_i a_w) = 0$$

derived from satisfying the boundary conditions at the coaxial line surfaces (Marcuwitz, 1951).

$$\alpha_i = x_i^2 - k^2 \qquad x_i \sim 2k(d - a_w)/i \qquad\qquad i = 1,2,3..... \qquad (3.3.26)$$

Some of the incident TEM power is transferred through the slot into the TM_{oo} surface wave mode and some radiation is emitted into free-space. The TM_{oo} mode is reflected backwards and forwards between the end-face and the ground-plane resulting in an infinite series of terms which may be expressed in a closed form assuming 100% reflection at the ground-plane.

$$E^T_{\rho\nu s} = E_{\rho\nu s} \left[\frac{e^{-(\alpha+j\beta)z} + \Gamma_e e^{(\alpha+j\beta)(z-2\ell)}}{1 + \Gamma_e e^{-2l(\alpha+j\beta)}} \right]$$

$$H^T_{\psi\nu s} = H_{\psi\nu s} \left[\frac{e^{-(\alpha+j\beta)z} - \Gamma_e e^{(\alpha+j\beta)(z-2\ell)}}{1 + \Gamma_e e^{-2\ell(\alpha+j\beta)}} \right] \qquad (3.3.27)$$

Notice that a dissipative attenuation coefficient α has been included here and this will be determined later on in Section 3.3.4. α has only a second-order effect on the input impedance solution but is very important in the efficiency and Q calculation.

The continuous spectrum of modes may be written as

$$E_{\rho\nu R}(\zeta) = \frac{j\gamma}{k_{\nu R}} [a_{\nu R} J_1(k_{\nu R}\rho) + b_{\nu R} Y_1(k_{\nu R}\rho)] e^{-j\gamma z}$$

$$H_{\psi\nu R}(\zeta) = \frac{\omega\varepsilon_o \varepsilon_\nu}{\gamma} E_{\rho\nu R}(\zeta) \qquad (3.3.28)$$

The coefficients $a_{\nu R}$, $b_{\nu R}$ may be determined by applying the boundary conditions to the fields at $\rho=a$ and $\rho=b$ and then by normalising a_{2R} to unity,

$$a_{2R} = 1 \qquad b_{2R} = J_o(k_{2R}a)/Y_o(k_{2R}a)$$

$$a_{3R} = \frac{\pi k_{3R} b \varepsilon_r k_{3R}}{2k_{2R}} [J_1(k_{2R}b) + b_{2R} Y_1(k_{2R}b)] \, Y_o(k_{3R}b)$$

$$- \frac{k_{2R}}{\varepsilon_r k_{3R}} [J_o(k_{2R}b) + b_{2R} Y_o(k_{2R}b)] \, Y_1(k_{3R}b)$$

$$b_{3R} = [J_o(k_{2R}b) + b_{2R} Y_o(k_{2R}b) - a_{3R} J_o(k_{3R}b)]/Y_o(k_{3R}b) \qquad (3.3.29)$$

The radiation spectrum and the TM_{oo} mode are mutually orthogonal to each other and the representations (3.3.27) and (3.3.28) are exact.

The variational method (Marcuwitz, 1951; Harrington, 1967) is now applied at the annular slot plane A, $a_s \leq \rho \leq c$, $0 \leq \psi \leq 2\pi$ to evaluate the reflection coefficient Γ which will give the impedance of the antenna. In this calculation it is assumed that the trial field $E_{\rho A} = 1$ in the annular slot region A, which is a good approximation for a small slot size c-a. The fields in the region z>0 and z<0 are assigned unknown excitation coefficients S_w, S_{wi}, S_{as}, $S_{aR}(\zeta)$ and these are determined by equating the transverse electric fields to the aperture field in the slot and applying orthogonality.

$$S_w E_{\rho w}^T + \sum_{i=1}^{\infty} S_{wi} E_{\rho wi} = \begin{cases} 1 & a_s \leq \rho \leq c \\ 0 & \text{elsewhere} \end{cases} \qquad (3.3.30)$$

$$S_{as} E_{\rho \nu s}^T + k \int_o^{\infty} S_{aR}(\zeta) E_{\rho \nu R}(\zeta) \, d\zeta = \begin{cases} 1 & a_s \leq \rho \leq c \\ 0 & \text{elsewhere} \end{cases} \qquad (3.3.31)$$

Multiplying eqn.(3.3.30) by $H_{\psi w}^T$ and integrating over the coaxial cross-section gives

$$S_w = \frac{c - a_s}{60 N_w^2} \frac{1}{1 + \Gamma} \qquad (3.3.32)$$

where

$$N_w^2 = \ln(d/a_w)/60$$

Now multiplying eqn.(3.3.30) by $H_{\psi wi}$ and integrating over the coaxial cross-section gives

$$S_{wi} N_{wi}^2 = 2\pi \int_{a_s}^{c} \frac{j\omega\varepsilon_o}{x_i} [J_1(x_i\rho)Y_o(x_ia_w) - J_o(x_ia_w)Y_1(x_i\rho)] \rho d\rho$$

(3.3.33)

where

$$N_{wi}^2 = -j \frac{4\omega\varepsilon_o\alpha_i}{x_i^4} [\frac{J_o^2(x_ia_w)}{J_o^2(x_id)} - 1]$$

Similarly, multiplying eqn.(3.3.31) by $H_{\psi\nu s}$ and integrating over $a \leq \rho < \infty$, $0 \leq \psi < 2\pi$ gives

$$S_{as} N_s^2 = 2\pi \cdot j \frac{\omega\varepsilon_o\varepsilon_r}{k_{2s}^2} \int_{a_s}^{c} [a_2 J_1(k_{2s}\rho) + a_3 Y_1(k_{2s}\rho)] \rho d\rho$$

(3.3.34)

and multiplying eqn.(3.3.31) by $H_{\psi\nu R}$ and integrating over $a \leq \rho < \infty$, $0 \leq \psi \leq 2\pi$ gives

$$kS_{aR}(\zeta) N_{aR}^2 = \frac{2\pi j\omega\varepsilon_o\varepsilon_r}{k_{2R}} \int_{a_s}^{c} [a_{2R} J_1(k_{2R}\rho) + b_{2R} Y_1(k_{2R}\rho)] \rho d\rho$$

where

$$N_{aR}^2 = -\frac{-\gamma[a_{3R}^2 + b_{3R}^2] 2\pi\omega\varepsilon_o}{k_{3R}^3 k}$$

(3.3.35)

The continuity of the transverse magnetic fields is now enforced at $z=0$ to give

$$S_w H_{\psi w}^T + \sum_{i=1}^{\infty} S_{wi} H_{\psi wi} = S_{as} H_{\psi\nu s}^T + k \int_o^{\infty} S_{aR} H_{\psi\nu R}(\zeta) d\zeta$$

(3.3.36)

Now multiplying eqn.(3.3.36) by $E_{\rho A}$ and integrating over the slot region gives

$$\frac{1 - \Gamma}{1 + \Gamma} \frac{(c - a_s)^2}{60\ln(d/a_w)} + \sum_{i=1}^{\infty} S_{wi}^2 N_{wi}^2$$

$$= S_{as}^2 N_s^2 [\frac{1 - \Gamma_e e^{-2\ell(\alpha+j\beta)}}{1 + \Gamma_e e^{-2\ell(\alpha+j\beta)}}] + k^2 \int_o^{\infty} S_{aR}^2 N_{aR}^2 d\zeta$$

(3.3.37)

$(1-\Gamma)/(1+\Gamma)$ is the relative admittance of the antenna and can be written as

$$\frac{1 - \Gamma}{1 + \Gamma} = G_s + jB_s + Y + jB_w \qquad (3.3.38)$$

where G_s is the relative conductance of the slot due to the radiation spectrum

B_s is the relative susceptance of the slot due to the evanescent spectrum

Y is the power transfer term for the TM_{oo} mode

D_w is the relative susceptance of the slot due to evanescent terms in the coaxial line.

$$G_s = qk^2 \int_o^1 S_{aR}^2 \; N_{aR}^2 \; d\zeta \qquad (3.3.39)$$

$$jB_s = qk^2 \int_1^\infty S_{aR}^2 \; N_{aR}^2 \; d\zeta \qquad (3.3.40)$$

$$Y = qS_{as}^2 \; N_s^2 \; \frac{1 - \Gamma_e \; e^{-2\ell(\alpha+j\beta)}}{1 + \Gamma_e \; e^{-2\ell(\alpha+j\beta)}} \qquad (3.3.41)$$

$$jB_w = -q \sum_{i=1}^\infty S_{wi}^2 \; N_{wi}^2 \qquad (3.3.42)$$

where $q = 60 \; \ln(d/a_w)/(c-a_s)^2$

The components of the input impedance given above are computed individually and their contribution to the input impedance is now discussed.

The value of B_w is shown in Fig.3.3.8 for a 50 ohm coaxial line launcher with a small annular slot, computed from eqn.(3.3.42). The actual capacitance of the slot is given by $1/(B_w \cdot \omega)$ and is constant at 0.024pF over the frequency range shown. Values of B_s and G_s are shown below in Fig.3.3.9 for three types of material coating. It can be seen that B_s and G_s are an order of magnitude greater for a purely dielectric material than for a magnetic material and in the latter case, B_s is comparable to B_w. These terms are incorporated into eqn.

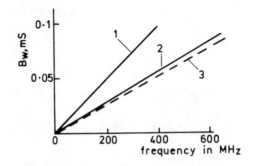

Fig.3.3.8   Computed values of B_w against frequency for d=3.5mm, a_w= 1.5mm and c=2.5mm, a_s=1.5mm. (1) computed from eqn.(3.3.42), (2) computed from Marcuwitz (1951).

(3.3.38) and the input impedance is computed in Fig.3.3.10 for two types of material.

It is immediately apparent that the purely dielectric material gives an unacceptably low input resistance at resonance (<1 ohm for F=4) and would be very difficult to match into. This confirms the early exper-imental findings of James and Burrows (1973) discussed earlier. The hybrid material with ε_r=μ_r gives a higher resistance due mainly to the higher transverse wave impedance of the TM_{oo} mode and partially to the higher radiation loss. B_s tends to detune the antenna slightly, al-though the major contribution to this detuning effect from the quar-ter-wave resonance condition arises from the complex nature of Γ_e. If $B_s + B_w$ is small then the condition for resonance is

Imaginary part of $(1+\Gamma)/(1-\Gamma) = 0$

that is, $2\beta\ell - \phi = 2\pi$
or $\ell/\lambda_g = 1/4 + \phi/4\pi$

Since ϕ is negative, the monopole length must be reduced by $\phi/4\pi$ to retain the resonance condition.

G_s has little effect on the impedance at resonance but can play a much larger part at the anti-resonance condition $\ell \sim \lambda_g/2$.

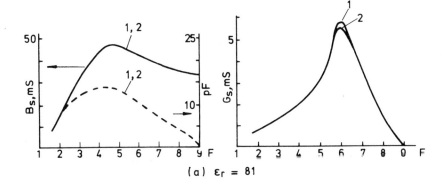

(a) $\varepsilon_r = 81$

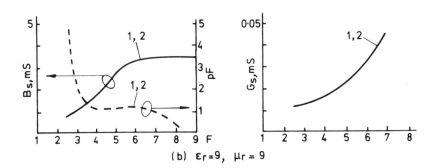

(b) $\varepsilon_r = 9, \mu_r = 9$

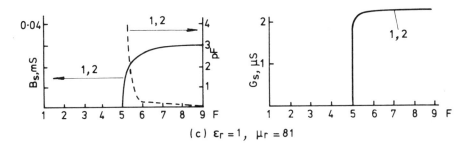

(c) $\varepsilon_r = 1, \mu_r = 81$

Fig.3.3.9 Computed values of B_s and G_s for a coating of thickness 20mm and wire diameter of 1mm fed by a coaxial cable.
(1) c=0.25b, a_s=0.15b. (2) c=0.25b, a_s=0.2b

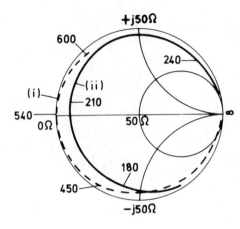

Fig.3.3.10 Computed input impedance of a coated monopole fed by a 50 ohm coaxial launcher. (i) ε_r=81, F=4, ℓ= 38mm;(ii) $\varepsilon_r=\mu_r$=9, F=4.5, ℓ= 78mm.

3.3.4 Antenna parameters

The analysis of Section 3.3.3 has shown how to calculate the input impedance of the coated monopole and the resonance condition but the more fundamental antenna parameters such as Q and efficiency have yet to be determined. A detailed consideration of material losses has now to be made so that these parameters can be estimated for a wide range of F factors. The following perturbation analysis assumes that the material loss factors are small. Writing

$$\varepsilon_r = \varepsilon_r{}' - j\varepsilon_r{}'' \qquad\qquad \mu_r = \mu_r{}' - j\mu_r{}''$$

$$= \varepsilon_r{}'(1 - j \tan \delta_\varepsilon) \qquad\qquad = \mu_r{}'(1 - j \tan \delta_\mu)$$

then $\tan \delta_\varepsilon$, $\tan \delta_\mu \ll 1$

The inclusion of $\tan \delta_\varepsilon$ and $\tan \delta_\mu$ into the transcendental eqn.(3.3.5) for guide wavelength would not perturb the solution significantly. This is a reasonable assumption for materials of practical interest, particularly since only low-loss material is suitable for height- reduction applications.

Thus for small losses the power dissipated per unit length of coating (P) is

$$P = 2\pi\omega \left[\tan \delta_\varepsilon \; \varepsilon_o \; \varepsilon_r' \int_a^b (E_{z2s}E_{z2s}{}^* + E_{\rho 2s}E_{\rho 2s}{}^*) \; \rho d\rho \right.$$

$$\left. + \tan \delta_\mu \; \mu_o \; \mu_r' \int_a^b H_{\psi 2s}H_{\psi 2s}{}^* \; \rho d\rho \right] \tag{3.3.43}$$

where * indicates complex conjugate. The power lost per unit length of conductor is

$$P_c = 2\pi a \; R_s \; H_{\psi 2s}H_{\psi 2s}{}^* \Big|_{\rho=a} \tag{3.3.44}$$

where R_s is the characteristic surface resistance of the conducting monopole and is approximately $(\omega\mu_o/2\sigma)^{1/2}$
where σ is the conductivity, assumed to be large.

$$P_c = \frac{2\pi a \varepsilon_o \varepsilon_r^2}{\mu_o} \; R_s \; k^2 \; [a_2 J_1(k_{2s}a) + a_3 Y_1(k_{2s}a)]^2/k_{2s}{}^2 \tag{3.3.45}$$

The attenuation coefficient α which appeared in eqn.(3.3.37) for the input impedance is given by

$$\alpha = (P_c + P)/2P_s \sim P/2P_s$$

$$\text{for } P_c \ll P$$

P_s is the TM_{oo} modal power

$$P_s = \text{Re} \cdot 2\pi \int_a^\infty E_{\rho\nu s} \; H_{\psi\nu s}^* \; \rho d\rho$$

$$= -N_s^2 \tag{3.3.46}$$

where Re denotes the 'real part of'.

If Γ_e is near to unity, then the transverse electric and magnetic cavity fields have a z-dependence of $\sin(\pi z/2\ell)$ and $\cos(\pi z/2\ell)$, respectively, and under the low-loss assumption, the stored electric and magnetic energies are approximately equal. The Q of the cavity is then given by

$$Q_c = \frac{2\pi\omega\varepsilon_o}{P} \left[\int_a^\infty \varepsilon_\nu \left(E_{z\nu s} E_{z\nu s}^* + E_{\rho\nu s} E_{\rho\nu s}^* \right) \rho d\rho \right] \qquad (3.3.47)$$

The Q given above will be lowered by the effect of radiation on the cavity action. On the first impact of the surface wave at the end-face, the incident modal power will be $(P_s - P\ell)$ and the reflected wave power is reduced to $(P_s - P\ell) \cdot (1-T)$ by the radiated power. This power is reflected back to the ground-plane and returns to $z=\ell$ reduced by the dissipation to $(P_s - P\ell)(1-T)(1-P\ell/P_s)$ and so on. This infinite series of terms for the total radiated and dissipated power readily summates to a closed form, giving

$$\frac{\text{power radiated}}{\text{power dissipated}} = \frac{T(P_s - P\ell)}{P\ell} \Big/ \left(1 + (1-T) \cdot \left(1 - \frac{P\ell}{P_s} \right) \right)$$

$$= r_r/r_\ell \qquad (3.3.48)$$

where r_r and r_ℓ are hypothetical resistances accounting for the two forms of power loss to the cavity.

The Q factor is now modified to account for the radiation losses to give

$$Q = \frac{Q_c}{1 + r_r/r_\ell}$$

The efficiency of the antenna is related to the resistances r_r and r_ℓ as follows

$$\eta = \frac{r_r}{r_r + r_\ell} \ (\times\ 100\%) \qquad (3.3.49)$$

or when expressed in dB, L_A

$$L_A = -10 \log_{10}(1 + r_\ell/r_r) \ dB$$

Computed values of Q and L_A are shown in Figs.3.3.11 and 3.3.12 and establish that for a given $\varepsilon_r \mu_r$ product, a hybrid material with $\varepsilon_r = \mu_r$ yields a more efficient antenna than purely dielectric material, for

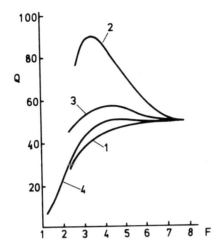

Fig.3.3.11   Computed values of Q

1	$\tan \delta_\epsilon = 0,$	$\tan \delta_\mu = 0.02$
2	$\tan \delta_\epsilon = 0.02,$	$\tan \delta_\mu = 0.02$
3	$\tan \delta_\epsilon = 0.01,$	$\tan \delta_\mu = 0.01$
4	$\tan \delta_\epsilon = 0.02,$	$\epsilon_r^\mu = 81, \mu_r = 1$

$\left. \begin{array}{l} \end{array} \right\} \epsilon_r = \mu_r = 9$

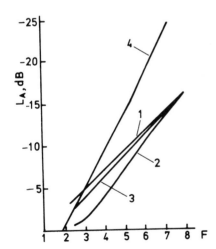

Fig.3.3.12   Computed values of L_A, for same parameters as Fig.3.3.11.

high F values. As F tends to unity, the purely dielectric material shows some advantage in this respect but this depends on whether the loss in the hybrid material is a dielectric or magnetic effect or a combination of both. This is also evident for Q where magnetic loss has a greater damping effect on the hybrid material than a numerically equivalent dielectric loss. For large F values, Q is seen to tend to the reciprocal of the sum of the loss tangents.

To verify the computed results, five dielectric antennas were constructed from deionised water enclosed in Perspex cases, ranging from very thin coatings with small F factors to very wide coatings with large F factors. The input impedances of the monopoles were measured and the bandwidths determined. The efficiency was measured using the 'Wheeler can' method (Wheeler, 1959). Bearing in mind that the measurement of very small input resistances is involved, large inaccuracies in bandwidth and efficiency were anticipated. Table 3.3.2 gives a comparison of the measurements and the computer predictions (indicated in brackets) of antenna performance. The loss factor $\tan \delta_\varepsilon$ for water was estimated using the Debye formulas as 0.02 (Debye, 1929). The slot size was c=2.5mm, a_s=1.5mm.

The above results have confirmed that the cavity analysis for the coated monopole antenna is a reliable technique over a wide range of F values and will now be used to design some VHF and HF antennas.

Table 3.3.2   Summary of measured and computed performance of water antennas. The square brackets indicate computed results.

Antenna type	Dimensions			F	T $=1-\|\Gamma_e\|^2$	r_o	f_o = resonant frequency	L_A	Δf %
	a	b	ℓ						
	mm	mm	mm			Ω	MHz	dB	
D_1	0.75	23.5	23	9	[0.00029]	0.4 [0.3]	381 [381]	9 [24]	2.6 [2.0]
D_2	0.75	15	37	6.1	[0.012]	0.4 [0.5]	339 [376]	10 [11]	2.4 [1.9]
D_3	0.6	16	89	3.2	[0.092]	0.4 [1.0]	257 [257]	1.4 [3.3]	9.7 [2.6]
D_4	0.6	12.5	125	2.3	[0.22]	2.5 [4.4]	255 [255]	0.7 [0.41]	5.5 [7.3]
D_5	0.6	11.5	160	1.9	[0.26]	8.5 [8]	253 [225]	0.15 [0.146]	9.9 [10.5]

3.3.5 Design considerations

From the computations made, it is evident that dielectric and magnetic materials can be used for height-reduction purposes but only at the expense of reductions in efficiency and bandwidth. Small reductions, up to say F=3, can be obtained fairly easily with reasonably thin coatings of commercially available dielectric or ferrite materials, with acceptable efficiencies. Larger F values however result in much thicker coatings and low efficiencies even with low-loss materials, which is due to the cavity action of the antenna.

The principal use of dielectric materials as coatings lies mainly above 100MHz due to the large thicknesses involved at the lower frequencies. At these frequencies, there are only a few ferrite materials available with low loss and this somewhat limits the choice of materials to these few ferrites or to the much wider range of dielectric materials. In Fig.3.3.13 the thickness of coating required for a range of F factors is plotted for various permittivities from 50 to 1000.

For example, to construct an 80MHz monopole antenna 14cm long would require a coating 4cm in diameter with a permittivity of 1000. This would be unacceptable from both volume and weight considerations for a

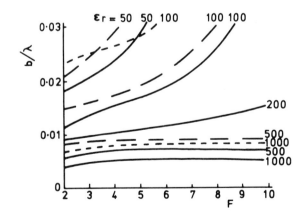

Fig.3.3.13   b/λ versus F factor for dielectric materials.
——— b/a=20, – – – b/a=10, ----- b/a=4

portable radio application. Fig.3.3.14 shows the loss factor L_A and the Q corresponding to the values of Fig.3.3.13 and for this particular antenna, the loss would typically be about −15dB for a bandwidth of 0.2%.

The input impedance of this antenna would be very small, certainly less than 1/4 ohm, but certain feeding techniques can overcome this problem. This is demonstrated in Fig.3.3.15 for an experimental water antenna, where a much higher impedance was obtained by feeding it at some point along its length.

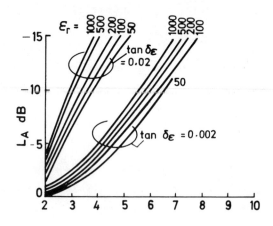

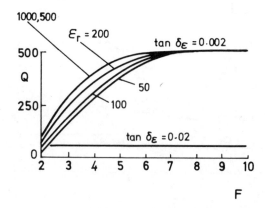

Fig.3.3.14   Loss factors and Q for dielectric-material-coated mono-
    poles.

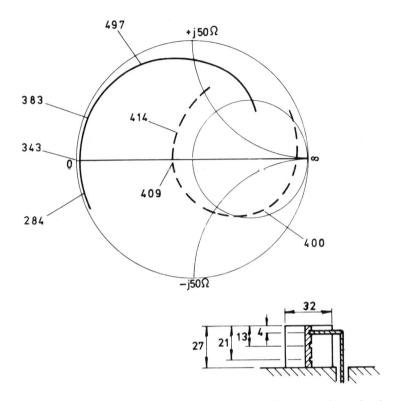

Fig.3.3.15   Increasing input resistance by tapped-in feed.
——— base-fed ----- tapped-in feed.
Dimensions in mm,   frequencies in MHz.

This slightly detuned the antenna and decreased the bandwidth somewhat but clearly is a simple technique for improving the match at the
input and has been used in the past on helical antennas (Hiroi and
Fujimoto, 1976).

Below 100MHz, several ferrite materials are available and these have
definite advantages over dielectrics, particularly if the permittivity
is comparable to the permeability, as is the case for some ferrites.
Firstly, the coating thickness for a given F value and $\varepsilon_r \mu_r$ product is
much smaller than for a similar dielectric material as demonstrated in
Fig.3.3.16; the loss factors and Q are also smaller as shown in Fig.3.
3.17.

234

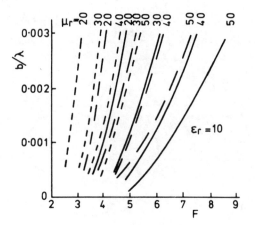

Fig.3.3.16   b/λ versus F factor for ferrite materials. ε_r=10 in   all
    cases.
    ———— b/a=20   — — — b/a=10   ----- b/a=4

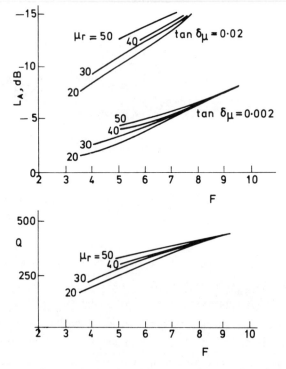

Fig.3.3.17   Loss factor L_A and Q versus F factor for ferrite   materi-
    als. ε_r=10.

Secondly the ferrite material has a much higher input impedance for the annular slot feed, as shown in Fig.3.3.18, which simplifies the feeding arrangements.

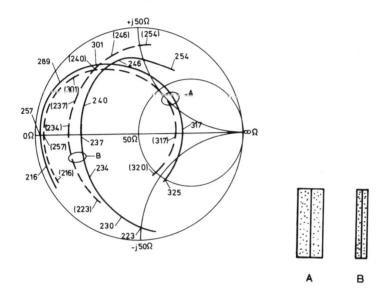

Fig.3.3.18   Measured and computed input impedance of ferrite and dielectric coated monopoles fed by annular slot.
   Case A: ε_r=80
   Case B: ε_r=10, μ_r=12
   Inset shows comparative sizes of antennas at 237 MHz. Bracketed values indicate computed frequencies in MHz.

Antenna B was constructed from a set of toroids available commercially, with ε_r=10, μ_r=12, tan δ_ε=0.017, and is compared to the water antenna D3 of Table 3.3.2. Both antennas have an F factor of about 3 but the inset Figure shows the comparative sizes of the two antennas. The ferrite antenna had a higher loss factor at -3.8dB, a Q of 40 and an efficiency of 40%. The measurements are not strictly comparable to the computed charts due to the toroidal construction of the device.

With this particular material, it is feasible to make an 80MHz VHF antenna of the same length as the dielectric version previously discussed but with a thickness of only 2cm. This is more acceptable for a portable application but typically one would expect a loss of -10dB

for a bandwidth of 2% which could limit its usage in certain bad reception areas.

An HF antenna was also constructed out of ferrite toroids, 4 cm
wide with μ_r=50 and ε_r=10 (James and Henderson, 1978). Its performance is shown in Fig.3.3.19, giving an F factor of 5.7 at 25MHz with
an efficiency of between 12 and 30% and a bandwidth of about 1%. It
had an input resistance of 15 ohms at resonance which enables efficient matching to a 50 ohm feed to be carried out.

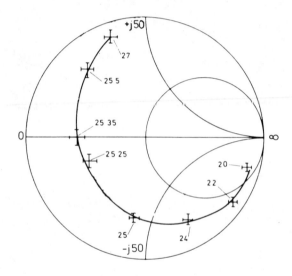

Fig.3.3.19   Measured Smith Chart of ferrite HF antenna.

When designing for a lower frequency of operation, the ferrites
available have a larger μ_r value making ferrite monopole antennas a
reality. One further antenna was constructed at 7MHz with a thickness
of 4 cm and this had an F factor of 6. The antenna had a considerable
weight and was probably too unwieldy for most portable applications
such as on vehicles for example. Antennas constructed using wire
winding techniques which resemble monopoles in shape, such as the
helix and the more recent counterwound/doubly wound antennas of James
et al.(1979) shown in Fig.3.3.20, possibly have more promise where
weight and cheapness are important system factors. Scaled-down ver-

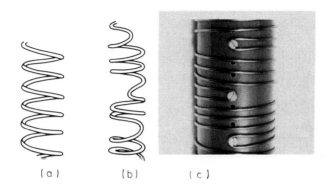

Fig.3.3.20   (a) Helix (b) Counterwound (c) Doublywound antenna

sions at UHF have shown that the counterwound and doubly wound   coils
have   an   efficiency   and bandwidth of about 30% for an F factor of 4,
compared with the helix which has a much narrower bandwidth   as   shown
in Fig.3.3.21. These figures should scale down to HF frequencies   and
in practice the counterwound antennas will not need a matching circuit

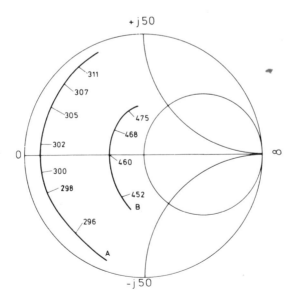

Fig.3.3.21   Smith Chart of helix and doubly wound antennas at UHF
    (A) helix (50mm long). (B) doubly wound (40mm long)

238

due to their high input resistance, thus incurring no further power losses.

The short coated monopole antenna has now been fully evaluated as a height-reduced antenna and it is now appropriate to examine how material loading techniques can be applied to size — reduce conformal antennas which are already small in terms of height.

3.4 Small conformal antennas

Conformal antennas are principally installed on the sides of vehicles such as aircraft, ships or armoured vehicles where more conventional antenna structures would not survive the environmental conditions. One of the earliest forms of conformal antenna was the top-loaded capacitor plate which consists of a short monopole loaded by a large metal plate and is still in use today. This antenna has been developed recently by Fort Monmouth (Goubau and Schwering, 1976) for use as a shock-proof vehicle antenna and, as shown in Fig.3.4.1, the space below the plate has been filled up by a dielectric material to increase the robustness. The antenna was fitted with an automatic tuning circuit which enabled a total efficiency of between 11 and 70% to be achieved over a 30-80MHz frequency range and demonstrates the usefulness of this simple antenna structure.

Armour plated disc

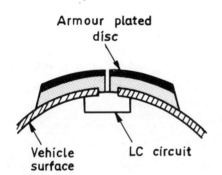

Fig.3.4.1   Low-profile VHF vehicle antenna

Vehicle surface   LC circuit

An alternative technique to top loading for the upper HF band has been suggested by Fenwick (1965) and consists of printing spiral coils onto dielectric substrates as shown in Fig.3.4.2. Being a resonator, this antenna has a very narrow bandwidth and the efficiencies are as

Fig.3.4.2   Low-profile spiral antenna by Fenwick (1965).

yet unknown. Other commonly used low-profile antennas are the inverted L- or tranlines, suitable for helicopter applications at low frequencies, and various kinds of cavity backed slots, most of which are
described in the glossary.

The most recently exploited conformal antenna is the microstrip
patch which has become very popular over the past few years due to the
cheapness of manufacture. Microstrip was invented around 1950 as a
planar transmission line but its use as an antenna did not develop
until about 1970. The basic theory and operation of microstrip antennas are now well-established (James et al., 1981) but here their use
as electrically small elements will be considered. The rectangular
patch is the simplest type to evaluate and the basic structure is
shown in Fig.3.4.3, along with a circular patch. The antenna consists
of a metal patch printed onto a dielectric substrate material and is
fed by either a coaxial feed as shown in the Figure or in line by a
printed-on microstrip line. The rectangular patch antenna is operated
at resonance where the size of the patch is approximately half a wavelength in material ($\lambda_g/2$). The physical action of the patch is basically cavity-type, characterised by a narrow bandwidth response. It
can be made an odd multiple of $\lambda_g/2$ but the radiation pattern will be
multi-lobed. The circular patch functions in a similar way and by
making its diameter close to λ_g, omni-directional pattern coverage
can be obtained as shown in Fig.3.4.3.

In order to reduce the size of the patch, a high-permittivity substrate has to be used and the efficiency will accordingly decrease.
This loss in efficiency arises from two sources: firstly the copper

240

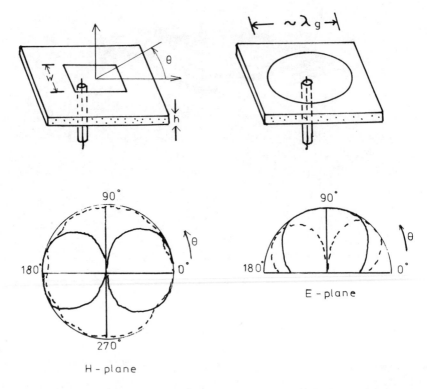

Fig.3.4.3   Microstrip patch antennas and radiation patterns.
——— rectangular   ----- circular

loss in the ground-plane and on the patch surface and secondly, the
dielectric loss in the substrate, defined by the loss tangent $\tan \delta_\varepsilon$.

The antenna efficiency η as defined for the coated monopole, eqn.(3.
3.49) is given by

$$\eta = \frac{r_r}{r_c + r_D + r_r} \qquad (3.4.1)$$

where r_r is the radiation resistance of the end-face, r_c and r_D are
the equivalent resistances accounting for power dissipation due to
copper loss and dielectric loss, respectively. η may alternatively be
represented in terms of the Q factors corresponding to these resistances. As an example, design formulas are given here for the $\lambda_g/2$
rectangular patch. The circular patch can be similarly designed using

circular eigenfunctions for the cavity fields.

$$\eta = \frac{Q_c Q_D}{Q_c Q_D + Q_c Q_R + Q_D Q_R} \quad (\times 100\%) \qquad (3.4.2)$$

$$Q_R = \frac{\pi r_r}{4 Z_m(\varepsilon_r)}$$

$$Q_c = \frac{78.6\sqrt{f}\ Z_m(1)\ h(\text{in cm})}{P_m} \qquad \text{for copper}$$

$$Q_D = \frac{1}{\tan \delta_\varepsilon} \qquad (3.4.3)$$

f is the frequency in GHz; $Z_m(\varepsilon_r)$ is the impedance of the microstrip line derived from quasi-static formulas

$$Z_m(\varepsilon_r) = \frac{120}{\sqrt{2(\varepsilon_r+1)}}\ [\ln(\frac{8h}{w}) + \frac{1}{32}(\frac{w}{h})^2 - \frac{1}{2}\frac{\varepsilon_r-1}{\varepsilon_r+1}(\ln(\frac{\pi}{2}) + \frac{\ln(\frac{4}{\pi})}{\varepsilon_r})]$$

$$\text{for } \frac{w}{h}<1$$

$$Z_m(\varepsilon_r) = \frac{60\pi}{\sqrt{\varepsilon_r}}[\frac{w}{2h} + 0.441 + 0.082(\frac{\varepsilon_r-1}{\varepsilon_r^2}) + \frac{(\varepsilon_r+1)}{2\pi\varepsilon_r}(1.451 + \ln(\frac{w}{2h}+0.94))]^{-1}$$

$$\text{for } \frac{w}{h}>1$$

$$P_m = [1 - (\frac{w}{4h})^2][1 + \frac{h}{w}] \quad \text{for } \frac{w}{h} \leq 2$$

$$P_m = \frac{2\pi[\frac{w}{h} + \frac{w/(\pi/h)}{w/(2h) + 0.94}][1 + \frac{h}{w}]}{[\frac{w}{h} + \frac{2}{\pi}\ln(2\pi e(\frac{w}{2h} + 0.94))]^2} \quad \text{for } \frac{w}{h} \geq 2$$

The radiation resistance r_r of the end-faces of the patch has been calculated using approximate formulas

$$1/r_r = w_e^2/90\lambda^2 \qquad \text{for } w_e < 0.35\lambda$$

$$= w_e/120\lambda - \frac{1}{60\pi^2} \qquad \text{for } 0.35\lambda \leq w_e < 2\lambda$$

$$= w_e/120\lambda \qquad \text{for } w_e \geq 2\lambda$$

where w_e is the equivalent width of the line given by

$$w_e = 120\pi h/(Z_m(\varepsilon_r)\sqrt{\varepsilon_e})$$

The wavelength in the material (λ_g) is related to ε_e by

$$\lambda_g = \lambda/(\varepsilon_e)^{1/2}$$

where

$$\varepsilon_e = \frac{1}{2}(\varepsilon_r + 1 + (\varepsilon_r - 1) \cdot (1 + 10h/w)^{-1/2})$$

The bandwidth of the antenna, Δf, is given by

$$\Delta f \simeq \frac{1}{Q} (\times 100\%)$$

where

$$\frac{1}{Q} = \frac{1}{Q_D} + \frac{1}{Q_c} + \frac{1}{Q_R} \qquad (3.4.4)$$

given by eqn.(3.4.3).

Values of efficiency and bandwidth, computed from (3.4.1) and (3.4. 4) for a square resonant patch are given in Fig.3.4.4 for a wide range of substrate permittivities.

As the permittivity of the substrate increases, the resonant length of the patch decreases as ε_r and the efficiency and bandwidth slowly decrease. With a substrate of permittivity 100, tan δ_ε of 0.002 and thickness of 0.0075λ, for example, the dimensions of the patch are reduced by a factor of 10 but the efficiency is reduced to 12% for a bandwidth of 1/2%. As for the coated monopole, the Q factor tends to a value of $1/\tan \delta_\varepsilon$ as the dimensions reduce and for a high efficiency the small microstrip patch will be extremely narrowband, if tan δ_ε is small. For use as a small antenna in the VHF communications band, the microstrip patch will require a large-permittivity substrate material $(\varepsilon_r > 10)$ in order to achieve a reasonable size reduction and will consequently be inefficient unless tan δ_ε is small. At microwave frequencies, however, the dimensions involved are relatively smaller and

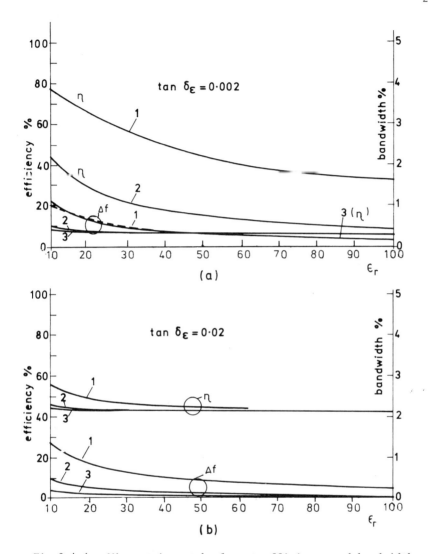

Fig.3.4.4   Microstrip patch element efficiency and bandwidth
(1) h = 0.0225λ   (2) h = 0.0075λ   (3) h = 0.0033λ

existing plastic substrates ($\varepsilon_r \sim 2$) enable reasonably   efficient   antennas to be constructed.

A practical example of using small microstrip antennas for   personal
communications is now given to demonstrate the usefulness of the technology.   A post-loaded rectangular microstrip antenna (P-MSA) has been

244

developed for small size UHF equipment. The P-MSA is an antenna modified from an ordinary quarter-wavelength rectangular microstrip antenna (O-MSA) and is designed to have two apertures excited by one
feed and have higher gain than the O-MSA. The design of the P-MSA is
briefly decribed as follows. (Kuboyama et al., 1985).

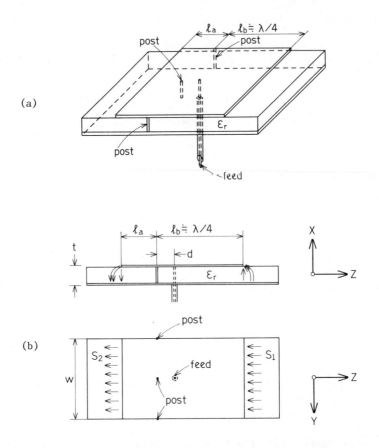

Fig.3.4.5.   P-MS Antenna: (a) antenna structure and (b) side view and
top view.

The antenna structure of the P-MSA is shown in Fig.3.4.5 with the
coordinate system. The P-MSA shown here has three posts replacing the
shorted end of the O-MSA and an extended patch of length ℓ_a, which
forms a radiating aperture at its end. The location of the posts

placed on the sides of the patch, length ℓ_b, essentially determines
the resonance frequency. The posts act as reactance loadings in the
two-plate guided line, so that the length of the antenna can be made
shorter than that of the O-MSA.

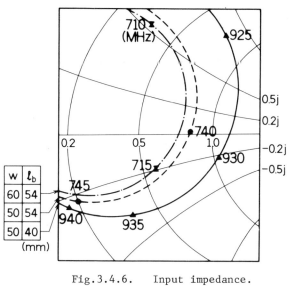

Fig.3.4.6.   Input impedance.
$$\left(\begin{array}{l}Z_o=50 \text{ ohm}, \ell_a=25\text{mm} \\ F_p=4\text{mm}, \; t=0.8\text{mm}, \; \Delta Z=5\text{mm}\end{array}\right)$$

The input impedance characteristics with respect to the length ℓ_b
and the width w are shown in Fig.3.4.6. The matching condition can
easily be obtained by adjusting the position of the feed point, F_p.
It was found experimentally that the resonance frequency F_r is related
to both ℓ_b and w and is given by the following equation, provided that
w is equal to or smaller than a quarter wavelength:

$$F_r = \frac{C}{4 \times (\ell_b + \alpha w)} \times \frac{1}{\sqrt{\varepsilon_e}} \;, \qquad (3.4.5)$$

where C is the velocity of the light and ε_e is an effective permittivity (Schneider, 1969), in which the effect of the fringing field
along the edge is taken into account. The resonance frequency F_r cal-

246

culated by taking α=0.22 in eqn.(3.4.5) agrees very well with measured
results as shown in Fig.3.4.7. The length ℓ_b can be reduced by widening w for the same resonance frequency. With the parameters shown in

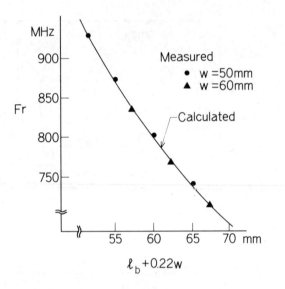

Fig.3.4.7.   Resonance frequency
versus antenna dimension.
$(\ell_a=25mm,\ F_p=4mm$
$t=0.8mm,\ \Delta Z=5mm)$

Fig.3.4.7, the length ℓ_b of the P-MSA became about 8% shorter than
that of the O-MSA. The relative bandwidth increases in proportion to
w, although the variation is small. The extended length ΔZ of the
ground plane from the radiating aperture affects the resonance frequency to make it lower as shown in Fig.3.4.8. This can be attributed
to the effect of fringing field which enlarges the radiation aperture
as ΔZ increases. However, ΔZ = 10 mm is the maximum; there is almost
no frequency variation for ΔZ ≥ 10 mm. As discussed later, the optimum ΔZ is about six times the thickness t of the substrate.

Radiation patterns on the X-Y plane are shown in Fig.3.4.9, where

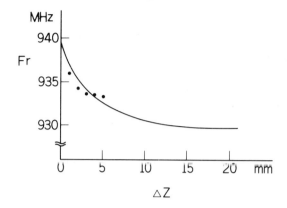

Fig.3.4.8.   Resonance frequency versus ΔZ.
(ℓ_a=25mm, ℓ_b=46mm, F_p=4mm)
t=0.8mm, w=30mm, F_r=930MHz

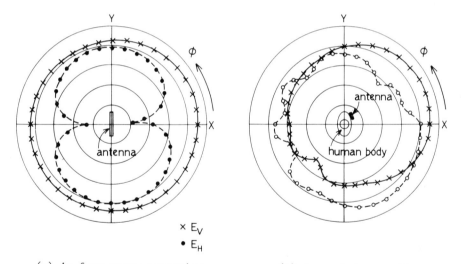

× E_V
• E_H

(a) in free space operation   (b) in-pocket operation

Fig.3.4.9.   Radiation patterns normalized with half-wavelength dipole
level.
(ℓ_a=17mm, ℓ_b=50mm, F_p=6mm, t=1.2mm, w=30mm, ΔZ=5mm, F_r=930MHz)

the vertical electric field E_θ pattern is seen nearly omnidirectional,
while the horizontal electric field E_ϕ pattern is a figure-eight
shape, as expected.

248

Fig.3.4.9 (b) shows the radiation pattern when the equipment is placed in an operator's pocket. The maximum level can be seen slightly increased from that in the free space. This resulted from the magnetic current radiation superposed in front of the operator with its image radiation due to the human body.

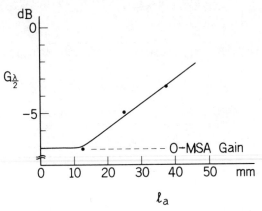

Fig.3.4.10.　$G_{\lambda/2}$ vs ℓ_a.
(ℓ_b=46mm, F_p=4mm, t=0.8mm,
w=30mm, ΔZ=5mm, F_r=930MHz)

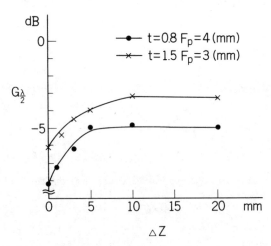

Fig.3.4.11.　$G_{\lambda/2}$ vs ΔZ,
(ℓ_a=25mm, ℓ_b=46mm, w=30mm,
F_r=930MHz)

The gain $G_{\lambda/2}$ with respect to the halfwave dipole is shown in Fig.3.
4.10, where the gain increases in proportion to ℓ_a under the condition
$\ell_a \geq \ell_b/4$. The gain $G_{\lambda/2}$ vs ΔZ is shown in Fig.3.4.11. The gain increases with ΔZ, but up to $\Delta Z = 5$ mm for $t = 0.8$ mm and 10 mm for $t =$
1.6 mm. It can be said that $\Delta Z = 6t$ is long enough to obtain the
maximum gain. Fig.3.4.12 illustrates the gain G_t (relative to that
for $t = \lambda_g/128$) vs t, where the gain G_t shows an increase up to $t = \lambda_g$
$/128$ (λ_g: the wavelength in the microstrip structure) and becomes
constant for $t \geq \lambda_g/128$. Thus t is chosen to be greater than or equal
to $\lambda_g/128$. The measurements here were made by putting a small oscil-
lator on the back of the microstrip antennas tested.

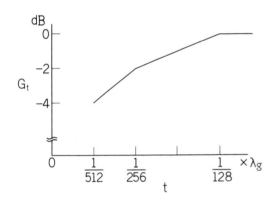

Fig.3.4.12. G_t vs t.
$\left(\begin{matrix}\ell_a=25\text{mm}, \; \ell_b=46\text{mm},\\ w=30\text{mm}, \; F_r=930\text{MHz}\end{matrix}\right)$

$t=\lambda_g/128$ corresponds
to $t=1.6$mm at 930MHz
with $\varepsilon_r=2.2$.

It is often encountered in practice that the antenna element is constrained to be mounted within a small volume (L × T × W, where $L \leq \lambda_g$
$/2$), and yet the antenna gain is desired to be as high as possible.
The procedure to choose the best design parameters for such a case is
as follows:

(1) Set $t = \lambda_g/128$ when $T \geq 128$. Set $t = T$ otherwise.
(2) Set $w = \lambda_g/4$ when $W \geq \lambda_g/4$. Set $w = W$ otherwise.
(3) Find ℓ_b from eqn.(3.4.5) after F_r and w are determined.
(4) Choose $\Delta Z = 6t$ whenever it is possible.
(5) Finally, $\ell_a = L - (\ell_b + 2\Delta Z)$.

The maximum gain can be obtained from the parameters chosen in the
above five steps.

3.5 Other uses of the coating technique

The previous Sections have been devoted to a cylindrical coated monopole structure and the small microstrip patch used as an electrically small antenna; their characteristics have been fully evaluated. Besides electrically short antennas, coating techniques can be used in a variety of ways to enhance a particular characteristic of a specialised antenna which is not necessarily small. The addition of dielectric material to regions of an antenna surface can make that region electrically larger and this property can be used to improve directionality in radiation patterns or improve bandwidth of operation. Several examples of such applications will now be described.

3.5.1 Conical log spirals

The conical equiangular log spiral antenna, Fig.3.5.1, is used for applications requiring hemi-spherical coverage over a wide bandwidth. Ramsdale (1983) has reported that dielectric materials can be incorporated over the structure to improve this bandwidth. This is illustrated in Fig.3.5.2 which gives experimental results using two types of materials, with permittivities of 4.7 and 6. In the Figure, it can be

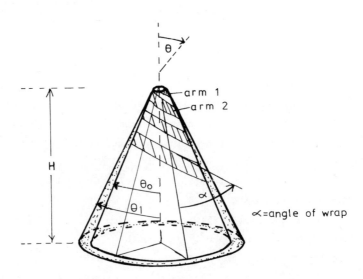

Fig.3.5.1   Construction of conical equiangular spiral antenna.

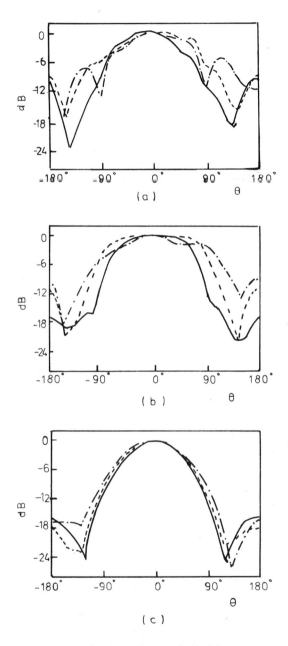

Fig.3.5.2   Largest circularly polarised field component for spiral
  (α=70°) with dielectric cone, θ_0=15°, θ_0=20°.
  ——— no dielectric. ----- ε_r = 4.7. —.—.— ε_r = 6
  (a) 1.5GHz   (b) 1.0GHz   (c) 0.5GHz.

seen that improvements can be achieved in the beamwidths of the antenna patterns at a particular frequency, by coating with dielectric
materials. In practice, the angle of wrap α must be optimised for
different types of coating, to achieve the best antenna beamwidths.
The uncoated antenna has the best performance when $\alpha=60°$ but this has
to be increased to 70°-80° with the dielectric coatings. In the Figure, $\alpha=70°$ in all cases and so the uncoated case is unoptimised, thus
reducing the apparent advantage of using dielectric covers somewhat.
Even so, the beamwidth can be increased by about 10° to 15° at 1.0 to
1.5GHz respectively, over the uncoated case, and the bandwidth of
operation can consequently be extended.

3.5.2 Radar reflection suppression

An interesting new antenna concept was introduced by Amin and James
(1981) which also uses the wire coating technique. There are numerous
applications where radar sets have to be located very close to long
wire communications antennas at HF/VHF, which can give unwanted radar
clutter. The aim is to reduce the reflections from these wire antennas by coating them with a layer of material which is lossy in the
radar bands. It is essential in doing so, that the performance of the
antenna at the operational frequency remain unimpaired and the material chosen must have a small dissipative loss in that frequency
range. Hexagonal ferrites (Von Aulock, 1965) exhibit these frequency
selective properties, shown diagramatically in Fig.3.5.3.

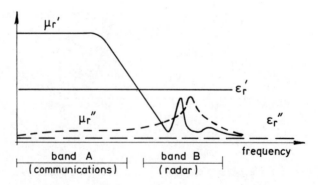

Fig.3.5.3   Material characteristics of a hexagonal ferrite as a function of frequency.

The permeability loss μ_r'' is small in the antenna frequency range of operation (A), but increases rapidly in the radar band (B). Because the permeability and permittivity are both greater than one in band (A), some slight reduction in height is necessary to retain resonance at the HF/VHF operational frequency.

The coated antenna must satisfy several conditions to achieve good absorptive properties. For a simple planar absorber, these conditions are that

$$\varepsilon_r' = \mu_r'$$

$$\varepsilon_r'' = \mu_r''$$

for minimum reflection. ε_r', ε_r'', μ_r', μ_r'' must all be high for a thin coating. There are no such simple criteria for cylindrical coatings but exact conditions can be derived (James and Amin, 1981) for both TM and TE type polarisations of incident radar fields.

The radar cross-section of the coated antenna σ defined as

$$\sigma = 4\pi r^2 \left| \frac{E_{scattered}}{E_{incident}} \right|^2 \quad \text{as } r \to \infty$$

is reduced by a factor R by the ferrite coating.

For the cylindrical coating, R can be found using analysis based on the spherical expansion of plane waves and is given by

$$R = -20\log_{10} \left| \sum_{n=0}^{\infty} \frac{\eta_n (-1)^n S_n}{\eta_n (-1)^n S_{no}} \right| \quad \text{where } \eta_n = \begin{cases} 1 \text{ if } n = 0 \\ 2 \text{ if } n \neq 0 \end{cases}$$

$$S_n = [Q_n J_n(kb) - J_n'(kb)]/[H_n^{(1)'}(kb) - Q_n J_n'(kb)]$$

For TM polarisation,

$$Q_n = [J_n'(k_1 b) + T_n H_n^{(1)'}(k_1 b)]/[J_n(k_1 b) + T_n H_n^{(1)}(k_1 b)] \cdot \sqrt{\frac{\varepsilon_r}{\mu_r}}$$

$$T_n = J_n(k_1 a)/H_n^{(1)}(k_1 a)$$

$$S_{no} = J_n(ka)/Y_n(ka)$$

and for TE polarisation

$$Q_n = \frac{J_n'(k_1b) + T_n H_n^{(1)}{}'(k_1b)}{J_n(k_1b) + T_n H_n^{(1)}(k_1b)} \bigg/ \sqrt{\frac{\mu_r}{\varepsilon_r}}$$

$$T_n = J_n'(k_1a)/H_n^{(1)}{}'(k_1a)$$

$$S_{no} = \frac{J_n'(ka)}{H_n^{(1)}{}'(ka)}$$

where $k_1 = k\sqrt{\varepsilon_r\mu_r}$

At HF/VHF the coating size is very small electrically and only a slight reduction in height has to be made. Such an antenna was constructed from toroids of ferrite and the R factor measured as shown in Fig.3.5.4.

Good agreement is observed between theory and experiment bearing in mind the difficulties involved in the measurement of μ_r which was done using Birks' method (1948). The communication antenna had an F factor of 1.3 and the efficiency was reduced by 92% due to losses in the coating,which is acceptable for most applications.

If a single layer of ferrite coating is used then the optimum absorption response is obtained when the thickness is about quarter wavelength in the material but this is a narrow-band response. A broader response can be obtained by applying different hexagonal ferrites in layers to the antenna,and using this technique it has been found that a −10dB reflection loss R can be achieved over a 20% bandwidth for a thickness of 2mm, with two different ferrites (James and Amin, 1981).

3.5.3 Electromagnetic probes and sensors

In electromagnetic interference measurements, isotropic broadband sensors are required to detect impulsive field strengths. Long coni-

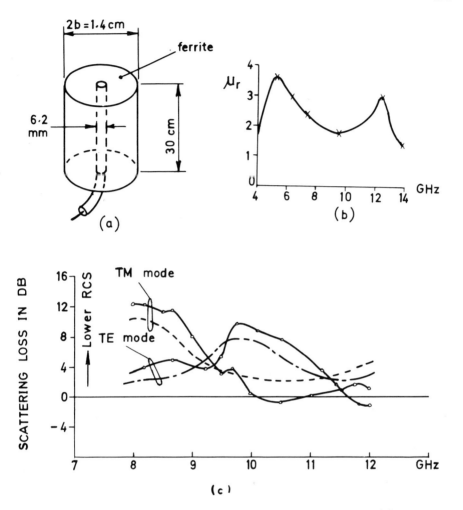

Fig.3.5.4   Cylindrical ferrite monopole: (a) construction, (b) magnetic
  parameters as a function of frequency, (c) scattering loss   compared
  to metal rod of same diameter.
  —₀— measured   ----- computed

cal antennas, TEM horns or long dipoles have been used in the past but
at the lower frequencies,   these become very large and it is difficult
to achieve omnidirectional patterns at the higher   frequencies.   Kanda
(1978) has used a relatively short monopole   antenna,   having a resistive loading,   for this purpose and has shown that such an antenna can
have improved patterns and be physically much smaller.   The probe   was

designed to work over 200MHz to 50Hz and is several wavelengths long
at the higher frequencies. If a simple monopole were to be used, the
field patterns would split up into lobes at these frequencies and be
unacceptable for use as a probe. When the monopole is designed with a
tapered resistive loading as indicated in Fig.3.5.5 then much improved

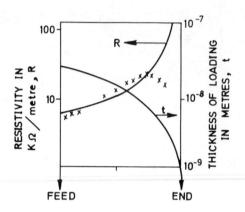

Fig.3.5.5   Resistive loading as a function of length along antenna.

patterns are obtainable. The analysis of Wu and King (1965) and the
moments method was used by Kanda to design such an antenna and it was
constructed out of a metallised glass rod 7.5cm long. Measurements of
the antenna patterns are shown in Fig.3.5.6 at 100MHz and 5GHz compared with a metal probe of the same length. At 5GHz the loaded antenna has a much improved pattern with no nulls and was found to have
a flat receiving response when used as a probe from 200MHz to 5GHz.
Such a probe has the capability of measuring fast EM pulses with mini-
mal pulse-shape distortion.

For a less demanding bandwidth requirement, the performance of short
electric wire probes can also be improved by dielectric loading. The
problem with electrically short probes, say $\lambda/10$ in length, is that
there is a severe power mismatch at the output. Birchfield and Free
(1974) have used water coatings to improve the sensitivity of their
measurement facility without the use of matching circuits. Figs.3.5.7
(a)-(c) indicate the improvement that can be achieved using this sim-

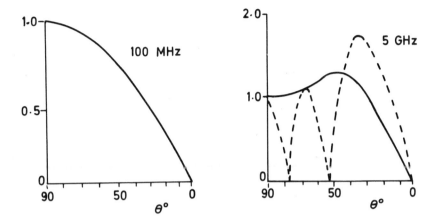

Fig.3.5.6 Measured radiation patterns of resistive probe compared
with those of a standard metal probe of the same length.
——— resistive rod. ----- metal probe

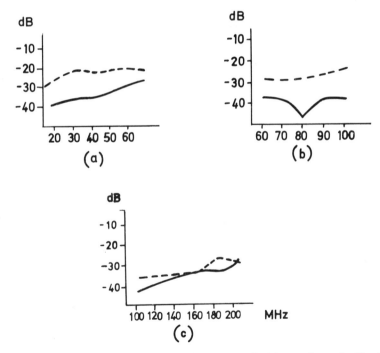

Fig.3.5.7 Received signal relative to half wavelength dipole.
(a) 50cm probe, (b) 30cm probe, (c) 15cm probe
----- coated probe ——— no coating

ple impedance matching technique. Although dielectric-material-coated monopoles have low input resistances at resonance, as demonstrated in Section 3.2, they do have a much improved impedance off resonance than their simple wire counterparts and this is the property that is being exploited in this work.

There are several applications, such as in underwater communications, where there is a requirement for a simply constructed antenna with some degree of directionality. Although antenna arrays could give this directionality, they would be inconvenient in practice and an alternative solution has been to use an eccentrically located wire inside a cylindrical dielectric coating.

In the case of underwater communications, trailing wire antennas are used which consist simply of a thin wire located inside an insulating dielectric coating. Wu et al. (1975) have derived formulas for the directivity obtained when the wire is placed off centre to the coating and is located in a lossy higher-permittivity medium, such as sea-water. Computations are shown in Fig.3.5.8 for two eccentricity ratios. As anticipated, an increase in eccentricity increases the directivity and typical radiation patterns shown in Fig.3.5.9.

More recently, Lytle and Laine (1978) have suggested using this technique to make miniature directional probes to fit down bore-holes

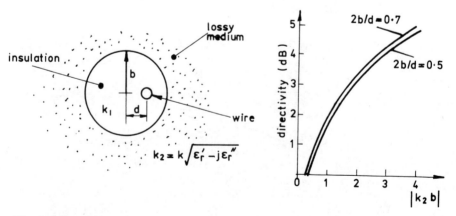

Fig.3.5.8 Directivity of insulated wire versus electrical thickness of coating.

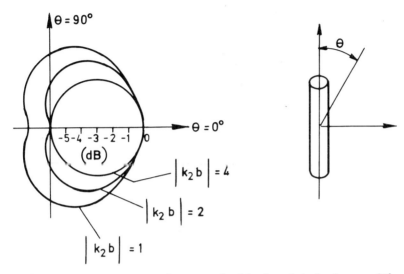

Fig.3.5.9   Field patterns of eccentrically insulated wire, with a/b= 0.1, 2b/d=0.7, referenced to a concentric wire.

for geophysical exploration purposes. They have used very − high − permittivity coatings,   typically ε_r=900-8000, and under these conditions the antenna performance is isolated from slight variations in the structure of the earth immediately surrounding the probe. For this new situation, formulas previously derived by Wu et al. do not apply and the performance of the new probe was predicted using a simple plane wave model, Fig.3.5.10, to derive rule-of-thumb estimations of directivity. It was found that in order to maximise radiation into region 3, D_2 had to be n $\lambda/2$ and D   about m $\lambda/4$, where n,m=1,3, 5... Further calculations were made on a point source in a long cylin-

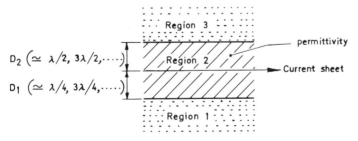

Fig.3.5.10   Plane Wave model for high − permittivity directional antenna.

der and the directional patterns obtained are shown in Fig.3.5.11.

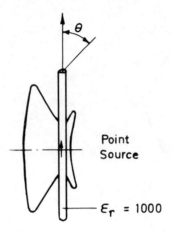

Fig.3.5.11 $|E_\theta|^2$ pattern of eccentrically located point source in a cylinder of high-permittivity material located in a medium of ε_r = 25, d/b=0.7.

Buettner (1980) has confirmed these findings experimentally by constructing a small directional antenna using a VHF ferrite material (ε_r =10, μ_r=13). The radiation patterns had a front to back ratio of 8.5 dB at 237MHz when measured in free-space. When used in granite underground, this directivity should increase slightly.

3.6 Summary comments

In the previous Sections many examples of loading dielectric or magnetic materials onto antennas have been given which have demonstrated the usefulness of the technique for enhancing various antenna characteristics, in particular for reducing height. The use of discretely loaded wire structures, as described in Chapter 2, should also be considered as an alternative design option for height reduction and it is interesting to compare their performances with material- loaded antennas. For narrow bandwidths, the self-resonant helix, Section 2. 2, is a good choice electrically, giving excellent efficiencies of about 80% for F=10. A short dipole of the same length but matched at the output by an external circuit would typically have only a 1-4% efficiency thus illustrating the careful design work that must be done before an antenna choice can be made for a particular application. F factors of this order would be very difficult to achieve with thin coatings of material and efficiencies of less than 1/2% would almost certainly be encountered.

For smaller F factors, the material coating method looks more attractive but even so produces relatively inefficient antennas. The efficiency of a matched short dipole with F=6.6, using a discrete lumped loading, is given in Fig.2.1.5 as about 20% whereas if the dipole were coated by a magnetic sleeve (about 0.6cm thick at 100MHz), an efficiency of about 5% would be likely with existing materials. The bandwidths of the antennas must be compared before a choice is made but it is apparent that lumped wire techniques are advantageous from an efficiency stand-point in most portable radio applications where fairly large height reductions are desirable.

The addition of material loadings to existing structures such as spirals and low-profile antennas has also been shown to be useful in enhancing radiation patterns or giving very moderate width reductions. The losses existing in material coatings although a disadvantage in small antenna applications can be put to good effect in the case of radar suppressed antennas. However, by far the most attractive applications of dielectrically loaded antennas is with those immersed in high-permittivity media, such as in geophysics, marine communications equipment and medical hyperthermia.

REFERENCES

Amin, M.B. and James, J.R., (1981). Techniques for utilisation of hexagonal ferrites in radar absorbers. Part 1: - Broadband planar coating.
Radio and Electronic Engineer, $\underline{51}$(5), 209-218.

Angulo, C.M. and Chang, W.S.C., (1959). A variational expression for the terminal admittance of a semi-infinite dielectric rod.
IRE Trans., $\underline{AP-7}$, 207-212.

Birchfield, J.L. and Free, W.R., (1974). Dielectrically loaded short antennas.
IEEE Trans., $\underline{AP-22}$, 471-472.

Birks, J.B., (1948). The measurement of permeability of low conductivity ferromagnetic materials at centimetre wavelengths.
Proc. of Phys. Soc.(London), $\underline{Vol\ 60}$, 282-292.

Blok, H. and Rietveld, J.J., (1955). Inductive aerials in modern broadcast receivers.
Philips Tech.Rev., $\underline{16}$(7), 181-212.

Buettner, H.M., (1980). Compact directional VHF antennas.
Electronics Letters,$\underline{16}$(25/26), 938-939.

Debye, P., (1929). Polar molecules. Chemical Catalogue Co., New York.

Fenwick, R.C., (1965). A new class of electrically small antennas.
IEEE Trans., $\underline{AP-13}$, 379-383.

Goubau, G. and Schwering, F. (Editor), (1976). Proceedings of the ECOM-ARO Workshop on electrically small antennas, held at Fort Monmouth, New Jersey, USA, 6-7th May, 153-157.

Harrington, R.F., (1967). Matrix methods for field problems.
Proc.IEEE, $\underline{55}$(2), 136-149.

Hersch, W., (1960). The surface wave aerial.
Proc.IEE, Monograph $\underline{363E}$, 202-212.

Hiroi, Y. and Fujimoto, K., (1976). Practical usefulness of normal mode helical antennas.

IEEE 1976 AP-S International Symposium Digest, 238-241.

James, J.R. and Burrows, R.M., (1973). Resonance properties of dielectrically loaded short unipoles.
Electronics Letters, 9, July, 300-302.

James, J.R., Schuler, A.J. and Binham, R.F., (1974). Reduction of antenna dimensions by dielectric loading.
Electronics Letters, 10, 263-265.

James, J.R. and Henderson, A., (1970). Electrically short monopole antennas with dielectric or ferrite coatings.
Proc. IEE, 125(9), 793-803.

James, J.R. and Henderson, A., (1978). Investigation of electrically small VHF and HF cavity-type antennas.
IEE International Conference on Antenna and Propagation, London, 322-326.

James, J.R. and Amin, M.B., (1981). Techniques for utilisation of hexagonal ferrites in radar absorbers. Part 2: Reduction of radar cross-section of HF and VHF wire antennas.
Radio and Electronic Engineer, 51(5), 219-225.

James, J.R., Hall, P.S. and Wood C., (1981). Microstrip antenna theory and design. IEE Electromagnetic Waves Series 12, Peter Peregrinus Ltd, Stevenage.

James, W., Drewett, R. and James, J.R., (1979). Experimental investigation of a new type of electrically small VHF antenna. Royal Military College of Science Tech. Note RT 114.

Kanda, M., (1978). A relatively short cylindrical broadband antenna with tapered resistive loading for picosecond pulse measurements.
IEEE Trans., AP-26, 439-447.

King, R.W.P. and Smith, G.S., (1981), Antennas in matter. MIT Press, Cambridge, Massachusetts.

Kuboyama, H., Hirasawa, K. and Fujimoto, K. (1985). Post loaded microstrip antenna for pocket size equipment at UHF.
International Symposium on Antennas and Propagation, Japan, 433-436.

Lytle, R.J. and Laine, E.F., (1978). Design of a miniature directional antenna for geophysical probing from boreholes.
IEEE Trans., GE-16, 304-307.

Madani, A., Le Rest, D. and Dubost, G., (1972). Antenne doublet cylindrique noyée dans une gaine de ferrite, cylindrique et de même axe.
Annales des Telecoms., 27, 430-449.

Marcuvitz, N., (1951). Waveguide handbook. (McGraw-Hill, New York)

McLachlan, N.W., (1934). Bessel functions for engineers. Oxford University Press, London.

Polk, C., (1959). Resonance and supergain effects in small ferromagnetically or dielectrically loaded biconical antennas.
IRE Trans., AP-7, S414-423.

Ramsdale, P.A., (1983). Dielectric loaded conical equiangular spiral antennas.
Third International Conf. On Antennas and Propagation, York, IEE Conf. Publication No. 219, 245-249.

Richmond, J.H. and Newman, E.H., (1976). Dielectric coated antennas.
Radio Science, 11(1), 13-20.

Schneider M.V. (1969). Microstrip line for microwave integrated circuit.
Bell Technical Journal, 48, 1421-1444.

Shevchenko, V.V., (1971). Continuous transitions in open waveguides.
Golem Press, Boulder.

Smith, C.E and Johnson, E.M., (1957). Performance of short antenna.
Proc. IRE, 35, 1026-1038.

Stovall, R.E. and Mei, K.K., (1975). Application of a unimoment technique to a biconical antenna with inhomogeneous dielectric loading.
IEEE Trans., AP-23, 335-342.

Stratton, J.A., (1941). Electromagnetic theory. McGraw-Hill, New York.

Tai, C.T., (1948). On the theory of biconical antennas.

J. Appl. Phys., $\underline{19}$(12), 1155-1160.

Ting, C.Y., (1969). Theoretical study of finite dielectric-coated cylindrical antenna.
J. Math. Phys., $\underline{10}$(3), 480-493.

Towaij, S.J. and Hamid, M.A.K., (1972). Radiation by dielectric loaded cylindrical antenna with a wall air-gap.
Proc. IEE, $\underline{119}$(1), 18-54.

Van Suchtelen, H., (1952). Ferroxcube aerial rods.
Electronic Applications Bulletin, $\underline{13}$(6), 88-100.

Vasil'ev, E.N., (1974). The use of integral equations in numerical solving of diffraction in problem of electromagnetic waves.
Proc of the 5th Colloquium on Microwave Communications, Budapest, ET-359 to ET-368.

Von Aulock, W.H., (Editor), (1965). Handbook of microwave ferrite materials. Academic Press, New York.

Wheeler, H.A. (1959). The radiansphere around a small antenna.
Proc. IRE, $\underline{47}$, 1325-1331.

Woodman, K.F., (1977). Dielectric-clad discone.
Electronics Letters, $\underline{13}$(9), 264-265.

Wu, T.T. and King, R.W.P., (1965). The cylindrical antenna with non-reflective resistive loading.
IEEE Trans., $\underline{AP-13}$, 369-373.

Wu, T.T., Shen, L.C. and King, R.W.P., (1975). The dipole antenna with eccentric coating in a relatively dense medium.
IEEE Trans., $\underline{AP-23}$, 57-62.

CHAPTER 4

Small Antennas On or Near a Conducting Body

INTRODUCTION

This is a problem which frequently occurs in the design of practical portable communication equipment and in other situations where a conducting body is in the near-field of an antenna system.

In the treatment of this problem, an antenna element and a conducting body are considered as one unified system, that is, the conducting body is not taken as a ground plane but as a part of the antenna system itself. In this chapter the portable communication equipment is modelled as an idealised rectangular metal box with an antenna operating in frequency range of 900 MHz, which is widely used for the mobile communications at present. In this frequency range, the antenna and the conducting body are not necessarily small as compared with the operating free-space wavelength λ. Examples where the length of the antenna is comparable to the size of a conducting body, housing a transmitter and a receiver, will be treated. The dimension of the antenna systems considered in this chapter are less than 1.1λ. Since the wavelength is about 30 cm, the total size of the antenna systems can be considered physically small.

In designing antennas for this portable communication equipment, it is necessary to find the characteristics of a wire antenna on or near a conducting body. The boundary-value problem invoked by a wire antenna and a conducting body in a unified system is totally beyond the scope of purely analytic methods and can only be solved by numerical approaches. To date, many publications have dealt with the problems of a wire antenna near or mounted onto a conducting body but only where the size of the latter is smaller than λ. A summary of some references is shown below, classified according to the shape of the conducting body and whether the wire antenna is located near the body or mounted on to it. A brief survey of the advantages and limitations of the method of moments for calculating electromagnetic radiation from complex conducting bodies may be found in Buchanan et al. (1979).

Type of conducting body	wire antenna (near/on)	Reference
Sphere	near	Butler and Keshavamurthy (1980)
	on	Bolle and Morganstern (1969) Tesche and Neureuther (1970)
Circular cylinder	near	Goldhirsh et al. (1971)
	on	Tsai (1973) Albertsen et al. (1974)
Plate	near	Wang et al. (1975) Hassan and Silvester (1977)
	on	Parhami et al. (1977) Newman and Pozar (1978)
Body of revolution	near	Glisson and Butler (1980)
	on	Fahmy and Botros (1979) Shaeffer and Medgyesi-Mitshang (1981)
Complex body	near	Hirasawa and Fujimoto (1982a)
	on	Knepp and Goldhirsh (1972) Miller and Deadrick (1975) Hirasawa and Fujimoto (1982 a, b)

References on the topic of wire antennas mounted on or near a conducting body

There have been two methods of analysis which could be applicable to the complex conducting body: the wire-grid method by Richmond (1966), Miller and Deadrick (1975), Hirasawa (1978) and Sato et al. (1979), and the surface current method by Knepp and Goldhirsch (1972), Albertsen et al. (1974), Sankar and Tong (1975), Wang (1978), Singh and Adams (1979) and Rao et al. (1982).

From the viewpoint of computer programming the surface current method requires three computer programs to calculate: (1) the surface current on the conducting body, (2) the line current on the wire antenna element and (3) the interaction between the wire antenna element and the conducting body. Its application to complex objects is quite difficult, and also it requires special treatment at the junction of the antenna element to the surface.

On the other hand, the wire-grid method requires only one computer program for the line currents, which represent all the currents on the antenna element and the wire model of the conducting body. Its application to complex objects is not so difficult, and the treatment of the junction of the antenna element and the conducting body is much easier. Although the wire-grid modelling of the conducting surface has fundamental limitations (Lee et al., 1976), which can sometimes cause problems (Miller and Deadrick, 1975), on the whole the wire-grid method has some attractive features from the viewpoint of computer programming, including shorter computation times. For these reasons, the wire-grid method is chosen here for finding the wire antenna characteristics on or near a rectangular conducting body, and how the limitations mentioned above can be overcome is shown in the next Section.

In Section 4.1 the assessment of the wire-grid method by Hirasawa and Fujimoto (1982a), in which a conductor surface is replaced by wires as a means of approximate computation, is given for antenna models such as (1) a loop antenna and (2) a dipole antenna placed very near a rectangular conducting body, and (3) a monopole antenna attached to a rectangular conducting body. The conducting body is assumed to have the size of portable communication equipment. The radiation pattern and the input impedance of these models are investigated for the various configurations of the wire-grid model which require the least computation time and also give satisfactory results. This will be very useful for the design of an antenna system for portable communication equipment.

In Section 4.2 the design of an antenna system for portable communication use, consisting of a thin wire antenna and a rectangular conducting body, has been investigated in detail by using the wire-grid method, as discussed in Section 4.1. The conducting body considered is not so small compared with the wavelength. In the past, a conducting body which is much smaller than the wavelength has been treated as an antenna element (Fujimoto, 1968) where the input impedance was calculated and the matching condition discussed. The detailed current distribution on the wire-grid model of a conducting body which is not so small compared with the wavelength has been calculated by Hirasawa and Fujimoto (1982b), and the input impedance and the radiation pattern are also obtained by considering currents on the conducting body. As far as the authors are aware, this is the first analysis that accounts for the effects of the current on the portable communication equipment upon the antenna performance such as input impedance and radiation pattern.

Types of wire antennas considered in Section 4.2 are (1) base-fed quarter-wave monopole, (2) base-fed half-wave monopole and (3) centre-fed half-wave dipole. Their current distributions, radiation patterns and input impedances are calculated. The computed current distribution will be useful in calculating radiation patterns and considering the hand-holding effects. Additionally it has been found that a deflection of the maximum radiation in the vertical plane can occur due to asymmetrical current distribution on the conducting body and this factor is important in the design of communication links.

Another example of a unified antenna/box system has been given in Chapter 2 where an inverted-L antenna is placed on the top-side of a portable equipment. There the current distribution on the antenna system and the radiation patterns are shown for that particular size of the equipment.

4.1   Assessment of wire-grid method

4.1.1   Method of Computation

The surface of the conducting body is approximated by the wire-grid model, as shown below. The model of the box and the antenna element are treated in a unified system and as a result the entire system is made up of wire elements only. It is assumed that the radii of all wires are much smaller than λ and the currents on the wires flow only axially. To find the unknown currents flowing on the wires the boundary conditions are enforced such that the total tangential electric field vanishes on the wire surfaces and the current is then computed by using the method of moments with piecewise sinusoidal expansion and weighting functions, as discussed in Section 2.1. Once the current induced on each wire is obtained, the input impedance and radiation pattern of the antenna can easily be calculated.

4.1.2 Configuration of the Wire-Grid and the Antenna Characteristics

Selection of the wire radius and complexity of the wire-grid will be assessed in this Section for a model of the portable radio equipment mentioned previously. Let us choose the wire-grid as shown in Fig.4.

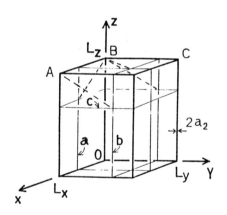

Fig.4.1.1. Wire-grid model.

1.1 (solid lines), and calculate the antenna characteristics. Since the current flowing on the edges is large, the edges of the rectangular conducting body are replaced by wires connected at the vertices. The surfaces of the body are replaced with equally spaced rectangular loops a, b and c; two of these intersect perpendicularly on each face of the body. Let MX, MY and MZ be the number of divisions of each face produced by the loops 'a', 'b' and 'c', respectively. For example, when MX=1 there is no loop 'a', and when MX=2, one loop 'a' divides the face into two equal parts. When MX=3, two loops 'a' are chosen, dividing the face into three equal parts.

Case (1): A Rectangular Loop or a Dipole near a Rectangular Conducting Body

A rectangular loop or a dipole near a rectangular conducting body, as shown in Figs.4.1.2 and 4.1.3, is considered, and it is investigated how the number of the wire-grids affects the input impedance, the

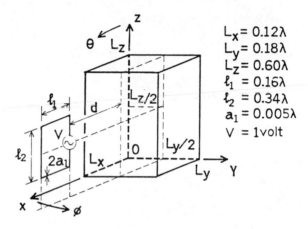

Fig.4.1.2.   Loop antenna near a rectangular conducting body.

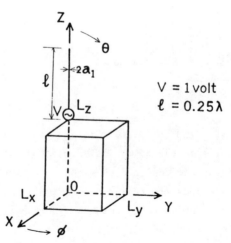

Fig.4.1.3.   Monopole antenna on a rectangular conducting body.

radiation pattern and the electric field in the centre (inside) of the body.

(i) Input impedance

Table 4.1.1 shows the input impedance calculated with various MYs and ds, where the radius of the grid wire is chosen as a_2 = 0.005 λ.

Table 4.1.1.   Input impedance (Ω).
(MX=MZ=1, a_2=0.005λ)

(a)   Loop antenna

MY	M'*	d = 0.1 λ	d = 0.3 λ	d = 0.5 λ
1	46	179.4 - j3.6	196.1 - j138.3	148.1 - j109.7
2	54	145.6 - j1.2	202.9 - j133.1	148.6 - j113.5
3	62	136.5 - j1.5	204.8 - j131.2	148.8 - j114.7
4	70	132.3 - j1.7	205.7 - j130.3	149.0 - j115.2
5	78	130.0 - j1.9	-	-
6	86	128.7 - j2.0	-	-
7	94	127.9 - j2.0	-	-

(b)   Dipole antenna

MY	M'*	d = 0.1 λ	d = 0.3 λ	d = 0.5 λ
1	41	58.5 + j92.2	121.0 + j41.6	87.0 + j29.4
2	49	41.0 + j80.3	121.2 + j47.2	89.1 + j28.0
3	57	36.8 + j77.0	121.1 + j49.0	89.9 + j27.6
4	65	34.9 + j75.5	121.2 + j49.9	90.2 + j27.4
5	73	34.0 + j74.7	-	-
6	81	33.4 + j74.3	-	-

*M' is the number of expansion functions.

It has been found that the values of MX and MZ do not have much effect on the antenna characteristics and so MX = MZ = 1 is assumed. As MY increases, the real part R_i and the imaginary part X_i of the input impedance converge to certain values, and from Table 4.1.1 we can find the value of MY = 3 (d = 0.5 λ), MY = 3 (d = 0.3 λ) and MY = 6 (d = 0.1 λ) for the loop antenna, and MY = 2 (d = 0.5 λ), MY = 3 (d = 0.3 λ) and MY = 4 (d = 0.1 λ) for the dipole antenna. To get an accurate value of input impedance, it can been seen that MY has to be increased as the wire antenna gets closer to the body.

Let us choose d = 0.1 λ, for which the input impedance changes very much with MY, and the relation between the input impedance and MY is calculated with three different a_2 s as shown in Fig.4.1.4. As a_2

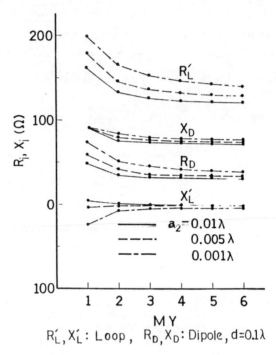

Fig.4.1.4.   Wire-grid radius and input impedance.

gets larger, the input impedance converges to a certain value with smaller MY. Therefore the chosen value of a_2 should not be too small, and $a_2 = 0.005\ \lambda$ is used in this Section.

To confirm the calculated results so far, the input impedance was measured as a function of d for the loop and the half-wave dipole in front of the conducting body $a_1 = 0.005\ \lambda$ and these measurements are compared with the calculated results as shown in Fig.4.1.5. The antenna system is placed on the centre area of the 1.8 m × 1.8 m ground plane under which the antenna is fed and the frequency 1000 MHz is used for the measurement. The agreement between the measured and the calculated results is very good, and it shows the possibility of modelling the rectangular conducting body by means of the wire-grid method.

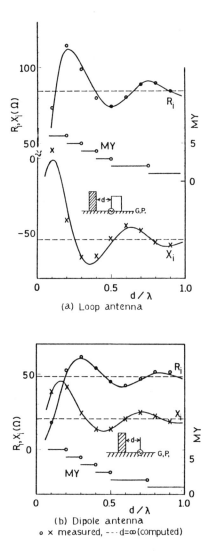

(a) Loop antenna

(b) Dipole antenna

o × measured, --- d=∞(computed)

Fig.4.1.5.   Input impedance.

(ii) Radiation pattern

The radiation patterns for d = 0.1 λ to 0.5 λ are not so sensitive
to the change of MY. The pattern for d = 0.1 λ changes most with MY
and is studied further. MX and MZ are kept equal to 1 and MY is
changed from 1 to 2 in Fig.4.1.6. Since the pattern for MY ≥ 3 is al-

276

most the same as the one for MY = 2, it is not shown here and indicates that MY = 2 is sufficient for an accurate radiation pattern with
$d \geq 0.1 \lambda$. Fewer wire grids are needed for the calculation of the
radiation pattern than for the input impedance.

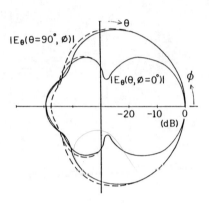

(a) Loop antenna

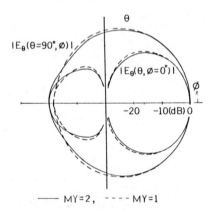

—— MY=2, ---- MY=1

(b) Dipole antenna

Fig.4.1.6.   Radiation pattern ($d = 0.1 \lambda$ MX = MZ = 1)

(iii) The electric field in the centre of the body

Although the electric field inside the solid conducting body is
zero, there may exist an electric field inside the wire-grid model of
the body, and the relation between the electric field in the body and
MY is investigated. Let MX = MZ = 1 with MY and d varied. The elec-

tric field in the centre of the body is obtained from eqn.(2.1.7), and is shown in Fig.4.1.7. The x and y components of the electric field

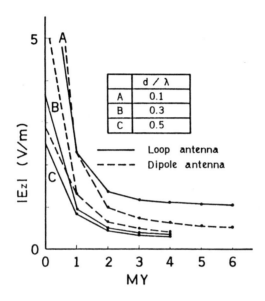

Fig.4.1.7. Electric field in the centre of the body.

(E_x and E_y) are zero and the magnitude of the z component $\left|E_z\right|$ is shown. When MY = 0 in Fig.4.1.7 the electric field is calculated at the point ($L_x/2$, $L_y/2$, $L_z/2$) in the absence of the conducting body. For both the loop and dipole antenna cases, the electric field inside the wire-grid model decreases as MY increases and has a tendency to converge to a certain value. Fig.4.1.8 shows the electric field in the centre of the body, the input impedance Z_i, the total number of the expansion functions M' (see eqn.(2.1.3)) and the execution time T as function of MY. Although the increase of M' from M'_1 to M'_2 makes the input impedance change very little, the electric field inside decreases greatly. This means that MY has to be increased substantially to make the electric field inside close to zero, but accurate results for the input impedance and the radiation pattern can be obtained, even if the electric field inside is significant. The calculation was made on the HITACHI M170 computer and the relation between T and M' is shown in Fig.4.1.8. It can be seen that T is nearly proportional to $(M')^2$.

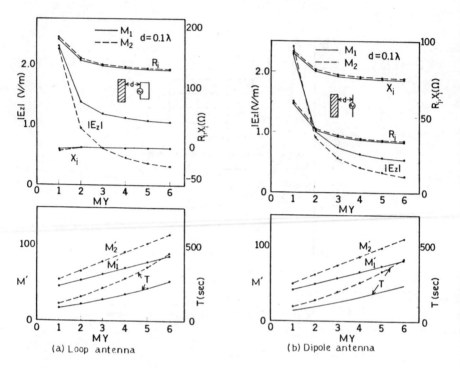

Fig.4.1.8. Electric field in the centre of the body, input impedance, expansion function and computation time.

Case (2): A monopole antenna attached to a rectangular conducting body

Let us consider a quarter-wave monopole antenna attached to the rectangular conducting body, as shown in Fig.4.1.3. The radius of the grid wire is assumed to be the same as the radius of the monopole antenna. The relation between the sizes of the wire-grid and the input impedance is now studied numerically and the radiation pattern is calculated.

(i) Input impedance

Fig.4.1.9 shows the input impedance versus the height of the body L_z $/\lambda$ for two cases (1) MX = MY = MZ = 1 and (2) MX = 1, MY = 2, and MZ =

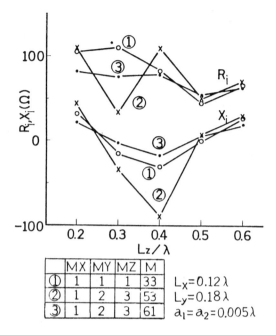

Fig.4.1.9.   Input impedance of monopole antenna.

3.   The difference between (1) and (2) is large for $0.2 \lambda \leq L_z < 0.5\lambda$; and is small for $0.5 \lambda \leq L_z \leq 0.6 \lambda$.   Therefore the wire-grid model in Fig.4.1.1 (solid line) may not be good enough to model the body around the feed point, so three wires (broken line) are added around feed point B and one wire (broken line) from point A.   Since L_y is twice as large as L_x, no new wires are placed at point C.   The curve ③ in Fig. 4.1.9 is the result of adding 4 extra wires to the model for curve ②. This eliminated the large variations in curve ②.

Table 4.1.2 shows the input impedance of the antenna for (a) $L_z = 0.25 \lambda$ and (b) $L_z = 0.525 \lambda$.   In Table 4.1.2 (a) the calculated values with the extra wires are in better agreement with the measured values. In Table 4.1.2 (b) the calculated results without the extra wires agree quite well with the experimental values as expected from Fig.4. 1.9.   This means that the z-directed current is quite large when L_z gets longer, and no extra wires around the feed point are needed.   The measured results in Table 4.1.2 (a) and (b) were obtained at 500 MHz

Table 4.1.2.   Input impedance (Ω) and field in the body (V/m)

$$(|E| = \sqrt{|E_x|^2 + |E_y|^2 + |E_z|^2}, \text{ MX} = 1)$$

(a) $L_x = 0.1\ \lambda$, $L_y = 0.2\ \lambda$, $L_z = 0.25\ \lambda$, $a_1 = a_2 = 0.0042\ \lambda$)

	MY	MZ	M'	$R_i + jX_i$	$|E_x|$	$|E_y|$	$|E_z|$	$|E|$
A	1	1	33	131.2 + j13.1	1.17	3.83	3.14	5.09
B	2	3	53	241.8 - j115.2	0.24	4.89	1.40	5.09
A'	1	1	48	100.2 + j8.0	2.23	1.38	0.96	2.79
B'	2	3	61	92.4 + j10.9	2.26	1.70	3.92	4.83
C	measured			81.4 - j10.7	-	-	-	-

(b) $L_x = 0.104\ \lambda$, $L_y = 0.155\ \lambda$, $L_z = 0.525\ \lambda$, $a_1 = a_2 = 0.004\ \lambda$)

	MY	MZ	M'	$R_i + jX_i$	$|E_x|$	$|E_y|$	$|E_z|$	$|E|$
A	1	1	33	45.8 - j2.3	9.42	15.7	1.72	18.4
B	2	3	53	48.7 + j2.4	1.40	6.54	1.09	6.78
A'	1	1	48	47.6 - j3.4	11.4	18.7	0.64	21.9
B'	2	3	61	49.4 + j2.2	2.57	9.00	4.41	10.3
C	measured			46.2 + j1.3	-	-	-	-

A' and B' : with extra wires

and 800 MHz, respectively. In Table 4.1.2 the calculated electric field in the centre of the body is also shown. The computation time for the results in Table 4.1.2 is 72 seconds (model A), 136 seconds (model B), 160 seconds (model A') and 214 seconds (model B').

(ii) Radiation pattern

Figs.4.1.10 and 4.1.11 show the radiation patterns of the two wire-grid models: (1) MX = MY = MZ = 1, and (2) MX = 1, MY = 2 and MZ = 3 (the extra 4 wires added). $L_x = 0.12\ \lambda$, $L_y = 0.18\ \lambda$ and $a_1 = a_2 = 0.005\ \lambda$ are assumed, and the cases for $L_z = 0.25\ \lambda$ and 0.6 λ are considered. For $|E_\theta|$ the difference between the results of (1) and (2) is very small, and the coarse model (1) is good enough. On the other hand, for $|E_\phi|$ models (1) and (2) show somewhat different results and in this case, the fine model (2) should be used.

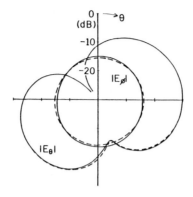

(a) Vertical pattern ($\phi = 90°$)

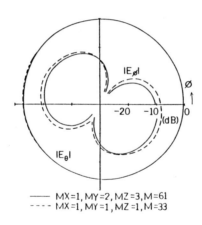

—— MX=1, MY=2, MZ=3, M=61
- - - - MX=1, MY=1, MZ=1, M=33

(b) Horizontal pattern

Fig.4.1.10.   Radiation pattern ($L_z = 0.25 \ \lambda$)

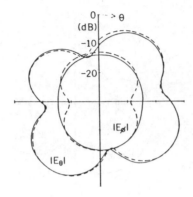

(a) Vertical pattern ($\phi = 90°$)

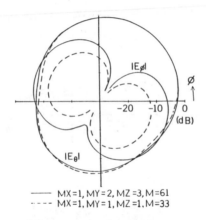

——— MX=1, MY=2, MZ=3, M=61
- - - - MX=1, MY=1, MZ=1, M=33

(b) Horizontal pattern

Fig.4.1.11.   Radiation pattern ($L_z = 0.6 \lambda$)

4.2 Various wire antennas on a rectangular conducting body

The wire-grid method discussed in Section 4.1 is used to model monopole antennas fed at various points and attached to a rectangular conducting body as shown in Fig.4.2.1. The antenna characteristics including the effects of the box are obtained by the method of moments.

The wire-grid model used is shown in Fig.4.2.2. Note that there are
six wires to model the feed point (B) at the vertex of the body. From

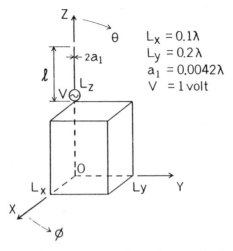

Fig.4.2.1.   Wire antenna on a rectangular conducting body.

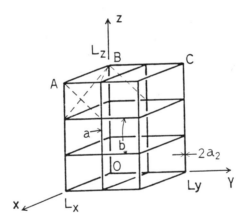

Fig.4.2.2.   Wire-grid model.

the practical point of view the radius of the antenna element a_1 =
0.0042 λ is chosen, and it is assumed that the radius a_2 of the grid
wires equals a_1. Let all the peaks of the expansion functions on the
wire-grid model coincide with the intersections of the grid wire, as
in Section 4.1. On the antenna element, 5 and 10 expansion functions
are used for a quarter-wave and a half-wave monopole, respectively.
Nine expansion functions are used for a half-wave dipole.

284

4.2.1 Current Distribution

The feed voltage V = 1 volt, L_x = 0.1 λ and L_y = 0.2 λ are assumed, and two cases (1) L_z = 0.25 λ and (2) L_z = 0.6 λ are considered. Types of wire antennas considered are

(i)   base-fed quarter-wave monopole (the base is the point B in Fig. 4.2.2)

(ii) base-fed half-wave monopole

(iii) centre-fed half-wave dipole (the antenna element and the body are not electrically connected at the antenna at the point B in Fig.4.2.2).

The size of the body and the types of the antenna elements are typical of the portable communication equipment commonly in use.

Case (1): L_z = 0.25 λ

(i)   Base-fed λ/4 monopole antenna (case (i))

The amplitude of the current distribution is shown in Fig.4.2. 3 (a). Since the length of the monopole is λ/4, the current amplitude maximum on the monopole occurs around the feed point, and is about 11 mA. This large current flows into the body (i.e. it is distributed into the six wires coming from the feed point). As a result, a relatively large current flows on every wire of the wire-grid model of the body shown in Fig.4.2.2.

(ii) Base-fed λ/2 monopole antenna (case (ii))

The current amplitude is shown in Fig.4.2.3 (b). Since the length of the monopole is λ/2, the current amplitude maximum on the monopole occurs around the centre of the antenna element. Consequently the current amplitude around the feed point becomes smaller, and is about 2.4 mA. Hence the current into the body is much smaller than that of case (i), and the current on the body is almost zero except in the neighbourhood of the feed point. If it is possible to reduce the current flowing into the body as in this case, the body has little influence on the antenna characteristics, and hence it is favourable to the design of the antenna system.

(iii) Centre-fed $\lambda/2$ dipole antenna (case (iii))

An idealized sleeve dipole antenna is considered here, and it is assumed that the antenna element and the body are not connected electrically. The calculated results are shown in Fig.4.2.3 (c). Although the current from the antenna element does not flow into the body, the current on the body is induced by the near field due to the current on the antenna element. This behavior can be seen in Fig.4.2.3 (c), and in this case the current on the body is less than the one in Fig.4.2.3 (a), but more than the one in Fig.4.2.3 (b).

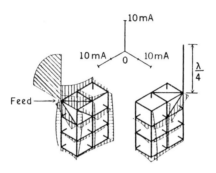

(a) Base-fed $\lambda/4$ antenna (case (i))

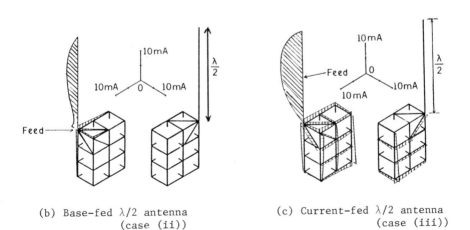

(b) Base-fed $\lambda/2$ antenna
(case (ii))

(c) Current-fed $\lambda/2$ antenna
(case (iii))

Fig.4.2.3. Current amplitude.

Case (2): $L_z = 0.6 \lambda$

(i) Base-fed λ/4 monopole antenna (case (i))

The current amplitude is shown in Fig.4.2.4 (a) where a current of 15 mA flows near the feed point on the antenna element, and a current of 14 mA flows on the wire coming down from the feed point. As a result most of the current flows down from the feed point and the rest is distributed on the five wires from the feed point. Hence these five wires have small effects on the input impedance. Unlike the case for $L_z = 0.25 \lambda$, the current on the body is mainly z-directed and the horizontal component of the current is almost zero except around the feed point.

(ii) Base-fed λ/2 monopole antenna (case (ii))

The current amplitude is shown in Fig.4.2.4 (b) where the current maximum on the antenna element occurs around the centre of the antenna element, and a current of about 2 mA flows into the body from the feed point, most of which goes down the body. The current on the conductor is very small and can be seen only around the feed point. As a result, the current flowing on the bottom two-thirds of the conductor is almost zero, and it can be imagined that the hand-holding effect may be very small.

(iii) Centre-fed λ/2 dipole antenna (case (iii))

The current amplitude is shown in Fig.4.2.4 (c). Since the antenna element and the body are not electrically connected, no direct current from the antenna element flows into the body, but the induced current on the body due to the near field of the antenna element is mainly z-directed and the horizontal current on the body is very small. The current flowing on the body is less than that in Fig.4.2.4 (a), but it is more than that in Fig.4.2.4 (b).

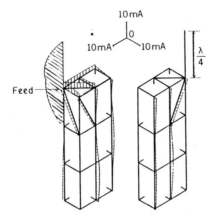

(a) Base-fed $\lambda/4$ antenna (case (i))

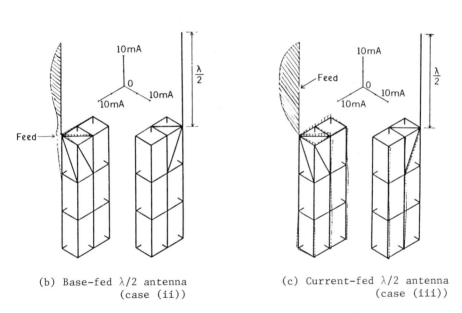

(b) Base-fed $\lambda/2$ antenna
(case (ii))

(c) Current-fed $\lambda/2$ antenna
(case (iii))

Fig.4.2.4.   Current amplitude (L_z = 0.6 λ).

4.2.2 Input Impedance

The input impedance Z_i (= $R_i + jX_i$) versus the length ℓ of the antenna element is shown in Fig.4.2.5. L_x = 0.1 λ and L_y = 0.2 λ are assumed, and the two cases for L_z = 0.25 λ and 0.6 λ are considered.

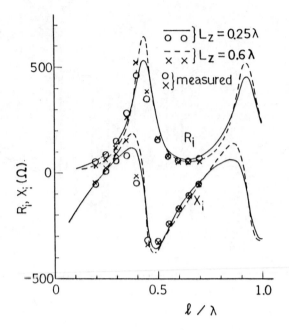

Fig.4.2.5.   Input impedance.

The input impedance change due to L_z is very small, as long as R_i and X_i are not close to their local maximum value. Also, $X_i = 0$ is obtained when ℓ becomes about 0.25 λ and 0.75 λ.

The measured input impedance for ℓ = 0.2 λ - 0.7 λ is also shown in Fig.4.2.5. The measurement is quite difficult due to the very nonsymmetrical structure, but the calculated and measured results agree quite well.

4.2.3 Radiation Pattern

Consider the same size of box as was used in calculating the current distribution. Assume L_x = 0.1 λ and L_y = 0.2 λ, and consider the two cases (1) L_z = 0.25 λ and (2) L_z = 0.6 λ. As before, the types of wire antennas considered are (i) base-fed quarter-wave monopole, (ii) base-fed half-wave monopole and (iii) centre-fed dipole. The radiation patterns $|E_\theta|$ and $|E_\phi|$ are normalized to the $|E_\theta|$ maximum.

Case (1): $L_z = 0.25 \lambda$

Fig.4.2.6 shows the radiation patterns for three different wire antenna elements where Fig.4.2.6 (a) - (c) are x-z plane, y-z plane, x-y

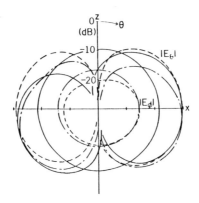

(a) Vertical pattern (x-z plane)

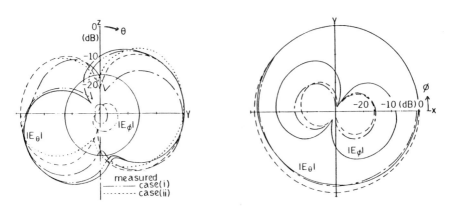

(b) Vertical pattern (y-z plane)   (c) Horizontal pattern (x-y plane)

Fig.4.2.6.   Radiation pattern (L_z = 0.25 λ).
(———— case (i), ----- case (ii) and -•- case (iii))

plane patterns, respectively. In Fig.4.2.6 (a) and (b) a deflection
of the pattern null in the vertical plane pattern is found; this is
due to the nonsymmetrical structure of the antenna system. The de-

flection is most notable in case (i) where the current on the body is the greatest among these three cases. The deflection of $|E_\theta|$ in the y-z plane pattern is larger than that in the x-z plane pattern. This is because the deflection is due to the horizontal component of the current on the body, the length L_y is twice as large as L_x, and consequently the y-directed current is larger than the x-directed one. The x-y plane pattern of $|E_\theta|$ (Fig.4.2.6 (c)) is almost circular except for case (i), for which the departure from the circle is about 4.5 dB at most.

The ϕ component of the radiation field E_ϕ is due to the horizontal component of the current on the body. For example, the y-z plane pattern (Fig.4.2.6 (b)) of $|E_\phi|$ is due to the x-directed current and the x-z plane pattern (Fig.4.2.6 (a)) is due to the y-directed current. In addition, the length L_y is larger than L_x. Hence the y-z plane pattern of $|E_\phi|$ is about 10 dB smaller than the x-z plane pattern of $|E_\phi|$. On the x-y plane pattern (Fig.4.2.6 (c)) if $L_x = 0$ (a rectangular plate), the pattern minimum of $|E_\phi|$ could occur in the directions of $\phi = 90°$ and $270°$. However, $L_x = 0.1 \lambda$, and the direction of the minimum $|E_\phi|$ is shifted about $25°$ from the y axis.

Case (2): $L_z = 0.6 \lambda$

Fig.4.2.7 shows the radiation patterns $|E_\theta|$ and $|E_\phi|$ on three different antenna elements. Figs.4.2.7 (a), (b) and (c) are the x-z plane, y-z plane and x-y plane patterns, respectively. Since L_z is longer than a quarter wavelength, the phase of the current flowing parallel to the z axis is not uniform. As a result the x-z plane and y-z plane patterns of $|E_\theta|$ (Fig.4.2.7 (a) and (b)) become distorted figure-eight patterns, and the effects of L_z appear most clearly in case (i), where the current flow on the body is greatest among the three cases. In case (i) the vertical pattern of $|E_\theta|$ will split as L_z gets longer. The deflection of the pattern null of $|E_\theta|$ from the axis is most notable in case (i) and is small in cases (ii) and (iii). On the x-y plane pattern of $|E_\theta|$ (Fig.4.2.7 (c)) the maximum shift from the circle (0 dB) is about 8.5 dB in the case (i), which is about 4 dB larger than that for $L_z = 0.25 \lambda$. This is because L_z is longer than $\lambda/4$,

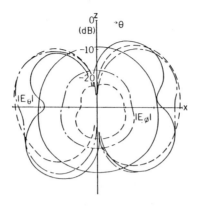

(a) Vertical pattern (x-z plane)

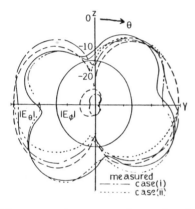

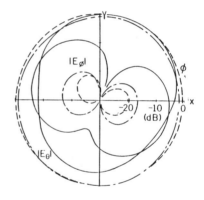

(b) Vertical pattern (y-z plane)　　(c) Horizontal pattern (x-y plane)

Fig.4.2.7.　Radiation pattern (L_z = 0.6 λ).
(———— case (i), ----- case (ii) and -·- case (iii))

and consequently the vertical pattern of $|E_\theta|$ starts to split into two.

The shape of the radiation pattern $|E_\phi|$ is similar to that for L_z = 0.25 λ, but in case (i) the x-y plane pattern of $|E_\phi|$ is not so small, and is even greater than that of $|E_\theta|$ in some directions.

The maximum gain of $|E_\theta|$ in the x-y plane is calculated with respect to the height L_z of the body and the length ℓ of the antenna element, and is shown in Table 4.2.1. As a result of the change in the length

Table 4.2.1   Maximum gain in the x-y plane (dB)
(with respect to a half-wave dipole)

	$L_z = 0.25 \lambda$	$L_z = 0.6 \lambda$
(i)	0.3 ($\phi = 45°$)	-3.4 ($\phi = 65°$)
(ii)	0.5 ($\phi = 60°$)	-0.7 ($\phi = 75°$)
(iii)	1.1 ($\phi = 60°$)	-1.4 ($\phi = 250°$)

L_z from 0.25 λ to 0.6 λ, the maximum radiation direction of the vertical pattern of $|E_\theta|$ is shifted from $\theta = 90°$, and the gain gets smaller. However, the gain decrease in the case (i), where the antenna element length is 0.25 λ, is most notable. This is due to the currents on the body.

4.3. CONCLUSION

In this Chapter, the size of the conducting body was assumed to be typically that of existing portable communications equipment, operated in the 900 MHz region. Because the dimensions were comparable to λ, this involved the use of the wire-grid method to calculate the radiation characteristics of both the antenna and the box as a unified system and gave more insight into the design associated with portable equipment, than work previously presented.

In Section 4.1 the wire-grid method was evaluated to find the characteristics of certain antennas such as (1) a loop antenna and (2) a dipole antenna, each placed very close to the rectangular conducting body and (3) a monopole antenna attached to the conducting body. It was found that the optimum positions of the grid wires were different for the cases of the wire antennas close to the conducting body and those attached to it. Also it was observed that more grid wires were needed to calculate the input impedance than to get the radiation pattern. Much computation time can be saved by choosing the grid positions for the body carefully.

In Section 4.2 the wire antenna element attached to a rectangular conducting body was considered in more detail and more emphasis placed on design considerations. The current on the box, the input impedance of the antenna and the radiation pattern were calculated by the wire-grid method, and their relations with the length of the wire antenna element, its feed point position and the size of the body were investigated. It becomes clear that the current on the body is largely dependent on the length of the wire antenna and its feed point position. In particular when the antenna element is $\lambda/2$, the current on the body is much less than that for quarter-wave antenna element. This suggests that the radiation pattern distortion and the hand-holding effect should be small with a half-wave antenna element. Also, when a quarter-wave antenna element is used, the radiation pattern changes greatly with the size of the rectangular body and this is a very important point to consider when the system of the portable communication equipment is actually designed. In calculating the input impedance of the antenna, again the effect of the rectangular body is taken into account and this can give more insight into the matching conditions encountered in practical situations.

In the past, a great many kinds of portable communication equipment have been used but their antenna systems have not been analysed in detail. Once the current distribution on the rectangular body is known, the radiation pattern and the input impedance are correctly obtained. This information is very useful when designing for portable communications equipment and enables characteristics such as body effects, matching and efficiency to be examined.

In this Chapter, we have concentrated on applications involving portable communications equipment but the analytical procedures and the results obtained can also be applied to many wire antenna/conducting body configurations where the dimensions are comparable to a wavelength (Nishikawa, 1983).

REFERENCES

Albertsen, N.C., Hansen, J.E. and Jensen, N.E. (1974). Computation of radiation from wire antennas on conducting bodies.
IEEE Trans., AP-22, 200-206.

Bolle, D.M. and Morganstern, M.D. (1969). Monopole and conic antennas on spherical vehicles.
IEEE Trans., AP-17, 477-484.

Buchanan, D., Perini, J., Chou, J., Schumon, H. and Hirasawa, K. (1977). Assessment of MOM techniques for shipboard applications.
Rome Air Development Center, RADC-TR-77-14.

Butler, C.M. and Keshavamurthy, T.L. (1980). Analysis of a wire antenna in the presence of a sphere.
IEEE Trans., EMC-22, 113-118.

Fahmy, M.N. and Botros, A.D. (1979). Radiation from quarter-wavelength monopoles on finite cylindrical, conical and rocket-shaped conducting bodies.
IEEE Trans., AP-27, 615-623.

Fujimoto, K. (1968). A loaded antenna system applied to VHF portable communication equipment.
IEEE Trans., VT-17, 6-12.

Glisson, A.W. and Butler, C.M. (1980). Analysis of a wire antenna in the presence of a. body of revolution.
IEEE Trans., AP-28, 604-609.

Goldhirsh, J., Knepp, D.L., Doviak, R.J. and Unks, R. (1971). Radiation from a short dipole or monopole near a thick conducting cylinder of resonant length.
IEEE Trans., AP-19, 279-282.

Hassan, M.A. and Silvester, P. (1977). Radiation and scattering by wire antenna structures near a rectangular plane reflector.
Proc. IEE, 124, 429-435.

Hirasawa, K. (1978). A study on reactively loaded grid-type corner reflector antennas.

Electronics and Communications in Japan, 61-B, 45-53.

Hirasawa, K. and Fujimoto, K. (1982a). On wire-grid method for analysis of wire antennas near/on a rectangular conducting body.
Trans. IECE Japan, J65-B, 382-389. (in Japanese).

Hirasawa, K. and Fujimoto, K. (1982b). Characteristics of wire antennas on a rectangular conducting body.
Trans. IECE Japan, J65-B, 1133-1139. (in Japanese).

Knepp, D.L. and Goldhirsh, J. (1972). Numerical analysis of electromagnetic radiation properties of smooth conducting bodies of arbitrary shape.
IEEE Trans., AP-20, 383-388.

Lee, K.S.H., Marin, L. and Castillo, J.P. (1976). Limitations of wire-grid modeling of a closed surface.
IEEE Trans., EMC-18, 123-129.

Miller, E.K. and Deadrick, F.J. (1975). Some computational aspects of thin-wire modeling in Numerical and asymptotic techniques in electromagnetics, R. Mittra, Ed., Springer-Verlag, New York, ch. 4.

Newman, E.H. and Pozar, D.M. (1978). Electromagnetic modeling of composite wire and surface geometries.
IEEE Trans., AP-26, 784-789.

Nishikawa, K. (1983). Analysis of a monopole antenna mounted on an automobile body by the wire-grid method.
Trans. IECE Japan, J66-B, 845-852 (in Japanese).

Parhami, P. and Rahmat-Samii, Y and Mittra, R. (1977). Technique for calculating the radiation and scattering characteristics of antennas mounted on a finite ground plane.
Proc. IEE, 124, 1009-1016.

Rao, S.M., Wilton, D.R. and Glisson, A.W. (1982). Electromagnetic scattering by surfaces of arbitrary shapes.
IEEE Trans., AP-30, 409-418.

Richmond, J.H. (1966). A wire-grid model for scattering by conducting bodies.

IEEE Trans., AP-14, 782-86.

Sanker, A. and Tong, T.C. (1975). Current computation on complex structures by finite-element method.
Electronics Letters, 11, 481-482.

Sato, G., Kawakami, H., and Funatsu, F. (1979). Design of metal-bar supported wideband full-wave dipole antennas with a reflector plate by moment method.
Electronics and Communications in Japan, 62-B, 65-74.

Shaeffer, J.F. and Medgyesi-Mitschang, LN. (1981). Radiation from wire antennas attached to bodies of revolution: the junction problem.
IEEE Trans., AP-29, 479-487.

Singh, J. and Adams, A.T. (1979). A nonrectangular patch model for scattering from surfaces.
IEEE Trans., AP-27, 531-535.

Tesche, F.M. and Neureuther, A.R. (1970). Radiation patterns for two monopoles on a perfectly conducting sphere.
IEEE Trans., AP-18, 692-694.

Tsai, L.L. (1973). Dipole antenna coaxially mounted on a conducting cylinder.
IEEE Trans., AP-21, 89-94.

Wang, N.N., Richmond, J.H. and Gilreath, M.C. (1975). Sinusoidal reaction formulation for radiation and scattering from conducting surfaces.
IEEE Trans., AP-23, 376-382.

Wang, J.J.H. (1978). Numerical analysis of three-dimensional arbitrarily-shaped conducting scatterers by trilateral surface cell modeling.
Radio Sci., 13, 947-952.

Index

298